CLASSROOM DISCIPLINE
IN AMERICAN SCHOOLS

CLASSROOM DISCIPLINE IN AMERICAN SCHOOLS

Problems and Possibilities
for Democratic Education

Ronald E. Butchart
and
Barbara McEwan
Editors

State University of New York Press

Published by
State University of New York Press, Albany

For information, address State University of New York
Press, State University Plaza, Albany, N.Y., 12246

Production by Diane Ganeles
Marketing by Fran Keneston

Library of Congress Cataloging in Publication Data

Classroom discipline in American schools: problems and
    possibilities for democratic education / Ronald E. Butchart
    and Barbara McEwan, editors.
        p.   cm.
    Includes bibliographical references and index.
    ISBN 0-7914-3617-9 (hardcover : alk. paper). — ISBN
0-7914-3618-7 (pbk. : alk. paper)
    1. School discipline—Social aspects—United States.   2.
School discipline—Political aspects—United States.   3.
Classroom management—Social aspects—United States.
4. Classroom management—Political aspects—Unites
States.   5. Constructivism (Education)—United States.
I. Butchart, Ronald E.   II. McEwan, Barbara, 1946–   .
LB3012.2.C53   1998
371.5'0973—dc21   97-10600
                                                   CIP

10 9 8 7 6 5 4 3 2 1

To
Josh Butchart
and
Matt McEwan

May your generation and the next
learn to create futures worth living.

Contents

Part III: Toward a Curriculum of Democratic Civility: Exploring the Possibilities of Critical Constructivist Discipline

Introduction

❑

Ronald E. Butchart

Controlling the behavior of students in contemporary U.S. schools has become a growth industry in the last two decades. School management experts of various persuasions huckster books, seminars, videotapes, programs, packages, and even computer software, with confident claims of educational peace and tranquility. Techniques and technologies proliferate.

One local entrepreneur, a veteran teacher with dreams of retiring on lucrative royalties from his handiwork, speaks to me confidently of the computer program he has written and tested that allows him, at a computer keystroke, to record every violation of every school and classroom rule by any child in his sixth grade classes at the moment of infraction. Control will somehow flow from precise record keeping, he is certain. A West Coast businessman has grander plans; for tens of thousands of dollars, he guarantees that his team will bring any school to heel, no matter its reputation. "I will not talk philosophy," he declared before the faculty at a school I visit. Order is everything. Even hardware is pressed into the battle for control. An advertisement in school administrators' journals offers what appears to be a standard traffic signal light wired to a receptor; when the noise in

1

cafeterias or other places where students assemble reaches a particular level, the light changes from green to yellow and then to red. Presumably, students are trained to monitor the light and to monitor their conversations accordingly. More likely, teachers, paraprofessionals, or other monitors are expected to wield whatever authority they have to restore the green light.

It is the published material, available in many media, that is most pervasive, however. A handful of authors stand out—Canter, Driekurs, Glasser, and Jones—but scores more are in print. Ironically, the ideas promoted by this growth industry directly contradict the cognitive perspective guiding most educational thinking in the last two decades.

Student discipline and classroom management have always been a concern for teachers, administrators, and teacher educators. Control has become a greater problem in the last half century, for troubling historical and socio-logical reasons that we do not attempt to explore here. Yet at the same time the problem has grown, and the public has become increasingly agitated, the educational dialogue *about* discipline and management has attenu-ated. In many ways, there is no longer a dialogue at all. Following much else in American civic life, dialogue has dissolved into market-driven claims delivered in scores of simultaneous monologues. And, like all aspects of mar-kets, those claims are increasingly devoid of ethical, moral, or social content and criteria. Like the discipline expert quoted above, we do not talk philosophy any longer when we speak of classroom order. And we do not talk with each other, but at each other.

We have three purposes in this book. First and fore-most, we hope to revive a moribund but critical dialogue among educators and between educators and com-munities. Ends and means are inseparable; talking phil-osophy is vital, nowhere more clearly than in the rela-tionship between the means we use to manage classrooms and children and the purposes we expect schools to serve. Our concern is to raise the social, moral, ethical, and

political issues that inevitably lie at the heart of every
management decision, issues that are sedulously ignored by most contemporary "models" of classroom
management and student discipline. We hope through
this volume to restore a dialogue regarding classroom
management that moves beyond the current tendency to
ask merely, "What works?" The question is never, "What
works?"—all manner of barbarity works, if the end is
orderliness alone. The question is, what works to assure
the sorts of civility and dignity that is essential in the
short term for effective learning, and vital in the long run
for democratic life? Our intention in this volume is to engage an inquiry into the ethical foundations of classroom
discipline and management.

The book's second purpose is to begin to suggest the
sort of research that is needed if this critical dialogue is
to flourish. Surprisingly, given the centrality of discipline
and management to classroom life, there is little research
that focuses specifically on discipline and management.
We have hundreds of studies of classroom life, of
curriculum, pedagogy, and nearly all other aspects of
schooling, yet very few ask penetrating questions about
how classrooms are orchestrated or inquire into the ends
served by various disciplinary means. Only by reading
between the lines, capturing the fleeting, uncertain
reflection of discipline as it appears in studies aimed at
other ends, do we gain insight into the varied modes of
discipline and management. We offer chapters drawing
from several research traditions, not as definitive studies,
but as suggestions of a few of the many leads this inquiry
might pursue. My observations, claims, and arguments
in this introduction need to be turned into research questions and explored through a variety of means.

Third, as a specific contribution to a revitalized dialogue, the volume builds a case against the modes of
discipline and management that have become the mainstream practices. Grounding our case in the fundamental
premise that, above all other ends, public education
exists to preserve and promote democratic social and

political life, the volume asserts that contemporary mainstream modes of classroom orchestration and student discipline are morally, ethically, and politically obtuse. In place of such bankrupt disciplinary regimes, we argue for a critical constructivist approach to classroom relationships, what we refer to as a curriculum of democratic civility. We offer one example of a curriculum of democratic civility to exemplify our argument, though we are certain that if educators and communities can create a rich, reflective, intelligent, and ethical dialogue about curricula of civility, many other approaches are possible.[1]

Classroom discipline is not a simple matter of one technique or technology versus another. Through classroom discipline, teachers enact social and moral relationships. The form of management enacted promotes particular social, moral, and political ends, usually unconsciously and unintentionally, but no less effectively. In any society, the ends promoted matter. What we seek through this volume is to promote school practices that in all their manifestations, from achieving competence in subject matter to achieving competence in ethical behavior, prepare young people for informed, reflective, responsible participation in the social and political life of a democratic society.

I referred above to mainstream disciplinary practices. Some of the contributors to the volume use similar language. By contemporary or mainstream discipline, we refer to modes of discipline and management dominated by practices derived from behaviorist dogma, practices dictated by bureaucratic routine, and practices characterized by teachers' "bags of tricks." We examine the contradictions between the results of behaviorist disciplinary training and the requirements for democratic citizenship. We explore the ways in which the bureaucratic disciplinary apparatus of structures and procedures, as well as "teachers' tricks," preclude questions regarding the ethical, moral, social, and political issues at the heart of daily classroom life, and lead teachers to rely on punishments, rewards, and other classroom bargains.

Mainstream discipline practices, we assert, may achieve a modicum of order, but they subvert intellectual growth, moral maturity, and democratic potential.

We argue further that some currently popular disciplinary techniques that appear to be constructivist share the same ethical and political problems as the more behaviorist models. For example, while elements of the work of William Glasser provide valuable guidance, at heart the program promoted by Glasser's Control Theory and his Quality Schools share many of the problems of other mainstream programs.[2] Mainstream discipline gains student compliance through threats or rewards; Glasser achieves compliance by cajoling. Both approaches theorize the learner as one to be manipulated rather than one capable of rational understanding. Glasser's higher moral claim rests on a reduction of coercion, yet the process of cajoling is only moderately less coercive, and no less reliant on irrationality, than gaining compliance through threats and bribery.

Glasser is, after all, a behaviorist at heart; he simply moves the source of behavior from external stimulus-response to internal stimulus-response, making his five basic needs the stimulus. No less than other mainstream modes of discipline, he ignores not only issues of democratic community and justice, but also issues of spirit. For a Glasserian, there can logically be no consideration of the morality of any particular conduct. One is simply a set of behaviors; which behaviors are called forth depends upon the degree to which one's basic needs are being met.

In a variety of ways, the authors here are attempting to point toward a curriculum of democratic civility based upon a critical constructivist approach to discipline and management. Constructivism holds that the most powerful learning arises in situations in which learners actively and intentionally "construct meaning" for themselves. It conceives learning as a participatory rather than passive activity; it relies on conscious, reflective efforts on the part of the learner.

A "pure" constructivism is always in danger of collapsing into radical possessive individualism when it deals with issues of society, power, and privilege, however. A critical constructivism provides constructivism with a moral core. Critical constructivism asks the learner to construct social meaning with careful regard for the common good and for democratic values. A constructivist discipline seeks to promote self-disciplined behavior by encouraging the learner to engage cognitively with her behavior to move beyond irrational actions; a critical constructivist discipline seeks to promote socially responsible behavior by encouraging the learner to engage cognitively with her behavior in regard to communal needs, moral imperatives, and democratic norms. A critical constructivist curriculum of democratic civility is vital, we believe, if public schools are to reclaim their long-neglected potential for democratic renewal.[3]

A variety of forces have led to our current subservience to mainstream disciplinary regimes. Among other things, university-based teacher education has largely abandoned the task of insisting that teachers and administrators reflect seriously and continuously on means and ends, preferring the more "measurable," and thus presumably more "scientific," task of training educators for schools as they exist. And schools-as-they-exist demand order and hold threats and promises of rewards over teachers to assure order. It is little wonder that teachers reproduce a disciplinary regime that is imposed upon them, particularly absent a professional preparation that intentionally prepared them with the skills to question ends and means, and a moral preparation that spoke a language of hope, courage, and commitment.[4]

Just as industrial processes continually deskill and reskill workers as a means to extend greater control over productive processes, teaching is being deskilled and reskilled in the interest of greater control over learning. As publishers, state departments of education, and business groups gain control over the deployment of curricular and pedagogical skills, "these skills are replaced by techniques for better controlling students."[5] The class-room management industry provides the packaged, teacher-proof techniques and technologies of control, presumably offering teachers greater efficacy, but in reality diminishing further the moral and political space teachers require to pursue their craft conscientiously.

The real sources of our subservience, however, lie outside the institutions of learning. The United States, along with much of the rest of the world, is being thrust headlong into a manufactured culture that in all of its primary social and technical relationships, from work to consumption to politics, is ruled not by democratic principles but by behaviorist technologies of control and manipulation. The behaviorists' preoccupation with the means to compel behaviors and their indifference to questions of purpose fit well with the demands of such a culture.[6] Contemporary behaviorist discipline and management regimes coolly reproduce and reinforce the technical, mechanistic relationships of contemporary technological production. The dominant modes of control arising from a market economy elevate efficiency, predictability and order to the status of virtues. Relationships, spirit, democracy, resistance, emotions, and other expressions of human volition and essence are consistently subordinated to the inexorable logic of the machine. Functioning at its best, the contemporary school, reinforced by mainstream disciplinary modes, will serve admirably to socialize the next generation to the brave new world emerging from the international economy.

The management of behavior—in contrast to a curriculum of democratic civility—deflects students and teachers from practicing the intellectual and moral skills and propensities requisite to a future as members of a democratic society. Those skills and propensities include authentic and frequent opportunities to debate issues of principle and justice, to become comfortable with argument, disagreement and conflict, to test competing truth claims, and to engage in moral inquiry. Mainstream modes of discipline and management abort those skills and propensities, instilling in their place passivity, irrationality, and a tolerance for manipulation.

Behaviorist and bureaucratic disciplinary regimes legitimate a morality of omniscient authority removed from accountability. Such authority generates resistances among the inmates of schools, yet it blunts the possibility of students practicing socially acceptable or politically responsible challenges to illegitimate authority, the quintessence of democratic life. Few acceptable lessons in justice, community, or compassion are likely to flourish under such regimes.

For these and many other reasons, contemporary modes of discipline are contradictory to the democratic ends of education. They are also internally contradictory. That is, contemporary classroom management takes lack of motivation and need for control as givens, never asking why motivation and behavior are problematic. There is virtually no such thing as an unmotivated four year old; young children are voracious learners. Yet the schools are full of unmotivated ten and twelve-year-olds. The death of voracious learning may, of course, result from natural, genetic processes that drain a child of a desire to learn, though we have little evidence of such a self-defeating genetic propensity. More likely, modern life has constructed children's lives in such a way that self-motivation is suffocated. Schools treat children much as wage labor systems treat workers, denying them control over the pace, direction and quality of their own learning, rationalizing and technicizing the processes of learning, and treating children like expendable factors of production. When the treatment of children as alienated labor power, or, alternatively, as raw material, results in boredom and submerged forms of rebellion, schools respond to the behavior, not to the causes, and respond to it in precisely the way the dominant form of labor mobilization responds to the behavior of workers—with threats and promises.

Mainstream modes of classroom discipline also appear to be counterproductive in the long term, even if we judge them only on their ability to maintain effective control and promote academic learning. While more research is needed, it appears that elementary schools have increasingly adopted behaviorist modes of control, with the result that secondary schools have been forced by students to move more and more toward what Linda M. McNeil and others have termed "defensive teaching." Apparently, what children learn under the discipline of behavioral manipulation is *not* how to behave as informed, reflective, responsible participants in the learning community of the school. Rather, they learn, through constant observation of the actions of adults in schools, to manipulate in their own turn. Through passive resistance, implicit negotiation, classroom bargains, and group sanctions, secondary students show the same contempt for reflection and cognitive growth that was modeled for them by teachers in elementary school classrooms that sought to manage rather than educate in the domain of civility. Behaviorist modes of control lose their effectiveness through overuse, in other words, leaving secondary teachers little recourse but to teach defensively, to "choose to simplify content and reduce demands on students in return for classroom order and minimal student compliance on assignments."[7]

The question facing educators and citizens in democratic societies is not the technical question, "How do we achieve continued economic growth?" but the moral question, "How do we encourage human growth in the face of inhumane technologies of control?" Similarly, the question posed by most classroom management texts is the wrong question. The issue is not, "How might one best attain and maintain classroom control?" The question is, "Toward what ends?" What sort of adults do we hope will emerge from the schooling we provide, not merely through the knowledge and skills we impart in the explicit curriculum, but perhaps more powerfully through the personalities, predelections, aspirations, and emotions we nurture through the implicit curriculum of the classroom's human relationships? Hierarchical relationships fostered through manipulation, humiliation, bribes, distance, and the primacy of technique and procedure stand an excellent chance of producing precisely the workers inured to "the logic of technical control," in Michael Apple's haunting phrase,[8] that the "competitive world order" demands. By their very nature, however, they will as certainly accelerate the anomie, despair, anger, incivility, narcissism, and irrationality that threaten the nation today.

We have forgotten, at our great peril, that the teaching of discipline, like all other aspects of teaching, is fundamentally moral, not technical, yet we reduce the moral process of teaching children to live disciplined lives, to a technical process of gaining control over children and classrooms.[9] Just as children do not enter the world knowledgeable about history, literature, or science, they also "do not enter the world compassionate, caring, fair, loving, and tolerant. . . . Rather, moral qualities are learned—acquired in the course of lived experience."[10] Yet moral qualities are not apt to be learned with any particular efficacy through techniques which are themselves of dubious moral value—manipulation, cajolery, punishment, bribery, and the other technical means advocated by advocates of "teacher tricks" or behaviorist approaches. Moral qualities are learned through models of moral action and moral reflection, through homilies and maxims, and through opportunities to imitate—and occasionally fail at—moral action. Classroom control rooted in moral principles requires justice, compassion, diligence, honesty, generosity, civility, tolerance, and forgiveness. What is enacted in many settings, however, is compassionless procedural justice, indignity, competitiveness, stinginess, impatience, and intolerance. The moral lessons that children learn from such settings should unnerve us.

Classroom discipline is inevitably a moral endeavor. It inevitably has an impact upon the moral development of children. Yet clearly the *form* of the discipline carries as much or more weight as the *content*. Forms of classroom discipline that do not promote, or perhaps even discourage, reflection on moral action may result in a tendency to behave "appropriately," but they are unlikely to result in moral development. Morality, in other words, does not arise simply from achieving "appropriate" behavior from young people. Domestic animals can be trained to behave appropriately, yet we do not refer to animals as behaving morally when they refrain from inappropriate behavior. To be moral behavior, the behavior must include reflection and cognition.[11]

That demands, in turn, that the "curriculum" that teaches discipline—the curriculum of civility—provide ample opportunities for reflection, cognition, and the practice of moral behavior. Classroom discipline that strives for moral development must give children "the latitude and flexibility to try actions based on new or different ideas, to assess the consequences of these actions, to ponder the goodness and rightness of what they are doing or contemplating doing, and to jointly reflect on their thought and action in concert with other students and teachers."[12] Modes of classroom discipline that subvert such processes of moral action and reflection are unacceptable in a moral society.

Mainstream management assumes that children are incapable of rationality, and must be controlled through various forms of enticement and manipulation. Constructivist discipline assumes that if children are capable of rationally mastering the complexities of language, symbols, and academic concepts, they are equally capable of rationally mastering the intricacies of responsible behavior. Barbara McEwan underlines the curious contradiction in schools today, the contradiction between, on the one hand, an emphasis in the academic curriculum on cognitive processes, reasoning, critical thinking, and reflection, all leavened with multiple pedagogical approaches reflecting greater sensitivity to differing learning styles and multiple intelligences, and, on the other hand, an emphasis in the behavior curriculum on non-cognitive stimulus-response processes, unreasoning obedience, unreflective docility, all delivered with no acknowledgement of differences in social background, learning styles, or intelligences.

In other words, all good teachers instruct, assess and reteach, using multiple approaches, in order to assist students to master the academic curriculum. We would have no confidence in the teacher who merely demanded mastery without instruction, assessment, and reteaching. Yet that same teacher is likely to simply demand particular behaviors, to engage in no assessment directed toward remediating flawed learning regarding socially responsible behavior, and to pose harsher demands when students fail to behave as demanded. In my experience in classrooms, that teacher is likely to react to a failure to learn the lessons in behavior by punishing. Teachers understand that students *do not know* the curricular material the teachers are presenting; they *expect* to teach facts, concepts, skills, and perceptions. Oddly, however, they expect that students do know the arcane skills, expectations, facts, concepts and perceptions of classroom life, the curriculum of behavior. They seek to *teach* academics through a variety of cognitive approaches, carefully monitoring, assessing, and instructing; but they make no effort to *teach* behavior. They expect that *announcing* a series of rules and consequences will result in mastery of the facts, concepts, skills, attitudes, and perceptions requisite to appropriate behavior.

That is the message that Lisa Delpit makes clear in her important work—that the curriculum of power, in her words, or the curriculum of civility or the curriculum of behavior, in my words, is a curriculum, and it needs instruction in precisely the same way that mastering math or gaining literacy or learning the tuba needs instruction.[13] While an occasional student masters math almost "naturally," or learns to read with virtually no conscious instruction, or takes to music effortlessly, most of us do not; similarly, while it often appears that many children know "right from wrong" naturally, the fact of the matter is that they have gained instruction that not all children gain.

Thus a constructivist discipline has the virtue of consistency. It extends the presumption of rationality to all aspects of educational life. It mobilizes pedagogical skills to solve the puzzle of social living just as they are mobilized to solve the puzzle of intellectual life. But this need not simply be consistency for the sake of consistency. In fact, findings from neurobiology also argue for cognitive, constructivist disciplinary practices. We now know that the mind is not a simple "blank slate" or empty vessel to be filled, nor an analogue to the digital computer, fixed at birth with set characteristics and capabilities. On the contrary, the mind constructs itself in response to external stimuli throughout our lives. Cognitive events that encourage reflection and connection-making promote mental growth and intellectual power; non-cognitive events—those that create fear, anxiety, or humiliation, or those that encourage unreflective, automatic responses—exert negative effects on mental growth. Thus, the choices we make as educators are not merely matters of taste, but deeply moral and ethical issues connected to the very capacity of minds to sustain democratic traditions and possibilities.

Public school teachers are often skeptical of calls such as ours to fundamentally alter their classrooms. They have heard too often from scholars and reformers claiming to have found the alchemy to perfection. Most of the authors of these chapters have been teachers; most of us currently work closely with teachers every day. We are mindful of the enormous difficulties posed by current social and political conditions as they work themselves out in schools—chronically overcrowded classrooms, particularly in districts serving children with the greatest needs; inclusiveness run amok; declining social civility, imported daily from adult communities into schoolhouses; a curriculum prone to fadism, subject to political whim, and overcrowded with non-academic, often anti-intellectual requirements.

Teachers are legitimately concerned to maintain basic order. They know full well that there is no learning in a disorderly classroom. Until they can be sure that change will not result in disorder, they will rely on what has achieved order in the past, if very imperfectly. They have just cause to fear that principals and other authorities will evaluate them negatively if their classrooms do not conform to the authority's notion of order.

It is important to note, then, that we are not calling for chaotic classrooms or a return to permissiveness. We all agree that social order is essential. The issue is not order versus chaos, though that is what *appears* to be the case when we criticize current discipline practices. The issue is which *route* to order achieves real learning, and which achieves only overt behaviors? Which sort of order leads to what sorts of learning about civility, self, community, and dignity? Which means comprise a curriculum of democratic civility, and which constitute a program of authoritarianism? Which is more likely to promote democratic social relations, and which is more likely to achieve the pacification and containment of children? Those are the central questions facing educators and schools.

We learn what we live. *Classroom Discipline in American Schools* calls on teachers and citizens to create classrooms and schoolhouses in which young people live a curriculum of democratic civility at the same time they are learning the curricula of intellectual and emotional mastery. It is our hope that through such classrooms and schoolhouses, young people will learn the life skills of leading courageous, just, committed, vibrant, democratic lives.

Notes

1. I have been able to identify only two curricula of democratic civility, or discipline frameworks, that are critical constructivist in orientation: see Alfred S. Alschuler, *School Discipline: A Socially Literate Solution* (New York: McGraw-Hill Book Company, 1980); and Forrest Gathercoal, *Judicious Discipline*, 3rd ed. (San Francisco: Caddo Gap Press, 1993).

The contrasting approaches of the two, a Freirian orientation versus a procedural justice orientation, only hint at the range of possibilities for a truly educational mode of classroom management. A third, Alfie Kohn, *Beyond Discipline: From Compliance to Community* (Alexandria, VA: Association for Supervision and Curriculum Development, 1996), while thin as a programmatic framework, and lacking political coherence, does rest on a constructivist foundation and raises excellent questions regarding mainstream practices.

2. William Glasser, *Schools without Failure* (New York: Harper and Row, 1969); Glasser, *Control Theory in the Classroom* (New York: Harper and Row, 1986).

3. On democratic renewal, as well as the multiple sources of the erosion of democratic skills and commitments, see especially Robert N. Bellah, et al., *The Good Society* (New York: Alfred A. Knopf, 1991).

4. Among other sources, see especially Daniel P. Liston and Kenneth M. Zeichner, *Teacher Education and the Social Conditions of Schooling* (New York: Routledge, 1991); Dennis Carlson, *Teachers and Crisis: Urban School Reform and Teachers' Work Culture* (New York: Routledge, 1992); and Linda M. McNeil, *Contradictions of Control: School Structure and School Knowledge* (New York: Routledge, 1986).

5. Michael W. Apple, *Education and Power* (Boston: Routledge and Kegan Paul, 1982), pp. 146–47.

6. Behaviorism traces its roots primarily to the work of B.F. Skinner, particularly *Walden Two* (New York: Macmillan Co., 1948). Among other critiques of Skinner, see Wilbur J. McKeachie, "The Decline and Fall of the Laws of Learning," *Educational Researcher* (March 1974): 7–11; and Edward G. Rozycki, "Reconsideration," *Educational Studies* 26 (spring/summer 1995): 11–22.

7. McNeil, *Contradictions of Control,* p. 158; see also Theodore Sizer, *Horace's Compromise: The Dilemma of the American High School* (New York: Houghton Mifflin, 1984); Arthur G. Powell, Eleanor Farrar, and David K. Cohen, *The Shopping Mall High School: Winners and Losers in the Educational Marketplace* (Boston: Houghton Mifflin, 1985); Michael Sedlak, et al. *Selling Students Short: Classroom Bargains and*

Academic Reform in the American High School (New York: Teachers College Press, 1986); Ralph W. Larkin, *Suburban Youth in Cultural Crisis* (New York: Oxford University Press, 1979); Robert B. Everhart, "Classroom Management, Student Opposition, and the Labor Process," in Michael W. Apple and Lois Weis, eds., *Ideology and Practice in Schooling* (Philadelphia: Temple University Press, 1983), pp. 169–192.

8. Apple, *Education and Power*; see also Apple, *Teachers and Texts: A Political Economy of Class and Gender Relations in Education* (Boston: Routledge and Kegan Paul, 1986).

9. My discussion of the moral implications of classroom discipline should not be read as an endorsement of the repressive claims to moral superiority or moral absolutism found in the New Right, or the efforts to resuscitate class-bound notions of "virtue." My thinking has been broadly informed by David E. Purpel, *The Moral and Spiritual Crisis in Education: A Curriculum for Justice and Compassion in Education* (Granby, MA: Bergin & Garvey, 1989); and James Q. Wilson, *The Moral Sense* (New York: Free Press, 1993).

10. Gary D. Fenstermacher, "Some Moral Considerations on Teaching as a Profession," in John I. Goodlad, Roger Soder, and Kenneth A. Sirotnik, eds., *The Moral Dimensions of Teaching* (San Francisco: Jossey-Bass Publishers, 1990), p. 132.

11. Fenstermacher, p. 135; see also Steven Selden, "Character Education and the Triumph of Technique," *Issues in Education* 4 (winter 1986): 301–12.

12. Fenstermacher, 135; see also Walter Feinberg, "The Moral Responsibility of Public Schools," in John I. Goodlad, Roger Soder, and Kenneth A. Sirotnik, eds., *The Moral Dimensions of Teaching* (San Francisco: Jossey-Bass Publishers, 1990), pp. 155–87.

13. Lisa Delpit, *Other People's Children: Cultural Conflict in the Classroom* (New York: New Press, 1995), esp. pp. 21–47.

Part I

Historical and Political Perspectives on Classroom Management

Absent from virtually all contemporary discussion of classroom management is the larger context—classroom management's own historical development, its meaning at various times and particularly its meaning today, and comparisons across time and space. Without that context, we understand too little of what it means to "manage" children in one way rather than other ways, yet advocates of various disciplinary regimes, and the few researchers who have seriously studied classroom management, have been content to ignore context and meaning.

The chapters in Part I introduce context. Each takes a different perspective, one historical, the other political, both examining aspects of intersecting economic and social contexts. They both argue, implicitly, that any mode of classroom management ultimately teaches much more than orderliness. Educators must attend carefully to the other lessons and messages, selecting those modes of discipline that achieve the order and civility necessary for teaching and learning while simultaneously reaching ends worthy of the best traditions of public schools, not merely those that achieve short-term control.

There is far more to context than just history and politics, however. As with all other parts of this volume, our intention is not to be exhaustive but suggestive, to open a conversation, not to shut it down. Our historical inquiry needs to be leavened with evidence from social history and closer attention to the fascinating alternatives that have flourished at various times. Our political perspective needs to attend to parallel analyses of other modes of discipline beyond those comprehended here. While we provide comparisons across time, the volume lacks the essential comparisons across space—evidence from other cultures and nations, understood culturally and politically, as well as educationally. These chapters invite anthropologists, sociologists, historians, and critical theorists to examine classroom discipline and management as closely as they have heretofore examined curriculum, administration, reform, pedagogy, and learning, for the matrix of management and discipline decisions, structures, and processes teach as much, if not more, and teach as powerfully, if not more powerfully, as any aspect of formal education.

1

Punishments, Penalties, Prizes, and Procedures: A History of Discipline in U.S. Schools

❏

Ronald E. Butchart

The entrepreneurs and academics who make their livings selling various approaches to classroom management and student discipline appear to have little interest in the history of their field. In nearly two centuries, they have published hundreds of handbooks, manuals, textbooks, and, more recently, video packages and other resources, intended to allay the discipline concerns of classroom teachers. Virtually none of them have engaged in sustained reflection on the sorts of management efforts that preceded their own. Most appeal to various teacher fears of unruly children, disorder or chaos, against which to contrast a peaceable future achievable primarily through one unique package or another.[1]

Their rhetorical strategy implies, usually quite indirectly, that there *is* a history to school discipline, but that the past was generally unenlightened compared to the strategies being touted, and certainly not worth rehearsing. At best, these writers may refer to the relatively recent past, occasionally referring to Skinner, either in praise or condemnation. The literature almost never considers earlier efforts to organize classroom life and to deal with social relations in schools.

That historical silence is curious on a number of grounds, not least of all because there has been a penchant until recent years for educators to compose laudatory histories that traced inexorable progress and improvement in educational governance, curriculum, pedagogy, student achievement, and human enlightenment.[2] That sort of "progressive" history has fallen on hard times recently, of course. Yet even before its demise, the legions of writers on school discipline were silent about their own history. More saliently, academic tradition demands historical reflection as part of a field's efforts to move ahead. Curriculum, school psychology, teacher education, administration, pedagogy, even the individual academic disciplines, each have a history that may be as contested as the substance of the field itself, but that still constitutes an essential context within which to understand problems and press for better solutions.[3] Those who speak of classroom management, however, are either ignorant of their historical context, or prefer not to share it with those to whom they speak.

Yet understanding the history of classroom management[4] is essential, not only for its intrinsic interest, nor just to avoid repeating the past. It is essential to move the field of classroom management from the arena of cheap huckstering and sloganeering to serious inquiry into the inevitable moral and political considerations implicated in every discipline decision. More importantly—since academic "fields" are worth little to teachers unless they contribute to better schools—some historical perspective is essential as teachers and schools struggle to improve.

Be forewarned, though. The history of discipline in schools does not indicate unambiguously which practices "work." Most practices work splendidly in one setting or another; most fail with nearly as much certainty in other places or times. Moreover, *what works?* is not the first question—works to achieve *what ends?* and *with what consequences?* are more salient, though we have time here to do little more than nod in their direction. Rather than easy "lessons" about programmatic failure or success, the story of classroom discipline uncovers assumptions, forces, institutional practices, professional habits, and cultural blinders at work in the choices made by schools and teachers. This history may provide guidance into the sorts of questions that must be asked; it will not provide convenient answers.

Pressed to describe the general outlines of a history of classroom discipline, many of us would probably point toward the decline in the use of corporal punishment in schools as a key organizing principle. We might not agree on a chronology for that decline, though most would place the process in quite recent years. In the popular imagination, and in the minds of some politicians, the disappearance of the rod is lamentable. Schools were safer, more orderly places with more learning going on when teachers ruled with the ferule or the paddle, according to common wisdom.

Yet the movement to abandon force in school discipline long antedates the twin whipping boys of modernism and progressive education. Successful efforts to limit corporal punishment date back to the 1820s and 1830s, led by conservative reformers who invoked the struggle for virtue as their primary justification. By the last quarter of the nineteenth century, some urban schools had banned corporal punishment entirely, and where it was not banned outright it had usually fallen into disrepute in urban districts.[5]

The question of corporal punishment seems to largely define the issue of school discipline, not only among the general public, but even in the slender literature on school discipline.[6] Imagining corporal punishment as the sum of classroom discipline is inadequate, however, and focuses our attention in the wrong direction.

This chapter will document a number of changes in classroom discipline. We will examine the various disciplinary doctrines that have commanded allegiance at various times, taking particular note of the contrasting constructions of authority within those doctrines, the ways educators and schools shaped and deployed disciplinary power at various crisis points, and the social forces at work in remaking disciplinary practice. We will attend as well to the slow accretion of what I shall call here disciplinary structures, intended to make order more predictable and efficient, but resulting ultimately in reduced teacher authority and institutional paralysis. Practices have changed. Their sources have changed. What has not changed is the peculiar irony of classroom discipline in U.S. education: Educators' longstanding mistrust of education itself as a means to achieve discipline. American schools long ago abandoned the foolishness of beatings, threats, and other non-cognitive means to achieve competence in literacy or understanding and insight in content areas, yet they routinely rely on punishment, penalties, prizes, and elaborate procedures to assure competence in civility or understanding and insight into the common good.

Nearly a century ago, Joseph S. Taylor provided one of the only exceptions to my observation that writers on classroom management pay no attention to history. His *Art of Class Management and Discipline* provides, in a dozen pages, a survey of management reaching from early Greek history to the turn of the twentieth century.[7] We shall be a good deal more modest, beginning with what might be called, by the end of the U.S. colonial period, traditional schooling.

Traditional schooling hinged on face-to-face encounters. School masters called upon individual students, or small groups of students, to recite lessons to which they had been assigned. During individual recitations, the rest of the school whiled away the time, in study or otherwise. The masters, maintaining haphazard surveillance while attending to recitations, relied on force and fear alone to maintain order, punish misbehavior, correct errors in lessons, and pass on to their charges an idea of the moral order of their society.[8]

The moral order in which such schools had been conceived was hierarchical and ascriptive, each strata holding absolute right over its social inferiors, including the right to remind them of their inferiority through physical violence. Notions of honor (and its inverse, shame) gave the society its moral core. Honor was a scarce commodity, meted out stingily by one's superiors. Authority and power were unambiguous and external, residing in the king and the nobility, and delegated through them to patriarchs in their families, and to masters, whether guild masters, slave masters, or school masters. The schoolhouse and the school master exemplified the moral order in terrifying relief to the children sent to them.[9]

That moral order was collapsing by the turn of the nineteenth century, however. The Enlightenment, American republicanism, the market revolution of the eighteenth century, industrialism and other factors coalesced in the United States to fundamentally reform traditional schooling and bring it into conformity with an emerging moral order founded on dramatically altered social relations. Two related but distinct reforms began early in the 1800s.

The first reform, institutionalized swiftly in urban centers, was bureaucratic discipline. It was demonstrated most effectively in Joseph Lancaster's monitorial schools early in the century. In place of discipline flowing from external, personal, patriarchal authority, as in traditional teacher-student relationships, Lancaster developed and deployed a form of disciplinary power that transformed relationships between teacher and student. Lancasterian and other forms of bureaucratic discipline sought to create an internalized, impersonal, bureaucratic authority. Students were no longer in a face-to-face relationship with the master, but in a group relationship with monitors—more advanced pupils who held rank not by ascription but by bureaucratically measured merit. Surveillance was continuous and multiple; each monitor was responsible for teaching, examining, and overseeing the study of a small group of learners of roughly equal ability and attainment; the master and higher monitors, in turn, surveyed the monitors and multiple groups. Posture, carriage, and deportment was precisely prescribed and closely monitored to assure attention and efficiency.[10]

Lancaster proscribed corporal punishment. In place of fear, he stimulated motivation by an elaborate system of rewards, prizes, and promotions, including promotion into and within the ranks of the monitors, signified publicly by a badge and chain to be worn about the neck. Each class was ranked against all other classes, and seated as a class by rank; within each class, each pupil was ranked against other pupils in the class and seated within the class by rank. In place of personal, patriarchal violence to assure obedience, Lancaster substituted sanctioned, teacher-directed humiliation of miscreants by other students.[11]

Notably, Lancaster designed this form of disciplinary pedagogy only for the children of the new industrial poor. It provided not only a rudimentary literacy and numeracy, but what Lancaster was sure was a proper moral training for the lower orders of urban society. Older notions of authority, virtue, and social morality were falling away, victims of ideas and material forces moving Western society toward free labor, free markets, and free markets in labor. New forms of social discipline were forged in that fire; Lancaster reproduced them through a form of disciplinary pedagogy that encouraged an internalized authority reinforced by omnipresent surveillance and examination, and that conceived of social relationships as competitive, zero-sum, and constantly reconstructed. If his reliance on public humiliation harked back to the shaming culture of a previous era, he simultaneously made all participants complicit in reaping the rewards of surveillance and reinforced the need for internalized vigilance.[12]

In other words, just as traditional discipline and classroom practices reflected a larger moral order, so Lancaster modeled for poor children aspects of the emerging moral order, and prepared them to participate in its birth. It was an order in which a modicum of mobility was available to the diligent and fortunate, but in which failure in the race

for position carried great psychic and material consequences—and those who succeeded did so at the expense
of those who failed.[13]

Lancaster devised a disciplinary pedagogy that
altered the nature and locus of authority and the angle
and frequency of surveillance, but that also embedded
new and elaborated disciplinary technologies in structures, procedures, rituals, and processes. Some of the
resulting disciplinary structures are obvious—the uses of
monitors to assure constant surveillance and application
on the part of the pupils; a reward system to embed
motivation in the processes rather than in the teacher,
his pedagogy, or the student's interests; the intricate
regulations and procedures to absorb energy and
channel activity. Other structures—particularly those we
have subsequently inherited and thus do not even notice
about us—are less obvious but just as important in the
elaborating and embedding of disciplinary structures.
These include continuous competitive, normative examinations and promotions, and the meritocratic structure
of the school, its classes, and its reward system.

Monitorial schools fell into disrepute in the second
quarter of the nineteenth century, yet, as we shall see,
central features of bureaucratic discipline remained and
were institutionalized in most nineteenth-century schools.
However, the movement to bureaucratic, non-monitorial
schools was mediated by the second reform in school
relationships.

The second reform began simultaneously with the
first American Lancasterian schools, but received its
articulation from a much broader range of reformers, and
took root more slowly and more permanently. Referred to
alternatively in historical literature as "soft pedagogy" or
"New England pedagogy," this reform was also a response
to deep structural transformations of the moral order, but
it came from and was more in tune with the aspirations
and anxieties of middle-class Protestant reformers.[14]

Like Lancasterian education, New England pedagogy
sought to instill an internalized authority. But the process

and nature of that internalization of authority differed markedly from Lancaster's formula. Rejecting external authority based on fear, but also rejecting an internalized authority based on impersonal bureaucratic surveillance, conservative Protestant reformers championed deeply personal, individualized relationships built upon emotionally intense, sentimentalized affection. Rather than an internalized authority built on an omnipresent surveilling other, these reformers devised a disciplinary pedagogy that constructed authority on emotional ties, guilt, and an interiorized self-surveillance. This "affectionate authority," like Lancaster's impersonal authority, was non-rational and was intended to generate automatic obedience responses, but whereas Lancasterian disciplinary pedagogy taught a possessive individualism responsive to external, market-driven cues, New England disciplinary pedagogy taught what David Hogan refers to as "affective individualism," responsive to internal cues codified as "conscience."[15]

We recognize features of this reform, for the reform successfully transformed both schools and families in the nineteenth century, casting them into forms that linger, at least in nostalgia, even today. The reform provided the moral and intellectual armament that overthrew Lancasterianism before mid-century. Its tenets infused nineteenth-century fiction, domestic advice, and reform literature. The ideal school, like the ideal family, exhibited love, affection, and deep emotional dependence upon the authority figure. The will was to be disciplined not by fear of pain, but by the fear of withdrawal of affection and withholding of love, and by expressions of disappointment in the miscreant.[16]

New England disciplinary pedagogy, then, reconstituted the teacher as an object of affection and sentimental veneration, a process facilitated by, and accelerating, the feminization of teaching. It rejected corporal punishment in schools except for exceptional situations, which often meant reserving it for the correction of working-class children whose home life presumably failed to prepare them for a gentler discipline. But it rejected as well bureaucratic discipline's reliance on emulation,[17] something that, to these reformers, smacked of an appeal to avarice, immodest personal advancement, and other base motives. In place of emulation and physical force, the reformers constructed a disciplinary pedagogy intended to "engage the interests of children by transforming learning into a pleasurable activity." They sought, in other words, to replace extrinsic with intrinsic motivation, the expansion of desire with the amplification of pleasure.[18] Simultaneously, conscience was mobilized; obedience and application became moral duties owed to the affectionate authority, and pleasure was to be gained through the satisfaction of duty.[19]

In both affectional discipline and bureaucratic discipline, the presentation and mode of internalizing authority, the modes of motivating, and the means to manage the classroom were built into the pedagogical activity and self-presentation of the teacher; in other words, they were designed into the particular structure of the disciplinary pedagogy. Other aspects of classroom discipline were embedded in new disciplinary structures. For example, nineteenth-century schools moved toward small, self-contained, graded classrooms, closely regulated school rituals and practices, and systems of promotions, retentions and demotions, wherever population densities permitted. Teachers experimented with various precursors to the modern report card and systems of merits and demerits. Object teaching began to supersede recitations, allowing both more learning-by-doing, and introducing whole-class teaching. Textbook authors sought to prepare curricular material that presumably heightened children's intrinsic interest and at the same time extended the moralization of the conscience.[20]

Smaller classes following strictly regulated practices facilitated surveillance, of course, while simultaneously reincorporating surveillance in adult authority, not in other learners as was the case in monitorial schools. Similarly, declining reliance on recitation and increased whole-class instruction increased efficient surveillance. Promotions, demotions, systems of merits and demerits, and other tangible rewards or punishments removed a portion of the burden of motivation, whether by fear or other means, from the teacher to external structures and rituals. Meanwhile, the reformers' disciplinary doctrines calling for appeals to the learner's interests and pleasure in doing his duty were promoted by textbooks that dressed their moral and academic fare in a garb calculated to capture interest. Yet those same resources were designed to stimulate sentiment, not rational inquiry, to promote belief, not skepticism. Such emotional goals, as contrasted with intellectual goals, provided one more disciplinary structure of consequence in understanding nineteenth-century education.

Bureaucratic pedagogy emerged nearly fully formed in a very brief period. It was elaborated rapidly through many urban areas, then shed its monitorial aspects after the 1830s. New England pedagogy, on the other hand, emerged more slowly and unevenly. Throughout the century, and even well into the twentieth century, hybrids of traditional pedagogy, bureaucratic disciplinary pedagogy and New England disciplinary pedagogy coexisted, particularly in small, rural schools. Symbols of traditional external authority—switches, whips, and paddles—rested prominently on the desks or hung from the walls of the same teachers who taught in bureaucratized classrooms yet sought to nurture affectional authority.

Reformers advocating New England "soft pedagogy" were responding to the apparent threat to Christian morality and ethics posed by market revolutions, industrialism, and democracy. They were fearful of an erosion of communal values and the elevation of avarice, ambition, and materialism over temperance, modesty, frugality, self-denial, and spiritual values—the elevation of possessive individualism over affective individualism. They sought to build classrooms shorn of features of competitive marketplaces and the mechanical regularity of factories. They conceived their work as the construction of bulwarks and sea walls against the moral onslaught of industrial capitalism, even as many of them promoted and profited from its economic and political consequences.[21]

Yet while New England Protestant pedagogy has a higher profile in recent scholarship, bureaucratic pedagogy had the greater impact on nineteenth-century schools. Its adherents, themselves Protestants, and probably as often from New England as those associated with affectional discipline, did not share their competitors' conviction that Christian values and marketplace values were antithetical. On the contrary, the champions of bureaucratic discipline celebrated capitalism, industrialism, and markets as quintessentially Christian and as central agents of the civilizing project. The bitter fruits of capitalism, industrialism, and markets—poverty, unemployment, oppression, and dependency—were paradoxical evidence of their divine inspiration, according to these educators. Success in the market depended upon Christian virtue, and social or economic failure indicated directly and powerfully the degree to which a people, or individuals, had failed to master Christian virtue. Moreover, the greater the degree of a people's virtue, the greater their degree of civilization. The challenge, then, was to prepare people for success in the market as a means to virtue and civilization, and simultaneously to increase their virtue as a means to success in the market and an increase in their degree of civilization.

Working within that perspective, Samuel Chapman Armstrong and other educators devised and promoted an important variant on bureaucratic pedagogy in the last third of the nineteenth century. Armstrong, the founder of Hampton Institute and mentor to Booker T. Washington, designed racialized disciplinary structures and pedagogies intended specifically for African Americans in the southern states after the Civil War. Affectional authority was out of the question for such learners; it suggested a mutuality if not exactly an equality between teacher and students that was intolerable. Nor was the mere internalization of authority adequate. Armstrong argued that African Americans needed individual and group internalization of the authority of a paternalistic, superior race. Further, traditional classical education was inappropriate; the market required black labor trained to be industrious, virtuous, aware of its need for the "civilizing influences" of the white race, and for patience to allow the gradual processes of Christianizing and civilizing to work themselves out.[22]

The work of Armstrong and others in southern black industrial education, extended to Native American education and education on foreign mission fields, laid the foundations of one variant of later progressive disciplinary power to which we will turn momentarily. These educators abandoned affective authority, with its strong emotional bonds. In its place they set the authority of sacrificial racial paternalism, modeled daily in their embrace of benevolent self-denial as principals and presidents of segregated institutions. No less reliant on the inculcation of guilt and dependence than affective authority, sacrificial racial paternalism established a disciplinary distance between teacher and student—a racial gulf and the implication of a virtually unsatisfiable moral debt owed to those making the sacrifice. Sacrificial racial paternalism also justified and argued for boarding schools, so sure were white educators of the cultural backwardness and moral bankruptcy of the target populations. Boarding schools expanded surveillance into the private lives of students, extending disciplinary power to nearly twenty-four hours a day. The elaboration of an industrial curriculum, involving many hours a day in manual labor and physical activity rather than in intellectual activity requiring the mutual attention of student and teacher, freed teachers for further surveillance and moralization.[23]

The experiences with industrial education in the last quarter of the nineteenth century prefigured some of the changes in disciplinary power that would occur after the turn of the century. Unsettling changes in the civic order, in productive relationships, and in market relationships, rendered affectional authority and affective individualism increasingly anachronistic, and exposed rigid bureaucratic discipline as unwieldy and nakedly authoritarian. Mass society, corporate order, the triumph of science, and the shift from markets for capital goods to consumer markets, all militated against the prevailing forms of classroom discipline. Racialized industrial education had demonstrated the potential power of differentiated disciplinary regimes engineered for the different destinies of various races and classes.

Interestingly enough, virtually no one who has studied education in the Progressive Era has documented a progressive form of classroom discipline. Yet classroom management underwent important changes in the early Progressive years, resulting in new forms of disciplinary pedagogy and new disciplinary structures that remained intact into the mid-1950s, and that can be referred to as progressive discipline and management.

To begin with, progressive teachers constructed a new form of authority. Authority did not arise from a moral psychology of love and familial nurture, but from a professional psychology of expertise, detachment, scientific study, and a hierarchal professional-client relationship. This is not to suggest that genuine affection did not develop within progressive classrooms; it is to say that such responses were not central to the professional aspirations of teachers, as they had been to an earlier generation; it is to suggest further that, when they were at their professional best, teachers were expected to make a radical separation between their feelings for particular children and professional judgments, including judgments regarding classroom management.

More dramatically, broad changes in progressive pedagogy entailed broad changes in discipline. Progressive schools rapidly sloughed off what remained of recitation. Teaching more frequently involved groups and whole classes. At least in the ideal, progressive schools involved greater movement, self-direction, activity, and learning-by-doing.[24]

Progressive educators were certain that those pedagogical changes would not merely result in better learning, but also in better classroom control. They sought to embed discipline in instruction itself, not in paddles, affection, or bureaucratic classroom practices. Misbehavior, many believed, stemmed not from sinful and willful children, but from the unnatural expectations that inflexible classrooms imposed upon children—expectations for silence, stillness, extended attention to single tasks, and the general corking of youthful exuberance. What was required, then—almost all that was required, according to the more romantic progressive reformers— was to free the child from artificial restraints and to provide her with access to a curriculum that interested her. The New England reformers' earlier insistence upon student interest and pleasure, then, was married to less structured, more active classrooms to create a new disciplinary pedagogy.[25]

On the other hand, the triumph of science and technique and the consequent eclipsing of religion in society and in schools moved progressive disciplinary pedagogy away from the New England pedagogues' expectations. Gone was the overt moralizing of textbook and classroom lecture. Faith in science and technique altered other aspects of classroom practice as well. In place of the admonition to monitor children's moral health, progressive educators were admonished to monitor physical health, comfort, and well being.[26] Classroom management manuals after the turn of the century spent nearly as much time on being alert to correct ventilation, adequate and properly adjusted lighting, appropriately calibrated seating, and other factors that might contribute to fatigue and thus to misbehavior, as they did to the means for dealing with rebelliousness, certain as they were that rebelliousness could be contained with the right techniques. And while firmly rejecting the rigid, mechanistic routinization of classrooms as practiced under bureaucratic pedagogy, they made fetish of efficiency and routine in all classroom activities.[27]

Surveillance, then, shifted once again. Child-centered, activity-centered classrooms freed the teacher from constant instruction and thereby broadened her scope for surveillance, although among romantic reformers, the hope was that a pedagogy stressing the child's interest would virtually remove the necessity for more than cursory surveillance. Further, the ascendancy of science and technique over moral regard reduced dramatically the need for and focus of surveillance. Difficult and contested moral judgments were replaced with scientific, measurable, tractable technical judgments regarding ventilation, light, and posture—judgments that might easily be given over to appropriate technology when the time came, embedding disciplinary power even further into structures and away from the moral authority of teachers.

Even before those technologies were in place, however, progressive educators were busy embedding other forms of disciplinary power in proliferating structures. The rapid expansion of school administration extended disciplinary power over teachers themselves, for example. That meant, in turn, more surveillance of teachers, resulting often, paradoxically, in a focus primarily upon classroom management.[28]

Similarly, progressive education added school psychologists and counselors to burgeoning corporate-style school bureaucracies. That was particularly momentous in regard to classroom discipline, for psychologists and counselors introduced a therapeutic view of behavior and discipline, and thereby radically redefined the issues. The therapeutic view privileged expert psychological knowledge, redefined misbehavior as mental maladjustment, and called for therapeutic interventions and mental hygiene. The issue was no longer willfulness, disobedience, or misbehavior; the issue was not even justice, equity, or democratic forms of social life, a consistently marginalized discourse in classroom management; the issue was stress, anxiety, and frustration, and finding ways of removing them from a child's life. The child was to be neither disciplined nor given a measure of control over her life; she was simply to be understood and her environment engineered and adjusted. Unnoticed by most, the mental hygiene movement radically redefined education as personality adjustment, largely abandoning whatever potential it had as a site for mass intellectual training for democratic citizenship.[29]

Progressive educators also institutionalized standardized testing and linked it to ability grouping and to a differentiated curriculum. The effects on classroom disciplinary relationships have not been adequately addressed. Grouping by ability and, just as often, by class and race, structured the dynamics of classrooms and schoolhouses. The implicit devaluing of students and curriculum in the lower tracks, and the differential dignity meted out by presumably scientific test scores and track assignments, doubtlessly add measurably to classroom discipline problems. Standardized testing relieved industrial education of the moral ambiguity of sacrificial paternalistic discipline, replacing its foundation in contested moral assertions of race and class superiority with scientific evidence of the same, to the satisfaction of white scientists and educators, at least.[30] Of course, standardized tests and differentiated curriculum were used in more obviously disciplinary ways as well, providing a supposedly neutral, professional means of identifying the causes of discipline problems.

Disciplinary structures first introduced in the nineteenth century were extended and standardized in the twentieth century—report cards, age grading, promotion or retention, for example. New structures were added as well that carried new disciplinary power: Carnegie units; consolidated schools; the sanctioned extra-curriculum, with its requirements for adequate grades and deportment; and perhaps most far-reaching, enforceable compulsory attendance laws. Each affected classroom relationships and classroom management, adding layers of bureaucratic regularity and oversight over both teachers and students, extending the distance between youths and adults, and proliferating opportunities for both success and failure, with the heightened disciplinary problems fostered by the codification of failure.

Arguably, however, the central changes in classroom management happened "on the ground," in classrooms. There, as already noted, progressives advocated a more open, flexible pedagogy. Just as the object method altered instructional relationships in the nineteenth century, so the project method defined new classroom relationships in the Progressive Era. Children's self-directed absorption in projects webbed to an integrated curriculum was expected to command classroom activity. If omnipresent, affective and bureaucratic authority dominated the nineteenth-century school, a less intrusive, professional authority deployed through the project method was expected to guide the progressive school. The child was the center, not the teacher; the child's ends and interests, not the curriculum, defined the day.[31]

For progressives from the child-centered wing of progressivism, discipline was unproblematic; given freedom, discipline would flow automatically from the child's interest.[32] Child-centered progressives essentially abdicated responsibility for discipline. Social reconstructionist progressives, on the other hand, dissented from the radical individualism of the child-centered progressives. They predicted that child-centered schools would result in purposelessness and a consequent increase in disruptive behavior. They advocated classrooms structured around lessons in social responsibility and the nurture of a social consciousness. That presupposed particular forms of classroom management and organization. However, social reconstructionists were disinclined to describe the forms of classroom management that flowed from their preferred reforms. Too little pedagogical practice patterned clearly on social reconstructionist doctrines ever emerged to develop a tradition of social reconstructionist disciplinary pedagogy. As a result, child-centered, social efficiency, and mental hygiene practices and traditions dominated the progressive literature on classroom discipline and progressivism's embedded disciplinary structures.[33]

Child-centered progressive educators imagined the possibility of self-authority. However, they assumed that self-authority could blossom untutored and undirected. They ignored questions of the relationship between self and society, and minimized issues of impulse control and legitimate expectations of social responsibility. They abjured the unconscious internalization of authority, but structured a disciplinary regime incapable of encouraging the conscious, critical construction of a socially responsibly authority. In its purest form, child-centered progressivism encouraged an impulsive, narcissistic form of possessive individualism well adapted to the marketplace's appeal to impulse, irrational desire, and a concern for style over content.[34]

Social efficiency progressives, by contrast, retained major features of earlier traditions, seeking more efficient, scientific modes of inculcating unquestioning obedience to social authority, adopting a language and a moral base not dissimilar from the "effective practices" discourse popular in the 1980s and 1990s. Issues of social control, explicitly so labeled, dominated their efforts. For these educators, appropriate classroom management was not determined by moral or intellectual criteria, but rather was deduced from presumably scientific criteria. Whatever could be demonstrated to efficiently assure implicit, automatic obedience was to be practiced.[35]

Mental hygienists, who made up a significant phalanx of the social efficiency progressives, appear not to have theorized authority at all, though an implicit theory drove their work. Their therapeutic world view placed all authority in the hands of psychologically trained experts whose task was to measure, calibrate and adjust individuals and settings. Stress-free, conflict-free, frictionless lives, orchestrated by benign managers, required no personal authority whatsoever, it seems, whether internalized unconsciously or constructed and embraced consciously.[36]

In the end, progressivism mobilized disciplinary power in the interest of a particular constellation of emerging social values and imperatives rooted not in democratic values, nor in earlier moral imperatives, but in emerging marketplace and productive relationships. The new moral order of the twentieth century privileged the authority of a scientific rationality deployed in the material and ideological interests of business. Classroom discipline continued to promote the uncritical internalization of external authority, though both the nature of that authority and the modes of internalization, were transformed. Overt moralizing was largely abandoned, while the moral economy of bureaucratically rationalized, hierarchical productive relationships increasingly defined the daily life of classrooms and schoolhouses. As enormous social, political, and economic power coalesced in the hands of the wealthy and in corporations at the expense of small producers, labor, and democratic processes, the dominant tendencies in progressivism responded by presenting to children, through the discipline of the schools, a world shorn of conflict and power, one in which narcissistic self-expression, unlimited individual ambition, and expert adjustment of environments constituted the ends of modern life. At progressivism's heart lay the expectation or hope—illogical and unreasonable from spiritual, environmental, psychological, and many other perspectives, yet no less seductive for all of that—that the unlimited expansion of demand for material goods produced by labor with little stake in the productive process could create the good life.[37]

Left unrealized by progressivism was the possibility of creating and deploying a disciplinary power bent toward the realization of democratic ends. Dewey hinted at such a possibility, though he failed to articulate its outlines, satisfied, ultimately, merely to criticize the romantic excesses of the child-centered heresy.[38] A democratic notion of classroom discipline would seek self-authority leavened with a social consciousness. Where child-centered and mental hygiene tendencies in progressivism essentially renounced responsibility for any instruction, democratic discipline would, following Dewey, understand that the child must be educated, must be instructed, even more urgently under conditions of enervated community, where moral authority increasingly rests in market-driven social decisions and image-making. A democratic discipline, like democratic education, would reject manipulation and demands for blind obedience, seeking instead rational inquiry into morally and ethically defensible exercises of personal and social authority.

The collapse of progressivism into an inchoate post-progressivism left a confused, contradictory, and flawed disciplinary legacy. Progressivism had abandoned the claustrophobic, guilt-based discipline of New England pedagogy, but rejected also its implicit moral critique of possessive individualism and market relationships. Progressivism retained aspects of the mechanical moral transmission belt of bureaucratic pedagogy and discipline, though it obfuscated moral issues under the pretense of science, leaving post-progressivism ignorant of clear means to discuss and critique the politics of moral intentions. Discipline was removed from the contested arena of ethics and politics to the sanitized laboratory of technique and science.

The moral core of progressive discipline lay in technical relationships, the authority of science and expertise, and—at least with regard to the triumphant wings of progressivism—demands for obedience to the state, to elites, and to markets. At times, particularly within its more romantic traditions, progressivism abdicated disciplinary power, but more frequently it deployed disciplinary power in increasingly sedulous forms. In some settings, authority was expected to flower internally in the absence of restraint and purpose, but more frequently authority remained external, to be internalized unconsciously through the operation of elaborated structures, rituals, and experts, beyond the grasp and critique of teachers and learners alike. Surveillance was broadened, rationalized and systematized, yet in the process it became increasingly diffuse and emptied of much of its disciplinary power.

The last four decades mark a watershed in the history of classroom discipline.[39] Prior to this period, educators invariably linked concerns for classroom behavior with visions of the larger social order. However classroom order might be constituted, writers explicitly held that such order was of benefit to the child, to the teacher, and ultimately to the future peace of the society. Virtually all discussions of student discipline spoke of broad social ends toward which the discipline was aimed.

Since the 1950s, however, disciplinary literature has fallen silent on the long term social objectives of school discipline, stressing instead the immediate control of students. The emphasis has shifted from ends to means and strategies. Rather than developing philosophies of discipline linked to visions of a preferred social order, writers have developed systems and models whose only criterion for success is their short-term goal of classroom order. Most of the models rely heavily on behaviorism, attempting to deploy rewards and penalties effectively in the service of authoritarian control. Others employ various degrees of constructivist discipline.[40] Few develop any clear conception of democratic social life, either as a short-term classroom goal or a long-term social objective. Both the behaviorist and the constructivist approaches attempt to reassert the authority of teachers, though the former does so primarily through the assertion of the right to punish while the latter attempts, imperfectly, to reconceptualize the teacher as moral authority.

Importantly, though, the current era marks a watershed in a second way. Earlier notions of classroom order can be seen at one level or another to be efforts to foster character traits and community norms consonant with emergent material and ideological realities, or realities that dominant groups hoped to promote. They were, in virtually all cases, built on the assumption of a producer society, one that valued diligence, thrift, deferred gratification, fidelity, industriousness, self-reliance, self-control, character, and the pursuit of worthy callings. They were, in short, based on a belief in a future and demanded impulse control.

In contrast, the notions of classroom order of the last half of the century are, overwhelmingly, efforts to provide schools with a prophylactic against the character traits created by a consumer society, one that privileges leisure, encourages debt, urges immediate gratification, promotes dissatisfaction, and treats human labor as a mere means to the end of consumption. Consumer markets, bureaucratic organizations, and perpetual deskilling and reskilling call for, and arguably create with devastating efficiency, people disposed to dependent relationships and possessive individualism, inured to the manipulation of taste, and prepared to accept the constant recreation of meretricious dissatisfactions—adaptable, manipulable, willing to seek satisfaction in consuming lifestyles rather than in consciously creating public and private lives. A consumer society has no interest in a future, but only in present consumption; it must, if it is to be successful, banish impulse controls.[41]

Such character traits, produced by the most powerful and seductive forces in civil society, are in direct contradiction to the character traits required for a producer society, as well as, importantly, the traits essential for effective classrooms. The last four decades, then, have been marked by frantic efforts to counter the character traits that children import into the school. Few of those efforts speak with any clarity about the sources of the problems they seek to neutralize; those that do offer an analysis that seriously confuses cause and effect, seeking the source of "permissiveness" and declining "virtue" in individual laxness and erroneous ideology rather than in material realities and their supporting ideologies.

Further, the structure and meaning of social authority came under increasing question at mid-century, culminating in rebellion throughout significant sectors of the traditionally powerless. An acute crisis of authority sabotaged efforts to turn schools into sites for the reimposition of social discipline. The rebellion has been contained and some of its gains have been rolled back in recent years. The conservative restoration carries with it clear outlines of a new form of disciplinary power. To be fully deployed, however, that power will require the dismantling of much of the disciplinary structure now in place (including prominently the very idea of a democratic common schooling through the instrumentality of public education), and the embedding of new rituals, structures, regularities, and procedures. Meanwhile, the strident calls for a renewal of virtue and social discipline seem unlikely to have their intended effects, for conservatives are as wedded to the contradictions within a consumption society—the endless expansion of demand based on possessive individualism—as those they vilify.

Ironically, perhaps tragically, throughout the last two centuries and more, the ends of classroom management have seldom included democratic imperatives. Yet, arguably, only those ends could ever have yielded a critical inquiry into legitimate authority and avoided the sedulous inculcation of external authority. Only democratic ends held any possibility of serving as a prophylactic for citizens and schools against the erosion of character and of learning essential to the success of a consumer society. Two centuries of employing disciplinary power in the interest of the power of the marketplace has dramatically blunted the potential for teachers and students to reimagine educational relationships more consonant with the imperatives of democratic life and human dignity.

Notes

1. An earlier version of this chapter appeared as "Discipline, Dignity and Democracy: Reflections on the History of Classroom Management," *Educational Studies* 26 (fall 1995): 165–84.

2. The classic critique of this tendency is Lawrence A. Cremin, *The Wonderful World of Elwood Patterson Cubberley: An Essay on the Historiography of American Education* (New York: Teachers College, Columbia University, 1965).

3. Among many others, see for example, Herbert M. Kliebard, *The Struggle for the American Curriculum, 1893–1958*

(Boston: Routledge and Kegan Paul, 1986); Paul Davis Chapman, *Schools as Sorters: Lewis M. Terman, Applied Psychology, and the Intelligence Testing Movement, 1890–1930* (New York: New York University Press, 1988); Jurgen Herbst, *And Sadly Teach: Teacher Education and Professionalization in American Culture* (Madison: University of Wisconsin Press, 1989); Larry Cuban, *The Managerial Imperative and the Practice of Leadership in Schools* (Albany: State University of New York Press, 1988); Patricia Cline Cohen, *A Calculating People: The Spread of Numeracy in Early America* (Chicago: University of Chicago Press, 1982); and David Warren Saxe, *Social Studies in Schools: A History of the Early Years* (Albany: State University of New York Press, 1991).

4. There are conceptual differences between *classroom management, classroom discipline,* and *student discipline.* Depending upon the discipline "model" one chooses, one or another might be seen as subordinate to another, or as implying different foci. For our purposes in this essay, however, I am collapsing the three terms, using all three to refer to the explicit practices followed to achieve the level of order and civility prerequisite to teaching and learning.

5. Barbara Finkelstein, *Governing the Young: Teacher Behavior in Popular Primary Schools in Nineteenth Century United States* (New York: Falmer Press, 1989), pp. 102–06; Kate Rousmaniere, "Losing Patience and Staying Professional: Women Teachers and the Problem of Classroom Discipline in New York City Schools in the 1920s." *History of Education Quarterly* 34 (spring 1994): 60–66; see also Joseph S. Taylor, *Art of Class Management and Discipline* (New York: A. S. Barnes & Co., 1903), esp. 65–68.

6. A substantial portion of the historical scholarship on school discipline published in the last two decades focuses primarily on the effort to rid schools of "the rod." That literature is remarkable for its interpretive absolutism. Its authors share a disproportionate horror of any use whatsoever of physical pain in correction; they share as well a revulsion against the reformers for their moderation in not seeking the total abolition of corporal punishment. See, for example, N. Ray Hiner, "Children's Rights, Corporal Punishment, and Child Abuse: Changing American Attitudes, 1870–1920," *Bulletin of the*

Menninger Clinic 43 (May 1979):233–48; Irwin A. Hyman and James H. Wise, eds., *Corporal Punishment in American Education: Readings in History, Practice, and Alternatives* (Philadelphia: Temple University Press, 1979); Donald Raichle, "School Discipline and Corporal Punishment: An American Retrospect," *Interchange* 8 (1977–78):71–83; and Robert A. Trennert, "Corporal Punishment and the Politics of Indian Reform," *History of Education Quarterly* 29 (winter 1989):595–617. In the broader literature, see also R. Brodhead, "Sparing the Rod: Discipline and Fiction in Antebellum America," *Representations* 21 (Winter 1988):67–96; Philip Greven, *Spare the Child: The Religious Roots of Punishment and the Psychological Impact of Physical Abuse* (New York: Alfred A. Knopf, 1991); Karen Taylor, "Blessing the House: Moral Motherhood and the Suppression of Physical Punishment," *Journal of Psychohistory* 15 (summer 1987):431–54; and Donald E. Greydanus, Helen D. Pratt, Samuel E. Greydanus III, Adele D. Hofmann, and C. Richard Tsegaye-Spates, "Corporal Punishment in Schools: A Position Paper of the Society for Adolescent Medicine," *Journal of Adolescent Health* 13, no. 3 (1992):240–46; see also Myra C. Glenn, *Campaigns Against Corporal Punishment: Prisoners, Sailors, Women, and Children in Antebellum America* (Albany: State University of New York Press, 1984).

7. Joseph S. Taylor, *Art of Class Management and Discipline* (New York: A.S. Barnes and Co., 1903), pp. 1–15.

8. Finkelstein, *Governing the Young*; W. H. Small, *Early New England Schools* (Boston: Ginn and Co., 1914); M. M. Mathews, *Teaching to Read, Historically Considered* (Chicago: University of Chicago Press, 1966); Clifton Johnson, *Old-Time Schools and School-Books* (1904; New York: Dover, 1963).

9. See, for example, Peter Berger, "On the Obsolescence of the Concept of Honour," in Stanley Hauerwas and Alasdair MacIntyre, eds., *Revisions: Changing Perspectives in Moral Philosophy* (Notre Dame, Ind.: University of Notre Dame Press, 1983), pp. 172–81. Bertram Wyatt-Brown, *Southern Honor: Ethics and Behavior in the Old South* (New York: Oxford University Press, 1982), provides a rich description of the culture of honor as it persisted in the American South until well into the nineteenth century.

10. David Hogan, "The Market Revolution and Disciplinary Power: Joseph Lancaster and the Psychology of the Early Classroom System," *History of Education Quarterly* 29 (fall 1989):381–417; Carl F. Kaestle, *Joseph Lancaster and the Monitorial School Movement: A Documentary History* (New York: Teachers College, Columbia University, 1973); Ronald Rayman, "Joseph Lancaster's Monitorial System of Instruction in American Indian Education, 1815–1838," *History of Education Quarterly* 21 (winter 1981):395-410; David Hamilton, "Adam Smith and the Moral Economy of the Classroom System," *Journal of Curriculum Studies* 12 (1980):281–98; and Keith Hoskin and Robert Macvie, "Accounting and Examination: A Genealogy of Disciplinary Power," *Accounting, Organization, and Society* 11 (1986):105–36.

11. Hogan, "Market Revolution and Disciplinary Power," 398–407, 411–12; Kaestle, *Joseph Lancaster and the Monitorial School Movement*; Finkelstein, *Governing the Young*, pp. 101–04, 121–22.

12. My thinking about Lancasterian education has benefited greatly from the early pages of David Hogan, "Modes of Discipline: Affective Individualism and Pedagogical Reform in New England, 1820–1850," *American Journal of Education* 99 (November 1990):1–56, particularly 1–16.

13. Hogan, "Modes of Discipline," 14.

14. Michael B. Katz, *The Irony of Early School Reform: Educational Innovation in Mid-Nineteenth Century Massachusetts* (Boston: Beacon Press, 1968), esp. pp. 115–160. David Hogan, who prefers the notion of New England pedagogy, dissents from Katz's interpretation of the meaning of "soft pedagogy;" see Hogan, "Modes of Discipline," 4–16. I find his arguments compelling, yet also incomplete, giving too little attention to the impact of republicanism as it shaped Americans' notions of individual freedom and dignity. I have not attempted here to explore that aspect of the reforms of the era, though my sense is that New England pedagogy was as much a reaction against Jacksonian forms of republicanism as against the moral consequences of the market revolution that engages Hogan.

15. Hogan, "Modes of Discipline," 14.

16. A rich historical literature explores the transformation of family relationships in the early nineteenth century; see, for example, Mary P. Ryan, *Cradle of the Middle Class: The Family in Oneida County, New York, 1790–1865* (Cambridge: Cambridge University Press, 1981).

17. *Emulation* has taken on a new meaning in the twentieth century. As used in the nineteenth, it did not refer to imitation of a positive model, but rather referred to the desire for superior place or status over others, to be won competitively. It means more than simple rivalry, then. For Lancaster and others, emulation was a positive impulse, related to the market and worthy of cultivation. For dissenters within the tradition of New England pedagogy, it substituted false, material ends for the loftier moral and intellectual ends for which the student should be aspiring.

18. Hogan, "Modes of Discipline," 13.

19. See, for example, Emerson E. White, *School Management: A Practical Treatise for Teachers and All Other Persons Interested in the Right Training of the Young* (New York: American Book Co., 1894).

20. Finkelstein, *Governing the Young*, 101–07; H. B. Wilbur, "The Object System of Instruction," *Addresses and Proceedings of the National Education Association* (1864):189–209; Ruth Miller Elson, *Guardians of Tradition: American Schoolbooks of the Nineteenth Century* (Lincoln: University of Nebraska Press, 1964). See also William R. Johnson, "'Chanting Choristers': Simultaneous Recitation in Baltimore's Nineteenth Century Primary Schools," *History of Education Quarterly* 34 (spring 1994):1-23.

21. Here, I am following the lead of David Hogan in rejecting Michael B. Katz's argument that New England pedagogues were merely ambivalent toward industrialism and urbanization, and that their reforms encouraged character traits functional to nineteenth century industrial and commercial society; see Hogan, "Modes of Discipline," esp. 4–8; Katz, *Irony*, 115–60. See also Carl F. Kaestle, "Social Change, Discipline, and the Common School," *Journal of Interdisciplinary History* 9 (summer 1978):1–18.

22. James D. Anderson, *Education of Blacks in the South, 1860–1935* (Chapel Hill: University of North Carolina Press, 1988), esp. pp. 33–78.

23. Anderson, *Education of Blacks in the South*; Anderson, "The Historical Development of Black Vocational Education," in *Work, Youth, and Schooling; Historical Perspectives on Vocationalism in America*, Harvey Kantor and David B. Tyack, eds. (Stanford, CA: Stanford University Press, 1982), pp. 180–222; Wilbert H. Ahern, "'The Returned Indians': Hampton Institute and Its Indian Alumni, 1879-1893," *Journal of Ethnic Studies* 10, no. 4 (1983): 101–24. It is worth noting that the disciplinary structure embedded within the industrial education curriculum was being developed simultaneously in northern white schools, though without an identical authority structure, and without the extended surveillance of boarding schools; see esp. Charles A. Bennett, *History of Manual and Industrial Education, 1870 to 1917* (Peoria, IL: Manual Arts Press, 1937).

24. Lawrence A. Cremin, *Transformation of the School: Progressivism in American Education, 1876-1957* (New York: Knopf, 1961).

25. The limitations imposed by a brief survey makes the above description far too arbitrary, of course. In fact, the progressive period produced a broad range of manuals on classroom discipline, running the gamut from refinements on bureaucratic discipline and efforts to fuse affectional and bureaucratic discipline, to more romantic proposals. Regarding the former, see, for example, Frances M. Morehouse, *Discipline of the School* (Boston: D. C. Heath & Co., 1914); Levi Seeley, *A New School Management* (New York: Hinds, Noble & Eldredge, 1903).

26. Two classroom management manuals, published within nearly a decade of one another, graphically indicate this shift. Emerson E. White, *School Management: A Practical Treatise for Teachers and All Other Persons Interested in the Right Training of the Young* (New York: American Book Co., 1894), in many ways the most complete expression of nineteenth-century New England disciplinary pedagogy, provides a closely argued defense of forms of discipline which carry moral lessons, and argues that all forms that contradict the moral aims of the school must be rejected. After a thorough

review of the means to classroom management available to a teacher, White turns in the second, and longer, section of his book to consider "Moral Training" as a fundamental purpose for schooling. By contrast, William Chandler Bagley, *Classroom Management: Its Principles and Technique* (New York: Macmillan Co., 1907), in a similarly weighty volume, never invokes moral considerations. His only focus in considering the range of disciplinary actions available to a teacher is social efficiency. The fundamental purpose for schooling, in Bagley's formulation, is the efficient preparation of the child for life in a civilized society.

27. See, for example, Bagley, *Classroom Management*; Norma Cutts and Nicholas Moseley, *Practical School Discipline and Mental Hygiene* (Boston: Houghton Mifflin Co., 1941).

28. Jeffrey Glanz, *Bureaucracy and Professionalism: The Evolution of Public School Supervision* (Rutherford, NJ: Fairleigh Dickinson University, 1991); David Tyack and Elisabeth Hansot, *Managers of Virtue: Public School Leadership in America, 1820–1980* (New York: Basic Books, 1982).

29. Sol Cohen, "From Badness to Sickness: The Mental Hygiene Movement and the Crisis of School Discipline," *Proteus* 4, no. 1 (1987):9-14; Cohen, "The Mental Hygiene Movement, the Commonwealth Fund, and Public Education, 1921–1933," in *Private Philanthropy and Public Elementary and Secondary Education: Proceedings of the Rockefeller Archives Center Conference Held on June 8, 1979*, edited by Gerald Benjamin (New York, 1980); Cohen, "The School and Personality Development: Intellectual History," in John Hardin Best, ed., *Historical Inquiry in Education: A Research Agenda* (Washington, D.C.: American Educational Research Association, 1983), pp. 109–37.

30. Among others, see Paul Davis Chapman, *Schools as Sorters: Lewis M. Terman, Applied Psychology, and the Intelligence Testing Movement, 1890–1930* (New York: New York University Press, 1988; Clarence Karier, "Testing for Order and Control in the Corporate Liberal State," *Educational Theory* 22 (Spring 1972): 159–80; and Karier, *Scientists of the Mind: Intellectual Founders of Modern Psychology* (Urbana: University of Illinois Press, 1986).

31. Regina Shaw Jones, "An Inquiry Into the Classroom Discipline Legacy from the Progressive Education Movement," (Ed.D. dissertation, Temple University, 1980), pp. 37-40. Jones provides interesting insights into disciplinary movements within progressivism, but ultimately her study is too narrowly and single-mindedly bent on finding one tendency that can serve to explain the crisis in school discipline since the 1950s. The study fails in its basic effort. On the project method, see also Neil Sutherland, "The Triumph of 'Formalism': Elementary Schooling in Vancouver from the 1920s to the 1960s," in Robert A. J. McDonald and Jean Barman, eds., *Vancouver Past: Essays in Social History* (Vancouver, B.C., Canada: University of British Columbia Press, 1986), pp. 175–210.

32. Jones, "An Inquiry Into the Classroom Discipline Legacy," 33–40.

33. Ibid., 91–98.

34. Ibid., 71–85.

35. See especially Bagley, *Classroom Management.*

36. See, for example, Norma E. Cutts and Nicholas Moseley, *Practical School Discipline and Mental Hygiene* (Boston: Houghton Mifflin Co., 1941).

37. Christopher Lasch, *The True and Only Heaven: Progress and Its Critics* (New York: W. W. Norton, 1991), though never dealing with education or school discipline, provides a dense analysis of the contradictions and ultimate futility of progressive ideology.

38. Mary Alice Blanford Burton, "The Disciplining of American School Children: 1940–1980. A Historical Study" (Ed.D. dissertation, University of Hawaii, 1987). Burton argues that by the 1940s and 1950s, democratic discipline was in fact being practiced in many schools. However, what writers often labeled as democratic discipline bore little relationship to democracy as a social and political process. More frequently, disciplinary regimes at the time sought to mobilize peer pressure toward the ends of classroom order, or simply added collective rule-making to a social structure already predefined and regulated without regard to democratic imperatives.

39. My discussion of the recent past will be brief. Much work remains to be done in exploring the multitude of disciplinary models produced in the last four decades. My effort here is simply to sketch the contours roughly.

40. Duke and Jones argue that since the 1960s, discipline writers have been split between those theories relying on punishment and those relying on communication between teacher and student. See Daniel Duke and Vernon F. Jones, "Two Decades of Discipline—Assessing the Development of an Educational Specialization," *Journal of Research and Development in Education*, 17 (4, 1984): 25–35. I would add that neither side of the split appear to have thought about educating the child consciously about authority, behavior, or the ends of either; both sides of the split sought merely to adjust the child to the classroom, either coercively or by winning the child's assent.

41. Jules Henry, *Culture Against Man* (New York: Vintage Books, 1965); Stuart Ewen, *All Consuming Images: The Politics of Style in Contemporary Culture* (New York: Basic Books, 1988); Ewen, *Captains of Consciousness: Advertising and the Social Roots of the Consumer Culture* (New York: McGraw-Hill, 1976); Christopher Lasch, *The Culture of Narcissism: American Life in an Age of Diminishing Expectations* (New York: Warner, 1979).

2

"Uncontrolled Students Eventually Become Unmanageable": The Politics of Classroom Discipline[1]

❑

Landon E. Beyer

Beginning and prospective teachers frequently express a cluster of perennial anxieties involving questions about how to deal with potential classroom disruptions. Typically, these questions include queries such as: How do I respond to disruptive students? What is the most effective way of generating and utilizing student enthusiasm? How do I deal with the diversity of student abilities, experiences, backgrounds, languages, and cultural values? What do I do if my classroom is not under control or if my students are not doing the work I require of them? An underlying fear when such questions are asked is that if students do not act in appropriate ways their learning will be compromised, and the quality of the teaching that is possible will be eroded. Sometimes this fear is tied to doubts about the sources of teachers' authority, and the basis on which they make decisions about curriculum, pedagogy, social relationships, evaluative activities, and so on. Often, too, such fear is exacerbated by the ways in which teachers are evaluated by principals or supervisors.

Such questions, fears, and doubts are understandable, perhaps even inevitable, especially for beginning teachers. In some way or another, those fears and doubts have to be addressed if teachers are to be effective. What is problematic is not the appearance of such questions, but the way educators—in public schools and institutions of higher education alike—typically go about responding to them. When confronted with questions like the ones mentioned above, educators have tended to look to the behavioral sciences, educational psychology, and related, school-based "here's what really works" management strategies to deal with disruptive episodes and to generate enthusiasm and "appropriate behavior" from students. In essence, we have regarded such questions as largely technical or managerial in nature, and thus susceptible to a variety of management strategies for their resolution. By creating a "treatment" for a particular (actual or antici-pated) unpleasant event in the classroom—by following steps a, b, and c to generate the desired behavior—it is often believed we can either prevent or respond ade-quately to undesirable student behaviors.

Such a framework for responding to teacher anxiety is consistent with dominant traditions of schooling and a significant amount of educational research. Those tradi-tions depict the school as a system within which people may be trained to offer the correct responses and behaviors, with regularities imposed upon both students and teachers designed to enforce compliance, couched in the values of efficiency, predictability, and control.[2]

An uncritical acceptance of "what works" within classrooms is problematic for a number of reasons. First, what "works" in one context, situation, or setting may not be generalizable beyond that particular context. Thus, while there may be some utility in noting "successful" practices in one situation, there is little reason to believe they will be equally successful, or even tolerable, in another. Such lack of generalizability makes the obser-vation of apparently successful practice a poor means of directing future actions. Second, and more important, to observe that some activity "works" always begs the important questions of "works for what?" or "for what purpose?" or "to what end?" Such an observation must, therefore, be accompanied by an important qualifier: what is the value of the condition or state that the activity accomplishes? Since it is always possible that what an activity works *for* is problematic or deleterious, the observation of a "successful" intervention does not mean that it is good or that it ought to be replicated. This in turn raises what is inevitably the central question for teachers: What ought I do in my classroom? To see teaching as a technical enterprise—dominated by "how to" questions and by a simplistic "what works" orientation—is to miss the normative, value-laden nature of questions related to curriculum, pedagogy, and evaluation.[3] Simply put, "what works" for a teacher can never be assumed to be synonymous with "what I ought to do."

There are several problems with thinking about teaching as a technical enterprise, and with the emphases on efficiency, predictability, and control that frequently shape the culture of schooling. These technical, efficiency-oriented perspectives also are problematic, especially in the long run, for responding to the sort of perennial questions and anxieties of teachers noted at the outset. This chapter addresses the political dimensions of classroom discipline as it is often understood and practiced, and offers an alternative perspective not only on the particular questions with which I began but on the values and ideas that undergird schools and classrooms. The perspective developed here highlights the normative, political dimensions of what are often considered technical or managerial difficulties. I begin by analyzing mainstream, behaviorist approaches to classroom discipline and the perspectives and values (overt or latent) they rely on and support. I then look at a conception of democracy whose major values and priorities are at odds with the assumptions built into mainstream approaches to classroom management. The chapter concludes with a democratic vision of classroom interactions and cultures, and their implications for rethinking classroom discipline.

Mainstream approaches to classroom discipline

We should note at the outset of this discussion that there is a fundamental contradiction between two under-standings of, and approaches to, "discipline." On the one hand, discipline refers to a disposition governing and guiding an activity that requires for its successful completion a certain quality of mind, diligence, and focus. Discipline in this sense is required if we are to take some activity seriously, or if we are to be effective in accomplishing something we find important and meaningful. In this sense discipline is something we bring to an experience that enhances its meaning, as when we speak of a disciplined approach to a craft, a sport, or an art. On the other hand, discipline is also used to refer to an action done *to* others who are unruly or disobedient, ranging from "time out" sanctions to corporal punishment. In this sense, discipline refers to constraints or punishments imposed on one person by another when the former fails to meet some external expectation or standard.

These two uses of the term discipline are different in many important, even crucial, ways. We need to be aware of these differences as teachers, in part because many people writing on the topic of classroom management fail to acknowledge those very differences. In the first sense of discipline discussed above, the activity in which the person engages is primarily self-initiated and self-regulated, and the person is engaged in that activity for the intrinsic value that is a part of the activity. In some ways, the activity and the person engaged in it are enmeshed, the one becoming a part of the other and even, at times, helping form the identity of the person. Photographers dedicated to their craft take on particular personality traits and develop especially sensitive visual perspectives that allow them to see the world differently—noticing combinations of color, shading, balance, and shape to which the rest of us are oblivious. A disciplined commitment to photography, or to any number of other activities and undertakings, becomes a part of who that person is, affecting his or her general activity and personality.

In the second case of discipline, by contrast, constraints of one sort or another are imposed from the outside. Rather than being intrinsically meaningful, this form of discipline is aimed at shaping activities in ways that the person with more power thinks appropriate or necessary. While this, too, may be effective in shaping personality and perception, it is done to the person involved, and is typically seen as an unwelcome invasion of one's personality. Whatever we may think of the value of these different types of discipline, it is important that we not move from one to the other as if they were interchangeable; many who write on the topic of classroom management fail to maintain that distinction, as we shall see.

Among the most mechanistic approaches to classroom discipline are those associated with one or another stimulus-response understanding of human behavior. Often associated with B. F. Skinner, this approach to shaping and predicting behavior is tied to a particular understanding of human beings and forms of intelligence.[4] Expanding on the idea that behavior is controlled through the appearance of stimuli that cause certain predictable responses, Skinner suggested that behavior could be reliably controlled through the use of positive and negative reinforcements.[5] By presenting stimuli that provide positive or negative reinforcements, teachers would be better able to shape their students' behavior. In following a consistent schedule of such reinforcements, making sure that they are effective and efficient, teachers may control student behavior and maximize learning. This is, among other things, the promise of behavior modification in schools.

Other, more recent works have aimed specifically at creating and maintaining a particular kind of environment in classrooms, and at avoiding problems of classroom disorder and ineffective learning. James Levin and

James F. Nolan, for example, in discussing principles for guiding classroom discipline, say that "teachers have the professional responsibility for assuming the role of instructional leader, which involves employing techniques that maximize student on-task behavior"; they also claim that "teachers who have . . . a systematic plan to manage misbehavior have classrooms characterized by a high percentage of on-task student behavior;" further, the authors contend that, "a preplanned hierarchy of management strategies increases the likelihood of appropriate student behavior."[6] For teachers to be effective classroom disciplinarians, then, they must be systematic in developing and implementing an efficient plan of hierarchical strategies that will ensure students are "on-task."

Levin and Nolan correctly point out that conceptions of appropriate classroom discipline are intertwined with conceptions of teaching. In identifying their own understanding of teaching, they rely on educational psychology, and in particular a form of behaviorism—the seemingly universal domain utilized in articulating mainstream conceptions of classroom discipline. Unlike more impositional models of behaviorism, however, they appeal to Adlerian psychological ideas to claim that "individuals cannot be forced either to learn or to exhibit appropriate behavior. . . . it follows that teachers change student behavior only by *influencing* the change, not *forcing* it."[7] They then argue that students' behaviors will change if the teacher's behavior changes in a conscious, deliberate way. Moreover, the ability of teachers to change students' behavior is increased "when teachers have a professional knowledge of instructional techniques, learning psychology, and child development and use it to guide the modification of their own behavior."[8]

More particularly, the authors define teaching as "the use of preplanned behaviors, founded in learning principles and child development theory and directed toward both instructional delivery and classroom management, which increase the probability of affecting a positive change in student behavior."[9] The authors' connection to educational psychology, and developmentalism in particular, is clear in these ideas. Equally clear is an indebtedness to forms of essentially behavioral/technical language that, importantly, helps to construct the paradigm out of which come this and other mainstream understandings of classroom management.

Consider another example of the interrelations among teaching and classroom discipline. In discussing ways to avoid misbehavior, William J. Gnagey provides the conventional wisdom about careful, precise planning:

> teacher training institutions insist that their students spend a great deal of time writing lesson plans with a lot of rich detail. Complicated taxonomies . . . and technologies . . . have been developed to make sure that the objectives of instruction are both clear and precise. Planning also includes some assessment of the readiness of the students; a description of the learning activities; a list of the necessary materials; and some way to summarize, evaluate, and make assignments for the next lesson.[10]

The author relies on a mechanistic, systems management orientation to teacher planning, which basically takes "the Tyler rationale" for granted without mentioning it by name (Tyler's name does not even appear in the references).[11] This appeal to an educational commonsense is accompanied by an isolation of the ideas and perspectives on which it draws, and an insularity with respect to curriculum debates that have taken place, and that continue. Gnagey suppresses disagreements over precisely such "commonsense" matters as the dominance of technicism in teaching, the justifiability of traditional "teacher training," the appropriateness of contemporary management ideology, and the separation of educational means and ends. The author even agrees with the old adage, "don't smile until Christmas": "It has been shown," Gnagey says, "that after a brief honeymoon period, classroom misbehavior rises rapidly to a peak. If the teacher practices effective management skills during this critical period, deviancy falls off and levels out. If not, misbehavior rates continue to rise until the class becomes virtually unmanageable."[12] To prevent such "deviancy," the author suggests several procedures to aid the teacher. These include the advice to:

1. Arrange the seating so *surveillance* is easy. . . .

2. Select a steering group to act as an early barometer of impending trouble. . . .

3. Scan the entire room frequently. If you allow your attention to be monopolized by one student or a small group, off-task behavior can quickly develop in other sectors of the class.

4. Look for concealment strategies. [Let students who misbehave, even if you do not make an issue of their misbehavior,] know immediately that *they aren't getting away with anything.*[13]

The picture of students and the image of teachers explicit in these pieces of advice are hardly uplifting. Students need surveillance and oversight, bolstered by close attention to those apt to misbehave; the teacher appears to be more of a member of a secret police than a guide or coach or fellow inquirer. The mainstream literature on classroom discipline does not consider the effects of the classroom environment and activities (as long as the students are "on-task," moving toward some hierarchy of pre-established ends or fulfilling certain needs), the culture of the school, or the students' own lives and difficulties, when discussing how to create and maintain "order" in the classroom.

Gnagey also recommends routinizing activities as a way of minimizing misbehaviors. "Taking roll, passing out supplies, breaking up into groups, and moving from class to class are all examples of administrative operations that can be routinized early. . . . Some instructional moves that can become routines include asking questions, praising answers, and giving directions."[14]

This routinization does several things. First, it trivializes and narrows student and teacher interaction in classrooms; second, it makes inquiry into significant issues appear valuable only to the extent that it contributes to a stable routine; third, it promotes the mechanization of interpersonal relationships among students and between students and teacher, adding a level of conformism to classroom activity; and fourth, it further distances students' interests and personalities from the learning process. These things lead to or exacerbate the alienation that many students feel in the classroom, and thereby contribute to a lack of "discipline" conceived as an intrinsically worthwhile activity felt meaningful by students. Yet when routinization and other strategies fail, there are other techniques to fall back on—including behavior modification. Gnagey, citing another researcher, advocates "the withdrawal or withholding of affection" as part of "the list of more tangible fines."[15] It follows that "a warm, affectionate relationship between teacher and students can make punishment more effective if it becomes necessary."[16]

Advocates of conventional classroom management appeal to a particular conception of professionalism for teachers. Professionalism, according to that view, consists of "the application of [a] specialized body of professional knowledge."[17] Thus, through managing behavior, teaching through mechanistic, Tylerian approaches, and pre-planning activities based on mastering the specialized knowledge available largely through developmental and learning theory, the teacher can be regarded as a professional. This perspective raises two questions. First, what bodies of knowledge or literatures are excluded when we focus on behavioral psychology and developmental theory as a basis for professionalism? And second, what other ways are there to conceive of professionalism in teaching? This latter question will be taken up in the final section of this chapter. For now it is enough to suggest that a technical or expert notion of teacher professionalism as applying specialized knowledge drawn from the domain of educational psychology has significant consequences for how we understand schooling and teaching—and for the proper classroom discipline to maintain.

An appeal to a technical or expert model of teaching and classroom discipline is often replicated in the very scholastic form in which books on classroom management are written. That is, those texts frequently embody specific, detailed, hierarchical modes that reflect the ideas they are conveying to teachers or prospective teachers. For example, Gnagey tells the reader of his text that "each chapter begins with a list of objectives that will alert you to the major points to be discussed. This list can also be used as brief essay questions with which to measure your own comprehension of the material after you have read it."[18] Each chapter also ends with a multiple choice quiz, with an answer key provided in the appendix.

I mentioned at the beginning of this section that discipline has at least a dual meaning: it is both something we do to provide an internally directed focus that enhances the meaning of an activity, and establishes a certain quality of mind, on the one hand; and it is an externally imposed sanction or reprimand, on the other. These dual meanings are often merged, sometimes in pernicious ways, as in this discussion of classroom discipline and its relationship to motivation:

> Let us think of *motivation* as the total of all the forces that cause a person to expend energy doing one thing rather than another. Let us say that *good discipline* refers to a situation in which your students are exerting an optimal amount of energy trying to *learn what you want to teach them* instead of wasting it in various other counterproductive activities. You can be called a *good disciplinarian* when you have learned to use the forces of motivation to keep your students moving toward *their academic goals* instead of misbehaving.[19]

The author moves from general questions about choices people make, to a view of the teacher as determining student activities, to the suggestion that, when successful, such teacher-dominated actions result in students moving toward "their" goals. This is a prime example of a management orientation in which students are seen as needing to be manipulated so that in channeling their energies in ways prescribed by the teacher, they come to see themselves as working for their own goals, within a context where "motivation" is seen as a neutral, personally disconnected force. While students do need to be able to discipline their activities in the self-directed sense of that term, the appeal here is to the externally imposed sort of discipline, but within the rubric, though not the reality, of the former understanding of discipline.

In a related way, classroom disruptions and unruly behavior are often seen through a pathological lens. That is, when a classroom event involving a student transpires that is bothersome or problematic for the teacher, the cause is commonly assumed to lie in the "pathology" of the student. This is sometimes the case, of course. Observing and responding to a classroom disruption via the adoption of this lens, however, locates problems within particular students, so that both other people and larger contexts are seen as "background information" that can be taken for granted or remain unnoticed. Other domains that may have been scrutinized to explain the disruption—for example, the particular curriculum being implemented, the pedagogical approaches of the teacher, the culture of the classroom, the class, gender, and racial realities of the school and the wider society, and so on— remain invisible and outside the realms of analysis and possible response or alteration. In short, utilizing a pathological lens when considering classroom decorum and its violation constrains the "unit of analysis" and narrows the range of questions that may be asked, as well as the responses that may be initiated.

In a similar way, ethical questions regarding the treatment of students are ignored or narrowed in scope in most discussions of how to maintain classroom discipline. For example, in discussing the negative repercussions of punishment, Gnagey says that "although students usually do not repeat behaviors that are punished, the fear and resentment that accompanies the administration of penalties may spawn new acts of anger and revenge for the teacher to deal with."[20] What is emphasized here is not the ethical question of inflicting punishment on students, but the consequences that student punishment may have for the teacher. Even the discussion of those consequences is framed in procedural and not ethical terms. This avoidance of ethical considerations is central to behavioral psychology generally, which asserts a hierarchy of needs that require fulfillment and where there are developmental stages thought to provide a natural progression outside of any important social context that might elicit moral questions.[21]

A certain skepticism regarding students' abilities and character is frequently present in many texts dealing with classroom management as well. In *Building Classroom Discipline*, C. M. Charles says,

> Many students are neither self-directed nor self-controlled, and they will not work well on their own for long even in the best activities. In such cases teachers must guide, exhort, help, monitor, provide feedback, entertain, and otherwise encourage students to do quality work. This role is traditional in teaching and its importance should not be slighted. *Let's be realistic: Most of us need a taskmaster, preferably a positive one, if we are to learn well in school.*[22]

No critical discussion of this observation follows that might lead us away from the utilization of a pathological lens. Instead we are provided with a list of ways to deal with such "realities."

Among the more popular school-based materials designed to foster classroom management and decorum are those developed by Lee Canter and Associates. In their guide for teachers, *Back to School with Assertive Discipline*, the authors outline an approach to classroom discipline that has been adopted by many schools.[23] Indeed, one author has called Canter's Assertive Discipline system "the most popular of all such systems" as well as "the most discussed."[24] We might well regard Assertive Discipline as expressing the conventional wisdom concerning classroom discipline.

Canter's Assertive Discipline plan has a series of interrelated components. First, the teacher must establish rules early on that students will be expected to follow at all times. As Canter says to the reader, "you need to get all of your students on *your* behavior track. Students need to know exactly what is expected of them."[25] Consistent with the technical or expert orientation to teaching (with its connection to bureaucratic processes and managerial oversight functions) that is connected to mainstream approaches to classroom discipline, Canter provides a "sample lesson plan" that contains an objective, a list of materials, and a procedure.[26] Each step is detailed and clearly laid out, consistent with his belief that the rules teachers provide for students should not only be specific but based on observable behaviors: "make sure that your rules are observable. Rules such as 'Be good' are too vague and not observable. Rules such as 'raise your hand and wait to be called upon before you speak' are observable."[27] Once the teacher's rules are clearly and firmly enunciated, students will understand which behaviors are appropriate and which are not in that particular classroom. Canter says, and often repeats, that the first rule of every classroom should be that students follow directions the first time they are given. There must also be unambiguous consequences for students if they do not follow the teacher's rules. As Canter puts it, "students need to be taught to be *responsible for their actions.* They need to realize that the choice is theirs: to follow the rules of the classroom and enjoy the rewards or to disregard the rules and accept the consequences."[28] The Assertive Discipline approach also recognizes the importance of establishing a reward system for students who follow the rules. The "positive reinforcement system," Canter tells the reader, "is the single most important tool you have to help students shape apropriate behaviors."[29]

Central to mainstream approaches to classroom discipline is the isolation of "behavior," "teaching," etc., and the assumption of rather mechanistic connections between one action and another, one person (teacher) and another (student): by employing action x, we induce behavior y. There are several unexamined questions involved here. Some of these are empirical in character: Does this purportedly causal connection really operate with all students in all classrooms, in the short and long run? What other effects—even unintended ones—are there for the students and the teacher? What are the consequences for the culture of the classroom and school more generally? Aren't there non-behavioral forms of learning? Other questions raised by the isolated, mechanistic understanding of classroom discipline are normative: What are the effects on students and teachers of using this form of language, these metaphors, those ways of thinking? How can we decide which values ought to guide our deliberations over appropriate classroom discipline? What kind of world are we preparing students to help construct and live in, and how do we justify that world-building process? What alternatives are there?

Beyond such empirical and normative questions, it is crucial that we ask what traditions people draw upon in articulating an approach to classroom management, and what traditions, forms of language, and value systems they exclude or discount. The assumptions and ideologies built into mainstream, behavioristic traditions influence what we regard as appropriate or normal or necessary, and correspondingly delimit the range of ideas and practices that are seen as appropriate. The reliance on particular traditions, paradigms, and forms of language— for instance, those conveyed by such phrases as "delivery systems," "on-task," "learning as changing behavior," and so on—results in ways of thinking and modes of discourse that themselves have at least tacit political connotations. They affect how teachers and others regard students, classrooms, schools, and the contexts in which they function. They suggest, as well, some unsettling ways of thinking about people, learning, and society.

The world enacted via mainstream understandings of classroom management is dominated by mistrust—the sense that students, like most of us, "need a taskmaster" if we are to function effectively in or outside of schools; that students must learn to be obedient, which will be facilitated if we can get them to think of others' directions as their own, resulting in a kind of duplicity. In addition to needing to be led by others, this world is one in which students must be constantly watched and supervised, managed and cajoled into the proper courses of action. The result for students is a decided powerlessness, a "followership" that often results in apathy and a with-drawal of their own interests and investments. And all of this in the name of celebrating a smoothly running, efficient, predictable, quiet classroom within which efficiency and predictability are central. It is consistent with this picture of classroom management that, in summarizing the available research on the modal classroom, Kenneth A. Sirotnik concludes, "we are implicitly teaching dependence upon authority, linear thinking, social apathy, passive involvement, and hands-off learning," all in a "virtually affectless environment."[30] Are these the qualities and values we really want for our children and for our schools?

Preparation for democratic living[31]

Virtually from their inception, public schools have been championed as central to democratic values and ideas. Yet the meaning of democracy as a concept, as well as its practical import for classrooms, continues to be contested by those with quite different perspectives and agendas. Educational reforms have been promoted as democratic when they raise standards in the name of enhancing our competitive edge in the global marketplace, when they highlight the importance of civic participation and service learning, or when they contribute to the sharing of a common cultural heritage involving historically important ideas, events, and people and thus provide a sort of cultural glue that holds Americans together. At a more general level, the meanings of democracy continue to be widely debated and discussed. From the call by members of the New Right to scale back if not abandon the Welfare State, which would allegedly hold individuals more accountable, to the embrace of the "new technology" and "post-capitalist" forms of economic arrangements that are said to make other political traditions obsolete, we mistakenly continue to use the term "democracy" as if it had one clear, unambiguous, universal meaning. But it does not. And much educational policy, as well as a sizable amount of classroom practice— including activities associated with classroom management—is, or might well become, shaped by our understandings of the imperatives of democracy.

We often associate democracy with the "founding documents" of our country such as the Constitution and Bill of Rights, as well as with the freedoms that those and other documents and court decisions protect. In addition, activities associated with elections—voting, running for office or supporting those who do, keeping abreast of current events and controversies, and so on—may be seen as central to the maintenance of democratic traditions and processes. Such documents and activities are, of course, central to what we might call the political-structural domain of U.S. society. At both individual and social levels, they protect our rights and make clear our obligations.

Yet democracy as a set of ideas, principles, and values has a more encompassing range than that associated with documents and electoral obligations, as important as these have been, for example, within South Africa. For democracy in a more global, normative sense can refer to the way we make decisions and enter into activities with others, how we treat and respond to those with whom we have interests in common, to how we understand ourselves, our relationships with others, and the kind of world we want to help construct. Democratic values and practices in fact can help construct our own identity, and our relations with other people and the worlds in which we live, while helping us find ways to work together in constructing a more humane, socially just world. At this level, we may think of democracy not as a subscribed set of practices but as a set of normative parameters that help us think about what those practices should be, and the appropriate ways to organize our lives.

Democracy centrally entails a set of moral commitments. These are made harder to see and act upon because of an entrenched individualism that is a part of our cultural heritage. This individualism fosters a view of people as "naturally" independent and autonomous, self-serving and self-motivated, concerned above all else about their own welfare or perhaps the welfare of their immediate family members. In addition, this perspective regards people as born with innate interests and desires, the expression of which often leads to conflicts which the state or government must prevent or somehow harmonize. Given the primacy of the individual, and the picture of people as naturally self-interested, we are to be allowed a freedom of expression and action that is attenuated only when its exercise may limit the freedom of others. Consistent with this individualistic orientation, the "negative freedom" to "be left alone" is often central to our conventional understanding of democratic life. Governed by constitutional and other guarantees that protect individual rights, striving to maximize our individual happiness and sense of worth, we form associations in large part because we believe they will protect our private interests.

In rejecting this emphasis on self-enclosed individuals who utilize freedoms that will further their own private interests, I want to suggest a different way to understand the meaning of democracy and the moral contours of democratic life. To begin, freedom means more than allowing individuals to undertake whatever actions they believe will serve their independently-calculated private interests. "Freedom of action," while in many situations obviously indispensable, tells us nothing about what *sort* of action we ought to undertake as a result of the freedom that is sanctioned. An emphasis on "negative freedom" is silent on the question of what we are supposed to do with the freedom thus created. As Benjamin R. Barber insightfully points out,

> Although we may use the imagery of laissez-faire as the key to our liberty, most people simply do not conceive of liberty in practice as being tied up with solitude, and endless choice. People feel free concretely not simply when they have choices, but *when their choices feel meaningful*; not when there is chaos and disorder in which anything is possible, but when what is possible is a set of life choices *ordered by ethical or religious values* they have chosen for themselves; not when they are left alone, but when they *participate in the free communities that permit them to define common lives autonomously and establish common identities freely.*[32]

Contrary to the emphases on individualism and negative freedom associated with some conceptions of democracy, any social group must structure its activities around certain values or others, in the pursuit of its own continuity. All societies are dedicated to creating principles of one sort or another in accordance with which people will live, that govern how they interact with each other and along what lines decisions will be made and carried out. It is through such principles and activities that we become people, and attain the sort of communal identity necessary for the development and exercise of freedom. We become people, in short, not through the expression of pre-given interests that are inherent in us as isolated, self-serving individuals, but through social contexts and interactions that help us *become* people. In and through engagement with other people, institutional structures, cultural practices, and political situations, people become who they are, and sometimes become other than they used to be. Individuals do, of course, need to be held accountable for their actions—from corporate executives who engage in leveraged buyouts that result in workers' losing their pensions, to government officials who break the laws of congress. Our character is more than a matter of individual orientation and action, but instead is related to the ways of life, cultural values and goods, economic patterns, and so on, that we are allowed to participate in. It is the *social* quality of experience and the values people acquire that in important ways shapes who we are and who we might become.

In *Democracy on Trial*, Jean Bethke Elshtain recognizes and understands the mistrust contemporary Americans have expressed in their elected leaders, in governmental institutions, and indeed in democratic practices as these continue to be lived out. She suggests as a response to this cynicism that we undertake to construct "a new covenant." The terms of this covenant simultaneously recognize the need for some form of common good while valuing disagreement. As Elshtain puts this:

> unless Americans, or the citizens of any faltering democracy, can once again be shown that they are all in it together; unless democratic citizens remember that being a citizen is a *civic* identity, not primarily a private sinecure; unless government can find a way to respond to people's deepest concerns, a new democratic social covenant has precious little chance of taking hold. . . . The social covenant is not a dream of unanimity or harmony, but the name given to a hope that we can draw on what we hold in common even as we disagree.[33]

Something other than self-referential contexts must provide a basis for moral choices as we live in and help rejuvenate social and communal bonds. Such contexts must be provided by communities concerned with the search for a common good. Such communities cannot flourish in societies where disparities of power, influence, and wealth are as large—and growing—as they are in the U.S.[34] Such disparities stifle or prevent the sorts of interactions that are required in order for public debate, reason, and analysis to flourish. If we are to participate as equals in the public space to make collective, morally informed decisions about the public good that can create social policies and practices, we must create opportunities for equal access in that space, recognize the importance of cultural values and ideas as these shape our consciousness, and consider the values by which we should be governed. Equally important is the need to develop empathy, nurturance, caring, and concern, as discussed by a number of important feminists,[35] and by those concerned with the interpersonal dynamics of cultural and political change.[36]

Democracy, considered as a way of life governed by moral values that generate particular kinds of interactions and practices, relies for its expression on the development of communities devoted to a public good, collectively articulated and enacted. The pursuit of such a common good is, of course, made more problematic by the emphases on individualism and negative freedom already noted. In arguing that education has a crucial role in the development of a participatory democracy that extends beyond the bounds of negative freedom as well as beyond electoral politics and our founding documents, I recognize the importance of reestablishing a sense of community within schools. Yet the values that are crucial for redressing inequalities and reestablishing participation and the sort of community required for the creation of a participatory democracy often continue to be forsaken in classrooms. It is important that teachers seeking to rekindle democratic values in their classrooms understand both how school practices deny those values currently, and the means by which those values may become more central to classroom activities.

The emphasis on reinvigorating participatory, normatively guided communities in schools is related to Freire's emphasis on "integration" with the world, rather than "adapting" to it. As Freire puts it, "integration results from the capacity to adapt to reality *plus* the critical capacity to make choices and to transform that reality."[37] To become an integrated person is not only to understand the social, physical, and political worlds in which we live and work, but to develop the attitudes, forms of consciousness, and outlooks that will allow people to take part in shaping and reshaping that world. This emphasis on critique of current realities, and on participating in the re-creation of our worlds, is a central part of the concept of democracy recommended here. It is a concept that is in opposition to the emphases on control, management, manipulation, and passivity that are embedded in mainstream approaches to classroom discipline.

As a way of life, democracy outlines how we are to regard and treat others, how we are to make choices, and how we can foster more widely shared decision making, in the process diminishing inequalities of power and status. As a moral and social force, democratic values provide frameworks and guidelines for how we live. "Democracy," Elshtain reminds us, "is not simply a set of procedures or a constitution, but an ethos, a spirit, a way of responding, and a way of conducting oneself."[38]

What I am proposing is a broadly based cultural vision for democratic practice in which daily activities and interactions, a search for the common good by people committed to egalitarian social relations, the reinvigoration of community, and an openness to dissent and difference, mutually support each other, and allow for new forms of social life and decision making. A democratic community must, accordingly, enable people to develop values and ideas that outline alternative possibilities, and that generate concrete practices that enact a moral vision. A democratic community encourages its members to become participants in open discussions that require concerted, collaborative actions in the name of social justice.

Teaching couched in such a conception of democratic life might then be seen as a deliberative process that attempts to balance and integrate an attention to the student, rich understandings of and skillful accomplishments in the world, and an awareness of the larger societal dynamics and life contexts in which students live and to which they will return as adults.

In working toward an education that is democratically empowering and cognizant of the harms and brutish outcomes of our current social context, we need to engage students in a meaningful and challenging education. This means an education that recognizes who the students are, helps them develop forms of knowledge and understanding that will enable them to become adult participants and fully engaged human beings within the kind of democratic setting sketched above. A progressive educational plan—especially for marginalized students— needs to understand students, their family, and the communities from whence they come. Simply exhorting "misbehaving" students to "take responsibility for their actions," as many advocates of classroom management do, in important respects misses the point. Provided little opportunity to take real responsibility for any set of actions in the school, and ignoring the real, material conditions surrounding their lives (as well as the ideological contexts and meanings within which they exist), such exhortations are hollow and misleading for students—especially those from marginalized populations. An alternative understanding of professionalism, teaching, and classroom culture is required in order for democratic relationships and responsibilities to become a real possibility in schools.

An Alternative Understanding of Classroom Discipline

Given the realities of many students' lives outside of schools, as well as the quality of the activities and interactions that are countenanced by mainstream approaches to classroom management and the corresponding view of teaching within the school, we might well see as understandable the kind of "deviancy" and "misbehavior" that management strategies try to root out. Indeed, that sort of deviancy may make good sense, given the internal dynamics of classroom culture and the conditions within which many students live. Misbehavior might even be seen as resistance to authoritarianism masked as behavior management—a resistance to be valued if not encouraged.

I noted earlier that the nearly wholesale embrace of behavioral psychology as the basis for mainstream approaches to classroom discipline denies the legitimacy of alternative bodies of knowledge or literatures. Consider again the language and images of behaviorist understandings: students become people whose interests and backgrounds are largely ignored, needing to be coaxed or cajoled to do the right thing, and punished if they do not; people who need to be kept "on-task," where that "task" is created and imposed on them by others; people requiring surveillance and monitoring, and who may need to be kept in line by informants, since they cannot be trusted; people who need to be told in detail what is expected of them, as well as the consequences if they do not comply; people who are expected to accept those externally-imposed tasks as their own; people, finally, who need to be manipulated, within an environment where externally imposed order, efficiency, and control are paramount.

Contrast these forms of language, those images, with the commitments and ideas undergirding a democratic orientation to social life: requiring a sensitivity to how we are to regard and treat others, not as means but as ends; fostering decision-making that is shared and communal, and where students become participants; diminishing inequalities of power and status in part through face to face interaction within genuine communities where difference is valued; honoring an ethos, a spirit, a way of responding that is related to the emphasis on developing an ethic of care and a capacity for love; and nurturing a capacity for seeking a common good.

I also suggested earlier that there are ways to conceive of professionalism in teaching that diverge from the technical or expert, efficiency-oriented models that are allied with mainstream understandings of discipline. Instead of thinking about professionalism in teaching as mastering a body of specialized, psychological and developmental knowledge that is available to only a few, and in opposition to the view of technical competence framed in terms of accomplishing ends that can be prespecified, we might focus on the centrality of praxis for teachers.[39]

Instead of technical expertise or managerial competence, professionalism framed by praxis calls forth the ability to make judgments on behalf of, and with, clients whose interests must not only be considered, but explored and even partially defined within the professional relationship. This requires of the professional not a specialized body of knowledge—and certainly not behavioral management knowledge—but an understanding of the situations in which the client lives and works, as well as an understanding and appreciation of the larger social conditions that help create those situations. Further, this understanding of professionalism remembers its essentially moral qualities and parameters, within which "to profess" is to make a claim, or to proclaim a vow to someone, or to acknowledge attachments. In reclaiming this view of professionalism as engaged practice based on the moral parameters guiding action and reflection, we keep alive the politically interested nature of the professional relationship, and the moral qualities associated with it.

This view of professionalism includes a realization that the bonds of attachment, of caring, and of community are central to the professional's activities. Working together, the professional and those whose interests he or she serves and helps protect may come to both recognize the source of problems and dilemmas as well as ways to overcome them. Such working together must integrate the immediate situation faced by the client as well as the larger social contexts that create it and the possibility of recreating the world in ways that help build a better one. These are the very activities and ways of life that serve the interests of the participatory democracy outlined in the previous section. Such attributes and understanding require the attitudes, involvements, and ideas that form the basis for community, the search for a common good, and structural changes necessary for the kind of equality that democracy requires. They provide alternative ways to consider the climate of classrooms.

In arguing for a different understanding of classroom dynamics, I do not want to forward a naive perspective of students (at any age level) as being always altruistic, other-directed, tirelessly selfless people who are committed to moral notions that would disrupt the power dynamics inherent in our society. Instead, I want to suggest that teachers can, and should, bring students into the classroom decision-making process in ways that respect students' potential autonomy and political identity, as well as their awareness of their own and larger worlds. This perspective moves us away from the manipulative, often cynical perspective that has infected mainstream classroom management ideas, while recognizing that the climate of the classroom provides an important arena for reflecting on the moral, intellectual, and political life of students in the present and future.

Many teachers not only understand these ideas but are implementing them in their classrooms.[40] In an essay dealing with her own struggles as a teacher in the Chicago schools to think through classroom dynamics, Mary Cunat makes several important observations about the moral and political aspects of day to day classroom life, observations centrally related to the dynamics of power in schools and their effects on students' and teachers' consciousness. Like most schools, Mary's has a rule about maintaining silence in the hallways and on stairways:

> There are three flights of stairs to quietly climb up and down. I have found there is only one truly honest and

democratic way I can handle this: by engaging my students in reflective dialogue about the rules. We discuss the value of following rules for the sake of appearances. I present my own difficulty with the situation. We think about our responsibility to the community. . . . We reflect on the personal responsibility of each individual in relation to me, their teacher, a relationship which most of them come to value. We reflect on the problems they will face should they decide to not respect this particular rule. Even though I cannot change the rule or my own personal discomfort, the students have a vital experience of reflection and evaluation. We are faced with such political and moral issues every time we trudge up and down those stairs. . . .

Far from seeing her students as people inclined toward mischievousness who need to be kept under surveillance, and for whom a hierarchical system of behaviorally oriented rules needs to be created, within an accompanying system of rewards and punishments, Mary treats her students as people who are capable of thinking for themselves. Not objects to be cajoled and shaped into manageable regularities, or underlings who need to climb on board the teacher's behavior track, they are people capable of quite sophisticated patterns of thought and interaction. And even their "misbehavior" can be a source of understanding:

Supposedly, verbally rewarding students who are following directions is a way to maximize desired behavior. Although I can utilize this strategy to quiet my class down, there is always an eventual clash with a few students somewhere along the line. I've come to understand that these "misbehaving" students are really a *gift* to show where the power struggles should and do occur. . . . Recognizing and discussing underlying issues within situations where conflict arises between students and any authority figure or structural constraint is part of democratic teaching. Developing a critical attitude toward school activities gives students an opportunity to experience and express their own voice and wrestle with their voicelessness.

A part of thinking differently about classroom discipline involves the teacher being able to let go of the "conventional wisdom" of teaching, professionalism, and classroom management. This means several things for the teacher that are both crucial and at least partially problematic. Among other things, a democratically organized classroom must foster the sort of community in which differences will be not only tolerated but valued— where people can share ideas without fear of rebuke or ostracism. This is a central aspect of participatory, morally infused democratic ways of life, and one that teachers as genuine professionals must actively help construct. It mandates teachers taking risks: trusting their students while understanding that students will not always do what teachers think they should, giving students the autonomy they need to make mistakes and find their own ways. This is facilitated by a sensitivity to students combined with a desire to help them explore and make sense of their worlds. As Katie Poduska, an elementary school teacher in rural Iowa, puts it,

In this context, the most important question that can be asked is "Why?" Such a question represents a need to discover the essence of a particular subject, the meaning and significance of our actions and theories. This is the true motive for learning. To call this forth from my students, I must also experience such a need. My "why?" does not stop with intensive research into a particular subject. My "why?" takes the products of the mental activity of my students and searches for connections to a larger community outside of the classroom. My "why?" enables me to provide glimpses of other possibilities for my students so that they themselves can build their own visions. When I focus on the "why?" of each activity that happens in my classroom, whether planned or unplanned, I am free from the limited vision of an established curriculum.

> What remains is a set of experiences carefully crafted
> by my students and me in which each of us identifies
> our own personal struggle. The curriculum then
> becomes a mosaic in which we all have an equal part,
> claiming ownership and celebrating its beauty. The
> curriculum is no longer a road map outlining a journey
> that I lead, while my students follow, providing inter-
> pretations of events along the way.

If we are to create a social environment in the classroom that will lead to the kind of democratic life sketched
in the previous section, we must abandon our usual
understanding of classroom discipline. A beginning is
provided by remembering the meaning-creating notion of
discipline, and its distinctiveness from the manipulative
and external form of control associated with behavioral
engineering, while keeping in front of us the question of
the sort of world our classrooms ought to be helping to
create. Acknowledging the moral components and
requirements of a new sense of professionalism, teachers
might come to see themselves as agents of change:
toward democratic forms of life in their classrooms that
can help alter larger sources of undemocratic influence.
Teachers will then become not technicians or managers
whose actions are governed by norms of technical competence, predictability, and efficiency, but people who see
teaching as a moral calling—a chance to "do good" for
their students and on behalf of reconstructing their
present and future worlds.

Notes

1. The quotation in the title is from William J. Gnagey,
Motivating Classroom Discipline (New York: Macmillan Publishing Co., 1981), p. 81.

2. See Landon E. Beyer, *Critical Reflection and the Culture
of Schooling: Empowering Teachers* (Victoria: Deakin University
Press, 1989).

3. See Landon E. Beyer and Michael W. Apple, "Values and Politics in the Curriculum," in *The Curriculum: Problems, Politics, and Possibilities* (Albany: State University of New York Press, 1988).

4. See B. F. Skinner, *Walden Two* (New York: Macmillan, 1948).

5. See C. M. Charles, *Building Classroom Discipline*, 4th edition (White Plains, NY: Longman), chapter 3.

6. James Levin and James F. Nolan, *Principles of Classroom Management: A Hierarchical Approach* (Englewood Cliffs, NJ: Prentice Hall, 1991), p. 1.

7. Ibid., p. 3, italics in original.

8. Ibid., p. 3.

9. Ibid., p. 4.

10. Gnagey, p. 62.

11. Ralph W. Tyler, *Basic Principles of Curriculum and Instruction* (Chicago: University of Chicago Press, 1949). For a critique of this tradition, see Herbert M. Kliebard, "Reappraisal: The Tyler Rationale," in William Pinar, editor, *Curriculum Theorizing: The Reconceptualists* (San Francisco: McCutchan Publishing Corporation, 1975), and Michael W. Apple, *Ideology and Curriculum* (Boston: Routledge and Kegan Paul, 1979).

12. Gnagey, *op. cit.*, p. 64, emphasis added.

13. Gnagey, p. 73, emphasis added.

14. Ibid., pp. 73–74.

15. Ibid., p. 94.

16. Ibid., p. 95.

17. Levin and Nolan, p. 4.

18. Gnagey, p. 7.

19. Ibid., p. 11, italics in original, underlining added.

20. Ibid., p. 17.

21. For a critique of developmentalism, see Shirley A. Kessler, "Early Childhood Education as Development: Critique of the Metaphor," *Early Education and Development* 2 (April 1991).

22. Charles, p. 131, emphasis added.

23. Lee Canter & Associates, *Back to School with Assertive Discipline* (Santa Monica, CA: Lee Canter & Associates, 1990).

24. Charles, p. 94.

25. Canter, p. 9, italics in original.

26. Ibid., p. 29.

27. Ibid., p. 9.

28. Ibid., p. 11, emphasis added.

29. Ibid., p. 13.

30. Kenneth A. Sirotnik, "What You See Is What You Get: Consistency, Persistency, and Mediocrity in Classrooms," *Harvard Educational Review* 53 (February 1983): 29.

31. Some of the ideas in this section are treated in detail in Landon E. Beyer and Daniel P. Liston, *Curriculum in Conflict: Social Visions, Educational Agendas, and Progressive School Reform* (New York: Teachers College Press, 1996).

32. Benjamin R. Barber, *An Aristocracy of Everyone: the Politics of Education and the Future of America* (New York: Ballantine Books, 1992), p. 25, emphasis added.

33. Jean Bethke Elshtain, *Democracy on Trial* (New York: Basic Books, 1995), pp. 30–31.

34. See "Workers' pay drops sharply despite rise in firms' profits," *Chicago Tribune*, Friday, June 23, 1995, section 1, p. 11, and Benjamin M. Friedman, *Day of Reckoning: The Consequences of American Economic Policy* (New York: Vintage Books, 1989).

35. See Jane Roland Martin, *The Schoolhome* (Cambridge: Harvard University Press, 1992); Nel Noddings, *Caring: A Feminine Approach to Ethics and Moral Education* (Berkeley: University of California Press, 1984); and Mary Jeanne Larrabee, *An Ethic of Care: Feminist and Interdisciplinary Perspectives* (New York: Routledge, 1993).

36. See Cornel West, *Race Matters* (Boston: Beacon Press, 1983); bell hooks, *Talking Back* (Boston: South End Press, 1989), hooks, *Outlaw Culture* (New York: Routledge, 1994).

37. Paulo Freire, *Education for Critical Consciousness* (New York: The Seabury Press, 1973), p. 4.

38. Elshtain, p. 80.

39. The ideas discussed here are elaborated in Landon E. Beyer, Walter Feinberg, Jo Anne Pagano, and James Anthony Whitson, *Preparing Teachers as Professionals: The Role of Educational Studies and Other Liberal Disciplines* (New York: Teachers College Press, 1989).

40. The excerpts included below are from Landon E. Beyer, editor, *Creating Democratic Classrooms: The Struggle to Integrate Theory and Practice* (New York: Teachers College Press, 1996).

Part II

Ethnographic and Personal Perspectives on Classroom Management

The chapters in Part II differ in tone and style from those in Part I, and differ, as well, from one another. We have chosen to give voice to multiple perspectives in this volume, respecting personal experience, seriously considered, as well as research anchored in traditional scholarly disciplines. Part II ranges from personal reflections on teaching, told in a confessional mode, to ethnographic analyses of classrooms, written in a scholarly mode. Using a variety of methodologies, these authors shift the angle of vision from the more global investigations of Part I to more intimate studies of specific places, where management and disciplinary regimes are enacted. Like the chapters in Part I, these chapters seek not merely to document practices, but more importantly to decode and interpret those practices. What does it mean to be a teacher managing a class in one way rather than in other ways? What does it mean to be a learner experiencing school life organized and regularized under one set of rituals, structures, and practices rather than under other sets?

The findings reported here are impressionistic and site-specific, surely. We need many other sorts of research and reflection on a full variety of disciplinary modes and sites. Yet, based on our own experiences in scores of classrooms and with hundreds of teachers, it is our sense that these portraits reflect the realities of many schools around the country.

In addition to the light these authors shed on class-room practices, and the moral and political relationships constructed within them, they also begin to suggest the importance of other institutional practices that, in turn, shape those classroom practices. Those practices, too, need close study—the constraints built into sanctioned classroom relationships, the tone and quality of administrative structures, traditions of authoritarianism within schools, the lack of time for reflection by teachers, among others.

Our intention ultimately, however, is not merely to compile research. Our intention is to challenge schools and educators at the classroom level to think seriously about discipline and management as it is now enacted, and to understand deeply the curriculum that is embedded in discipline and management practices, as a means to begin to imagine a more ethically and politically defensible classroom life. That process begins with the sorts of study represented here, but moves on to actions that change practices.

3

The Visceral Pleasures of the Well-Worn Rut: Internal Barriers to Changing the Social Relations of American Classrooms

❏

Jackie Blount

Confession[1]

The matter of ethical and appropriate school discipline has concerned me throughout my life. In seventh grade, for instance, I hid the teacher's paddle to prevent the swift and certain punishment of friends for behavior I thought justifiable. The teacher paddled me along with them. When I objected to the school's dress code for girls and wore clothing I considered appropriate, my misbehavior was the subject of a hastily organized assembly about obedience and proper attire where one teacher screamed for an hour about my flagrant disregard for the rules.

In spite of my insolence and to the surprise of friends and teachers, I eventually became a teacher. I knew I would defy the rule-bound, authoritarian models of my past and instead treat students fairly, never abusing them simply for the pleasure of exerting control. I would make my classes irresistibly interesting, formulate class rules *with* students, know about students' lives, and above all, I would be fair. Harsh, punitive discipline would not figure into my work. So when I landed my first teaching job and was required to attend workshops on Assertive Discipline, school discipline policies, and the types of classroom management that would merit successful teacher evaluations, I focused instead on how I would design hands-on activities for the physical science students I would meet in a few days. The discipline workshops, delivered by administrators who sported walkietalkies and monitored the halls and classrooms, offered little that I considered useful. I did what was required, such as posting a list of the classroom rules my students and I had formulated, stacking a few write-up slips in my drawer, and turning in a discipline plan to the main office explaining how I would handle escalating levels of misbehavior. I did all of these things, but with little enthusiasm.

The first week of classes went well aside from the overwhelming end-of-day exhaustion most teachers experience. During the second week, though, things changed. On Wednesday while the rest of third period happily manipulated simple machines, Alan tipped his dilapidated chair back, grabbed a lever/ruler with his pale, graffiticovered hand, and started rapping the desk. He shook his head wildly to an imagined guitar riff suggested by his loud humming. Why was Alan doing this? He had caught me off guard. After a moment's thought, I knew I had not provoked him since the rest of the class seemed interested in the material at hand. In an effort to preserve my dignity and his, I asked him gently and graciously to allow me to continue guiding the group activity uninterrupted.

Alan looked at me, but continued to hum louder, beat harder, and gyrate his head with ever-increasing histrionics. The other students slowly put their pulleys and wedges down, anxious to see who would win this familiar classroom battle of wills. I stared at him in astonishment and at once it hit me: I was no longer the rebellious student. Somehow I had become the teacher with a scripted role to play. Clearly, I had to demonstrate I could handle the part.

Hoping to defuse the crisis quickly, I quietly and firmly asked Alan again to allow me to finish leading the activities. He sprang from his chair, throwing it to the floor. He glared at me, waved a scrap of barbed wire broken from the security fence surrounding the school and yelled, "F—— no!" Numb with shock, yet with reflexes conditioned through years of my own schooling, I immediately sent for an assistant principal who ran to my class to get Alan and escort him away.

My blood pounded, my hands shook, and after he disappeared down the hall, I realized that Alan had posed a significant physical threat to me as well as to the rest of the class. Yet in spite of this bizarre drama and my resulting terror, I decided to act as though nothing had happened and to continue demonstrating the principles of levers. Somehow in that moment it seemed important to me to preserve the appearance of an efficient, smoothly functioning system, a well-managed class, an unflappable teacher.

My internal point of equilibrium had shifted, though. On one hand, I had felt a certain temporary satisfaction in resisting Alan's flagrant challenge and in proving to the rest of the class that I would not tolerate threatening outbursts. I knew how to act like a teacher. On the other hand, I had inflicted what would surely be a stiff punishment on someone I hardly knew, someone who had acted out in class for reasons I did not immediately understand. For a time, I could not trust my long-standing conviction that I would deal fairly and reasonably with students, but instead I felt as though I had become a widget in a mechanically efficient disciplinary system. What had happened?

Digging In

During the long commute home that day, I replayed the showdown with Alan in my mind, searching for the place where I could have prevented the final conflagration. I wanted better control of my classes so nothing of this magnitude ever happened again. But then, was control really what mattered most to me? Had I not resisted teacher control as an adolescent? Or had adulthood suddenly made me into a power-monger who could never again fully understand adolescents? Maybe as an inexperienced teacher I represented an easy mark for rowdy students anxious to wrest control from symbols of authority. Who would have control in my classroom?

I spoke about the incident with friends who encouraged me to look for a job in a safer place since in recent years my school had developed a reputation for student violence, discord, and assorted other image problems. Leaving this tough institution did not appeal to me, though, because I wanted to keep my job and figure things out. When I talked with the two or three teachers at work who could spare the time and would listen, they either responded, "Thank goodness Alan's not in my class!" or "Kids just aren't the same anymore—they don't have any values."

Should I blame Alan and his "lack of values" and thereby absolve myself of the responsibility for making my classes work well in the future? Or should I blame forces beyond either of us? In the mid-eighties when this happened, the media suggested that many school discipline problems could be attributed to external social problems. Newspapers featured stories about child poverty, the effects of divorce on children, homeless youth, ever-increasing rates of adolescent drug use, and a growing litany of social ills. By that time, reports of teen violence had become daily fare on national television, children had started bringing guns and knives to school, and teachers increasingly faced the threat of physical force from students.

As it turned out, Alan had ingested a combination of illicit substances before coming to my class. When I discovered this, I felt relief in knowing that the cause for his outburst lay outside my classroom. The temptation to limit my understanding of his behavior to this superficial analysis was overwhelming. On the other hand, though, I also knew he was searching for ways to cope with the boredom, lack of control and meaninglessness he felt in school; and to that extent, the school, and even my classroom, played an inescapable role in his behavior. Regardless of where I ended up placing the blame, however, I knew I would face future confrontations with him as well as other students and that I somehow needed to prepare myself.

I believed I had a problem requiring a solution, yet few solutions were evident around me. Some teachers passively accepted conditions in the school either by tolerating increasing levels of student violence or seeking jobs in reputedly safer systems. Those who favored active intervention tended to advocate strict, punitive, behaviorally-based schemes of controlling student actions. Ronald Reagan heralded the model of tough Joe Clark, the bullhorn- and bat-carrying principal who was later portrayed in the movie, *Lean on Me.* At my school, the recently installed barbed security fence protecting part of the building symbolized this get-tough policy. So did the active monitoring of hallways by walkie-talkie toting administrators.

Lee and Marlene Canter popularized another active intervention in the form of their Assertive Discipline program for student behavior management. Using this system, teachers would devise iron-clad sets of classroom rewards and punishments, communicate them clearly to students, and enforce them consistently. Student compliance, rather than reflection, would be rewarded by this scheme.[2] My school provided Assertive Discipline training for new teachers and required that we devise strict rules and consequences, communicate them to students, send copies home for parental approval, and then file them in the main office.

When I first arrived, these tough policies had just been implemented in an attempt to clean up the school's image tarnished by local media and grapevine reports detailing vandalism, violence, drugs, sex on campus, and other school problems. The image problem that carried the greatest weight in the minds of White district leaders, though unspoken, was the demographic shift in the student body. At the time, about fifty-five percent of the students were White, forty percent Black, and about five percent Asian, Hispanic, or Native American. Parents of the White students, who generally represented the wealthier residents of this industrial, racially segregated, southern town, threatened to pull their children out of the district and enroll them either in private schools or the surrounding county schools with almost exclusively White populations. The central office administrators and the principal felt pressure to create a sense of safety and order in the school to prevent further White flight.

In an effort to improve the school's image, the White principal devoted his time to meeting journalists from the newspaper and local television stations, hosting school board members, arranging discussions with White parents, speaking at meetings of local civic groups, and generally attempting to bolster the high school's reputation by promoting its successes, such as the state championship football team. Meanwhile, he required the Black assistant principals to handle the school's discipline problems with almost no assistance, few resources, and little time to meet with teachers to discuss and plan policies. When things went well, the principal's photo appeared in favorable newspaper stories. When things went badly, he left the assistant principals to take the blame.

The ten other new teachers and I then became concerned about a different image problem at the school: our own. We started to worry about how student behavior in our classes would affect our teacher evaluations. As per unwritten policy for new teachers at the school, we had each been assigned large classes with disproportionately high numbers of students who had been suspended or detained in the past. As first year teachers, we also faced constant observation and evaluation by the principal and central office staff who decided whether we should remain for another year or be fired. Even though we were embarrassed to admit this concern, we knew that we had to manage our classes—control students—to the satisfaction of district evaluators.

By the middle of the year, we understood those aspects of classroom management with which the administration was most concerned. Among other things, if we "wrote up" students and sent them to the office frequently, we would be closely scrutinized. I had written-up perhaps as many as six students by mid-year, a number I considered appallingly high. Each write-up felt to me like an admission that I did not know how to control my classes, that I was failing as a teacher in the ways that could affect the renewal of my contract. I also believed I was selling my educational soul by focusing any instructional energy on maintaining proper student behavior. I knew that most of the students in my classes were learning a great deal about physical science and many were coming to enjoy the subject for the first time in their lives. However, when evaluators appeared, it did not look like good classroom management if students spoke excitedly in class, moved about the classroom to get lab materials, or worked with their friends on cooperative assignments.

Rumor had it that Mary, another new teacher, had written up over sixty students by winter break. We worried for her and tried to figure out tricks that might help. Eventually, though, Mary figured out her own system that "worked" for her. She had discovered that students paid better attention to her lectures if she gave them assignments immediately afterward based on their careful attention to her words. She further noticed that students remained quiet and obedient if she gave them worksheets. As a result, Mary's spring semester passed with dramatically fewer write-ups as her students plowed through stacks of assignments and slept afterward. Walk-by evaluators noted attentive students focused on tasks at hand. To the evaluators, she had conquered her classroom management problems by the end of the year.

Tonya, a young, brilliant woman and another new teacher, wrote up the same number of students as I did.

Since our classrooms were next to each other, we often commiserated after school about the day's problems. We each attempted to make our classrooms more interesting and lively places. We tried to find out what was going on in our students' lives. We gave each other reality checks when we questioned our own judgment. Since I am White, she sometimes asked me to help her understand a few White students who treated her badly; and since she is Black, I likewise asked her to help me grasp why some Black students distrusted me. I could not have made it through my first year of teaching without her. Tonya, however, thought better of her public school teaching plans. She quit toward the end of the year to pursue a Ph.D. in biology. The students who had mistreated her missed her terribly when she left.

Mark, yet another new teacher, taught shop and worked with the football coach to train members of the highly touted football team. At first, Mark gained the respect of male students easily because of his size and muscular bulk. He did not need write-up slips. He enjoyed joking and playing with students, but as the months rolled by the students sometimes took control. Eventually Mark got frustrated with their behavior and, as students told it, he occasionally yelled, insulted, and humiliated them, spewed racist and sexist epithets, and sometimes even pinned them against the wall, inadvertently spraying them with chewing tobacco juice as he raged. Mark did not receive bad evaluations for classroom management, though. Students knew better than to cause trouble on the days that evaluators visited.

Each of the new teachers that year found ways to resolve the problem of controlling student behavior to the satisfaction of school administrators. We each did so in relative isolation, however, since there were few opportunities for collegial contact, for problem-solving sessions, for peer support, or for idea sharing. I felt fortunate to have cultivated a relationship with Tonya as well as with an excellent and more experienced teacher who generously agreed to mentor me. Otherwise, I felt cut off from professional contact with other teachers in the school. Our brief planning periods were staggered throughout the day, preventing common meeting times. Our lunch periods occurred in shifts and often we had to monitor the lunch room. Whenever scraps of time appeared during the day, most teachers scrambled desperately to prepare lessons, grade papers, handle the logistics of mandatory extracurricular assignments, or meet with students, parents, and administrators. At the end of the day, nearly every one of us suffered emotional and physical fatigue and could hardly bear additional meetings. On top of it all, most of us faced stacks of over a hundred papers to grade at home each night. Chronic exhaustion was a real and palpable problem for teachers at the school. It extinguished any hope for collegiality among the faculty.

Because of the intensely demanding workload as well as the social stamina required for maintaining relationships with 125 to 150 different students each day, most teachers sought ways to streamline their teaching efforts. Some devised a variety of systems for mechanizing the logistics of instruction and classroom management. One teacher arranged rows of students in alphabetical order to make gradebook entries efficient. Another gave up her dream of creating an original language curriculum and instead adopted textbook exercises verbatim. Most teachers opted for short answer or multiple choice tests and assignments to cut down on time-consuming essay grading. To reduce preparation time, some routinized the flow of each class period so that daily activities could be predicted with certainty. A few identified film and video resources that could stand in on days when they were simply too tired to pull together the next lesson; no saint in that arena, I was even known to have a few outstanding, gee-whiz science videos stashed away in case of such an emergency. We had to find ways to simplify our work or cut corners; otherwise we quickly burned out. Because of this burnout, some of the most inspired, original, and hardworking teachers left the classroom after serving only briefly. Students inevitably suffered.

In short, teaching was even more demanding than I had been warned. New teachers especially struggled to reconcile their earnest visions of becoming good teachers with the necessity of conforming to the narrow and specific demands of a highly structured, yet paradoxically chaotic, institution. During my first year, this struggle continually tested the limits of my creativity, drive, and situational judgment. Most new teachers abandoned their innovative classroom ideas to fall back on teaching as they had been taught. In spite of my initial missionary zeal, I sometimes found the lure of the familiar to be uncomfortably inviting.

Fortunately, I stumbled onto a practice that allowed me to gain enough daily perspective to forge ahead with my ideas. One day during the forty-five minute drive home, I noticed my cassette recorder in the passenger seat. I turned it on and spoke about the day's events, how they made me feel, what I thought about them, what I wanted to do differently, and how I could reevaluate my relationships with particular students. Since this process helped clear some of my daily confusion, I started making sense of my experiences in the classroom. I then began to decompress every day with the tape recorder and soon after kept a journal. That time for daily reflection eventually triggered critical breakthroughs in my understanding of teaching. I was then able to create unique ways of working with students and to foster a comfortable classroom atmosphere for all of us. I only needed a means of breaking free of my conceptions of what teachers do so I could think through each new situation in a contextually appropriate way. I needed to reflect, an activity unrewarded, scheduled out, and made unwieldy at school by the anxiety and exhaustion induced in most teachers by their heavy loads.

By the time I figured this out, Alan had dropped out of school. I regretted not having been very helpful in his life, but at least I had come to understand more about what had made his life difficult. Before he left he would sometimes confide in me, and when he thought no one else was looking or listening, he would even demonstrate his abundant scientific ability.

The Internal Culture of Schools

Although I began my teaching career determined to break free of the punitive disciplinary practices I had experienced in my own schooling, I soon felt pressured to adopt those same approaches. I labored to resist that compulsion, though, and as I did, I came to understand some of the social and structural constraints within which teachers have long had to operate, constraints that continue to make change in disciplinary practices difficult. Although the context of each school is unique, my teaching experiences exemplify some common aspects of contemporary school culture and illustrate important internal barriers to rethinking classroom management and changing the social relations of American classrooms. My experiences also demonstrate how even the most oppressive conditions and seemingly persistent barriers can sometimes give rise to noble and empowering change.

External Causes of Problems with School Order

Many teachers perceive that student behavior significantly affects their work. A recent government survey indicates that over a third of all teachers believe that disruptive student behavior interferes with their teaching. Further, some fifty-one percent say they have been verbally abused by students, sixteen percent have been threatened with injury, and seven percent have even been physically attacked by students.[3]

During the years I taught, a number of teachers quit or transferred because of disruptive, abusive, or violent student conduct. We knew that some students carried weapons. One day a young male brought a rifle and held an English class hostage while the rest of the school was quickly evacuated. In another incident, a student was stabbed to death near the campus in a dispute involving other students. The Klan repeatedly intimidated Black students by driving through campus in cars conspicuously full of firearms; and when Klansmen raised a white flag on the school's pole one afternoon, White and Black students armed themselves for racial confrontation. The presence of twenty-two police cars and a cautious early dismissal averted certain disaster. We did not need to read mounting nationwide statistics on youth violence to understand the phenomenon. The threat of student and community violence formed the unrelenting backdrop of our work.

These highly visible incidents represented only a portion of what occurred in the school. Students learned to choose their paths to classes after considering where confrontations might lurk. On days when tensions ran high, even the finest teachers felt they could accomplish little. Some teachers allowed clear and threatening disruptions in class to go unnoticed if they believed the perpetrators might retaliate with force. Other teachers attempted to crack down with military fervor because, they thought, "This is the only thing they'll understand."

There were numerous days that we all felt as though the school were under siege. Teachers and administrators struggled to extinguish one fire after another, sometimes literally. It was tempting to blame our vexing problems on external conditions. However, when the principal—who was known for his hands-off style of management, for appeasing wealthy White parents, as well as for making offhanded racist and sexist comments—resigned, the school climate changed. The level of campus unrest dropped noticeably and even the assistant principals could relax enough to smile and joke occasionally.

An astute, conscientious woman later assumed the interim principalship. She began by spending long hours with the assistant principals, listening to them, planning with them, and supporting them. She then met with the teachers one by one, adopting many of their suggestions. She attended meetings of every student group to hear student concerns and fears. She continued those meetings and made herself highly visible in the school. Nearly everyone marveled at her responsiveness, at how carefully she made her decisions and explained them. Even the football coaches, who had initially vowed to resist the authority of any woman, eventually came to respect and depend on this principal as well as to offer some of her greatest support. Perhaps most noticeable, though, was the dramatic drop in violent, disruptive, or abusive student conduct. Not coincidentally, teachers resorted to extreme punitive measures much less frequently as well. The school became a different place. Even though the community continued to suffer countless social, political and economic problems, the resort to external explanations for the school's problems rang hollow after we witnessed the transformation brought by this remarkable woman.

Hierarchical Organization

As a child, I viewed classrooms as self-contained social units, each as distinct as the presiding teacher. The principal existed mainly as the disciplinarian of last resort and was otherwise peripheral to my experience. When I started teaching, though, I quickly realized the extent to which teachers occupy a relatively low position in a much larger hierarchical structure and are held accountable to administrators much as students are immediately accountable to their teachers.

The teachers hired along with me understood the hierarchical power structure of the school and the system of reward and punishment that kept it in place. Most of us felt fortunate to have been hired in a tight job market and therefore believed our hold on these positions was tenuous at best. Like other teachers around the country, many of us came from meager circumstances.[4] Some had mobile home payments to make. Several struggled to keep up with rent. Other teachers in double-income families lived in modest country homes. Few of us had family or other resources available to tide us through crises in unemployment. We were economically vulnerable; that affected our willingness to take chances. Constant monitoring and evaluation chided us to perform according to administrative expectations. When the principal told us to control student behavior, we either complied or received lower evaluations, letters of reprimand, possible humiliation in faculty meetings, or—even more humiliating—a scolding in front of students. Ultimately, we could have lost our hard-won positions and faced future hiring prohibitions as poor recommendations followed us.

To avoid these frightening possibilities, most teachers endeavored to preserve the kind of classroom control described explicitly in the evaluation instruments used by classroom observers. We were to maintain a clean and orderly climate, keep students on-task, respond promptly and decisively to inappropriate student behavior, and convey to the administration our lessons in a standard format complete with student behavioral objectives. Evaluators would only record behaviors they could see or hear, and if the evaluator did not record something, it did not occur. Essentially, this system noted aspects of the classroom ecology that could be overtly observed and measured, such as behavior, while ignoring or discounting those more difficult to assess, though presumably more desirable, such as student meaning-making or intellectual growth.

As a final measure of accountability, administrators held teachers responsible for student performance on state-wide standardized achievement tests. In the nature of such examinations, to produce acceptable results teachers themselves needed to stay on-task, ignore explorations of interesting topics not evaluated by the tests, and to concentrate on conveying a series of specific facts deemed relevant by someone we did not know or whose expertise may have been questionable. For my physics classes, I was faced with the choice of foregoing my unit on the Theories of Relativity in order to teach computer savvy students how to use a slide rule—because questions about slide rules accounted for about three percent of the state physics test. Standardized tests obviated reflection on the deeper principles at work in the disciplines we studied as well as their meaning in our lives.

The principal and some central office staff monitored and evaluated our performance. Within the school district they maintained control of this system of reward and punishment, and thereby perpetuated the hierarchical distribution of power. Teachers in turn monitored and evaluated student performance, dispensing grades or punishments to maintain control. At each level in the hierarchical structure, compliance was defined in terms of observable behaviors rather than thought or understanding. Teachers and students who did not abide by this system faced negative consequences.

When the interim principal assumed her duties, she was vested with the same hierarchical, positional power as her predecessors. She decided, however, to relinquish some of that power so that others could contribute to the process of reforming the school culture. She encouraged flexibility rather than rigid adherence to rules. She observed teachers' classes and gave the results to the teachers to use as they saw fit rather than filing copies in the central office for future administrative consequences. She enticed students and teachers to reflect on their work by discussing the meaning of schooling. She de-emphasized the primacy of behavior by asking students and teachers why things happened as they did and expecting critical thought and rich dialogue in response. Although she began with positional power, she quickly reconfigured the school's power structure and distributed responsibility for the school's welfare among many. She demonstrated that the distribution of power in a hierarchical administrative structure could be negotiated and reshaped.

Institutional Inertia

When I arrived at the school, policy changes occurred slowly. The bureaucratic machinery of the district required that policies be drafted by administration-appointed committees, approved, budgeted, and staff development activities prepared before implementation could begin. The process usually took years. Older teachers at the school were fond of telling rookies that as soon as new initiatives were finally implemented, counteracting ones would already be in draft stage. "You might as well just keep doing what you've been doing because they'll change back to it eventually."

For many years, though, the aspect of the school machinery most impervious to change was the basic hierarchical distribution and control of power. When the first principal instituted Assertive Discipline training after routing the change through the proper channels, the distribution of power among teachers and administrators changed little. Administrators continued to delineate disciplinary parameters; thus, teachers could not establish classrooms rules beyond a limited range. Students were not encouraged to think through the consequences of their actions beyond simple binary possibilities. As a result, they were allowed little opportunity for complex thought that could have enhanced their ability to make empowering, socially responsible decisions.

In contrast, the interim principal demonstrated that the redistribution of power in the school was possible, that institutional inertia need not always impede thoughtful change. At the end of the school year, though, the school board chose not to hire her. Instead, it hired another principal who ushered in a new era of school discord. Despite impassioned pleas from teachers and students, the school board and superintendent were ultimately unprepared to relinquish or share any of their power.

Unreflective Pragmatism

Because of the first principal's expectations the year I arrived, teachers at the school searched for ways to make things work. Yet in spite of the urgency with which these expectations confronted us, there was little time provided in the work day to reflect carefully on how to solve these problems, let alone ponder the worthiness of the principal's goals. School efficiency practices established early in this century continued to shape our work in the 1980s. Such practices required that experts establish school goals, make curricular decisions for us, determine our tools for maintaining control, and mandate the modes of interaction among students, teachers, and administrators. These practices also dictated that we teach large numbers of students, cover great curricular territory, assign volumes of homework, assume extra duties, and work long hours.[5] In the rush to march lock-step through the state-mandated, standardized curricula and in the face of chronic and persistent overloads, teachers at the school responded to challenging new situations largely out of exhaustion. Some then re-enacted teaching methods witnessed in their youth. A few teachers devised novel solutions to problems, but once they were deemed successful, inquiry usually ceased. In the end, teachers' lack of critical reflection time further tightened the controlling grip by which the principal held us since it became more difficult for us to imagine alternatives to his default imperatives.

"Teachers teach as they have been taught," the old adage goes. In the case of disciplinary practices, a number of studies support the notion that teachers tend to perpetuate disciplinary styles modeled earlier in their lives. Students in teacher education programs often base their beliefs about learning and teaching on their own early school experiences.[6] They also frequently select class management strategies in alignment with the kinds of discipline they experienced in their families of origin. Those most likely to adopt punitive measures in their classrooms report higher instances of having been subjected to verbal or physical abuse as children.[7]

Time for critical reflection is necessary for breaking free of such unexamined patterns. Also, it is helpful to have resources and persons available to offer ideas or to assist in developing newer or more compassionate approaches to dealing with students. New teachers seldom seek the help of principals to figure out how to remedy problems.[8] This is not surprising considering that principals must often evaluate teachers. Novices instead turn to more experienced teachers for assistance, but often those teachers are overburdened and have little time to establish collegial, let alone mentoring, relationships. In short, there are few places for teachers to turn when they want to think through the inevitable challenges of their work. The structure of schooling makes it difficult even to turn inward for solitude and quiet thought.

From what I have seen and read subsequently, it appears that my experiences typify those of teachers around the country. Manifestly, numerous institutional constraints impede thoughtful reform in disciplinary practices. These impediments do not always prevent critical reflection and change, though, as I discovered when the interim principal at my school facilitated remarkable, though short-circuited, transformations in the school culture.

Digging Out

After leaving the public school classroom years later, I searched for ways to resolve the conflict I had felt between my desire to think well about school discipline and my lived experience of the constraints on teachers' work. Without the immediacies of raging Alans, I wondered why the matter of discipline had so thoroughly gripped my attention while in the classroom. A part of me believed that discipline is the instrumentality of hierarchical control. It keeps people in line, limits their options, and perpetuates hegemonic structures. At the same time, though, as I had developed individual relationships with students, gained confidence in my teaching ability, and felt increasing responsibility for students' long term growth, I knew that at some level I had come to value discipline. I felt I needed to create boundaries in my classes to focus attention on matters that class participants and I considered most important. I rejected the creation of rigid rules, though, and instead labored to adjust to the needs and expectations of individual students. If I had failed to establish some small measure of cooperation among students, the impulsiveness and social thoughtlessness of some would have eventually eroded any sense of collective purpose. We would have missed many opportunities to explore how our individual actions and intentions affected others and the class as a whole. My challenge then, as I had come to understand it, lay in the delicate daily navigation of the tricky terrain between authoritarianism and permissiveness.

My search for understanding eventually led to the writings of Nel Noddings whose philosophical discussions about caring offer a useful framework for analyzing and interpreting my classroom experiences. Noddings explains that caring, grounded in relatedness, receptivity, and responsiveness, finds expression in individual relationships where each person strives to meet the other morally. The caring relationship is asymmetrical in that the *one-caring* is engrossed in the needs and well-being of the *cared-for*. To the cared-for, the attitude and actions of the one-caring are of great importance and as a result, "the cared-for glows, grows stronger, and feels not so much that he has been given something as that something has been added to him."[9]

I knew that my teaching had worked best when I was able to establish and maintain respectful, thoughtful, and flexible relationships with each of my students. Rules became suggestions or guidelines open for negotiation as our unfolding relationships and ever-changing contexts necessitated change. Noddings contends that reliance on fixed rules and eternal principles of right and wrong, in contrast, divorces persons from considering the unique relational and situational contexts in which they must make ethical decisions. This separation ultimately dulls sensitivity to the needs and concerns of others and weakens the bond of a caring relationship. Essentially, educators who insist on strict, rule-bound discipline, such as that advocated by the Canters, may well diminish the possibility of establishing caring relationships in the classroom.

The interim principal had in many ways modeled the possibility of a caring educator. She spent considerable time and effort building individual relationships with as many persons in the school as possible, responding to their needs, and bending the rules frequently to serve the larger purpose of helping us each grow as members of the school community. She weighed her decisions carefully, always taking a deep-seated concern for her wide-ranging and newly developed relationships into account.

I also understood from my years of teaching that good teachers need time to reflect as well as some means of replenishing their energy for caring. Noddings explains that if the one-caring does not find ways to recharge, she grows tired and cannot sustain caring relationships well. Many of the structural constraints in teaching, such as overload, lack of collegiality, and scanty administrative support, effectively erode teachers' means of restoring their vitality, confidence, and sense of purpose. Without this support, many teachers feel that they must fall back on institutional structures to define their work relation-ships. When this happens, the value of each individual is lost to the goals of the larger structure.

The interim principal, through her caring leadership, offered teachers, administrators and students enough support and a safe climate so that we would not feel isolated or overburdened. Gradually, we each started to establish rich, interconnecting sets of relationships with other members of the school community. This process at times seemed less than magical as we stumbled along in learning to work with each other. In large groups, caring was often in short supply or sometimes proved inadequate by itself for solving some of our most vexing problems. Little by little, though, our increased levels of mutual trust led to the emergence of both planned and spontaneous democratic processes through which we could work out agreeable improvements together. Essentially, the interim principal's caring fostered a climate where democratic processes could flourish.

Whether or not the interim principal had read Noddings' ideas, she certainly cared about her work at the school, about us, and about helping the school to heal and grow. Sadly, I did not discover Noddings' or even Dewey's work until I had enrolled in a doctoral program. Before that, when I announced to students and faculty that I would leave my teaching position to attend graduate school, Ruth, my close friend and mentor, reacted angrily. She told me that I would eventually become like all the other education professors she had encountered: comfortable, filled with abstract and theoretical knowledge, and ultimately disconnected from the process of schooling. She maintained that the academics she had known had quickly forgotten what they had experienced in the classroom, if they had ever bothered to teach in the first place, that is. Soon, she warned, I would be just another university professor depicting teachers as compliant non-intellectuals in need of experts to tell them how to do their work. I would lose my teacher identity.

With Ruth's admonitions in mind, I have unearthed my tapes and journal notes to piece together this story about the complexities and difficulties of thinking well about discipline in schools. I am convinced that the best ending for this story would have been for me to have written it from the classroom. For this to have happened, though, I as a teacher would have needed a strong support system, time for reflection, and relief from chronic overwork, all important prerequisites of any sober effort to transform disciplinary practice. Short of that possibility, the best I can do is to remember and write as a person who has taught, who values the work of teaching, and who has wrestled with seemingly unresolvable value conflicts in thinking about discipline.

Notes

1. The following is a story about how my understanding of classroom discipline evolved. It is based on my recollections as well as tape-recorded notes and journal entries from my first few years of teaching in a medium-sized public high school in a southern, racially polarized, and economically depressed town. In contrast with traditional forms of academic discourse that require an explicit discussion of theoretical frameworks near the beginning of a work, this story will gradually unfold to better reflect how my thinking about discipline changed with my experiences.

2. Lee Canter and Marlene Canter, *Assertive Discipline: A Take-Charge Approach for Today's Educator* (Los Angeles, CA: Canter & Associates, 1976). For a journalistic analysis of the Canters' system, see David Hill, "Order in the Classroom," *Teacher Magazine* (April 1990): 70–77.

3. Wendy Mansfield, Debbie Alexander, Elizabeth Farris and Westat, Inc., "Teacher Survey on Safe, Disciplined, and Drug-Free Schools," National Center for Education Statistics (Washington, D.C.: Government Printing Office, 1991), 13.

4. Michael Sedlak and Steven Schlossman, "Who Will Teach? Historical Perspectives on the Changing Appeal of Teaching as a Profession" (Santa Monica, CA: The RAND Corporation, 1986), 27–35; Dan C. Lortie, *Schoolteacher: A Sociological Study* (Chicago: University of Chicago Press, 1975), 33–37.

5. For a discussion of early twentieth century efficiency measures in public schooling, see Raymond Callahan's classic, *Education and the Cult of Efficiency: A Study of the Social Forces that Have Shaped the Administration of the Public Schools* (Chicago: University of Chicago Press, 1962). Also, for a discussion of chronic teacher overloads, see Andy Hargreaves' "Time and Teachers' Work: An Analysis of the Intensification Thesis,"

Teachers College Record 94, no. 1 (1992): 87–108. Sid Womack documents the extra unpaid time teachers invest in their work in "No Extra Charge," *The American School Board Journal* 117, no. 7 (1990): 34, 37.

6. L.M. Anderson, "Learners and Learning," in *Knowledge Base for the Beginning Teacher*, M.C. Reynolds, ed. (New York: Pergamon, 1989).

7. Charles Kaplan, "Teachers' Punishment Histories and Their Selection of Disciplinary Strategies," *Contemporary Educational Psychology* 17 (1992): 258–265.

8. Kenneth M. Zeichner, B. Robert Tabachnick, and Kathleen Densmore, "Individual, Institutional, and Cultural Influences on the Development of Teachers' Craft Knowledge," in *Exploring Teachers' Thinking*, J. Calderhead, ed. (London: Cassell, 1987): 21–59.

9. Nel Noddings, *Caring: A Feminine Approach to Ethics and Moral Education* (Berkeley, CA: University of California Press, 1984).

4

Why is Michael always Getting Timed Out? Race, Class, and the Disciplining of Other People's Children

❏

Brian M. McCadden

After story time Mrs. Hooper[1] talks to the kindergarten children about the next item on the day's agenda. She rises from her seat at the front of the "meeting" space and moves a few steps to the bulletin board on the wall, upon which is tacked a column of laminated manila strips with words like "meeting," "outside," "lunch," and "story time" written on them in red magic marker. "Okay, class, we've been to meeting, we've been outside, we've been to see coach, we've had lunch and story." As she recites each activity, Mrs. Hooper removes the corresponding strip from the board and places it in a laminated pocket tacked to the board. Reaching for the strip marked "centers" she says, "Now, we are going to go to centers." The children, sitting on the floor in three semicircular rows facing Mrs. Hooper, arch their backs and edge forward just a bit in anticipation. Centers are their favorite part of the school day, besides outside time (recess) and coach (gym), of course.

Mrs. Hooper proceeds to talk about what she expects of the children at centers; how they should maintain good personal space, how they should use small voices, how they should work to be smarter, and how they should stay in their centers until the bell rings. "And what do you do then class?" Almost in unison the class chants, "Stop, look, and listen." "Oh, I do think that this is the best class I've ever had at Green End. You stop what you're doing, look at me, and wait for my signal to clean up your center and move on to the next one. Okay, Cam, you're first today for choosing centers. . . ." Mrs. Hooper calls off names alphabetically, with the first person called today rotating to the end of the list tomorrow, so that everyone gets a chance to be first.

As she runs through the procedure, she skips over Michael, who stays seated on the floor while the others move off to choose their centers and then proceed outside for recess. He sits in silent apprehension until the last few children are on their way out the door, then Mrs. Hooper says sternly, "Michael, you know what your job is at meeting. You know that I don't like it when people are talking and sprawling out and not listening when I am talking. We are going to have to sit here for five minutes and practice keeping our houses in order when we're up front." He had been disruptive during both story time and center directions.

I am standing at the back of the room holding the door for the children. As she passes me, Judith, one of the last children out, looks up and asks, "Why is Michael always getting timed out?"

Introduction

This vignette took place, and takes place, in Hanna Hooper's[2] kindergarten classroom at Green End Elementary School in Pinedale, North Carolina. It is representative of the types of management and disciplinary practices that Mrs. Hooper employs in her daily expression of teaching. While it would be an interesting and worthwhile exercise to unpack and examine these practices—structuring time, explaining standards and expectations, using positive reinforcement, tying consequences to actions, etc.—in this paper I want to focus on the last scene: I want to explore the question, "Why is Michael always getting timed out?"

My intention is not to attack or vilify Mrs. Hooper for the way she practices her craft. Indeed, it is nearly the opposite. In my two years as a participant observer in her classroom, I came to understand and appreciate the complexity of classroom management and the insufficiency of textbook solutions in the face of classroom contexts and real-time decision making. I also came to understand and appreciate Mrs. Hooper's ability to work in real time and to turn what seemed like chaos into "educative moments." Rather, then, than tear down her practice and provide lofty prescriptions or models, I want to contribute to the discussion on school discipline and classroom management by relating Mrs. Hooper's and my experiences as kindergarten teachers.[3] I believe that what happened in her classroom—the sorts of decisions made, identities constructed, patterns developed, disciplinary measures invoked—have much to tell us about the inherent difficulties involved in disciplining other people's children.[4]

Pinedale, North Carolina

While the issues of discipline and management are ambiguously tense enough on their own, they become exponentially so as more and more variables are introduced into the equation. One variable that stands out as particularly problematic in relation to discipline is that of race. And this is the focus of my paper. Here, Mrs. Hooper is a white teacher, while Michael is, as you may have guessed, a black child. The fear, loathing, and anxiety involved in the symbolism that a white power-holder disciplining a black, relatively powerless, person conveys cannot be underestimated. It is the sort of deep emotional dread that is not easily addressed, and that so often drives well-intentioned white educators to unintentionally hurt worse by trying to help more.

Pinedale, North Carolina is a suburban, generally professional, middle- to upper-middle-class community of roughly 40,000 people in the central part of the state. The population is 74 percent white, 18 percent black,[5] and eight percent "other," predominantly Hispanic and Asian. Mrs. Hooper's students mirror those percentages nicely, with eighteen white, three black, two Asian, and one Hispanic of twenty-four total students. The town promotes itself as socially progressive and fairly liberal-minded, and places a high value on education, as is evidenced in such things as strong parental involvement in school, heavy coverage of education in the local newspaper, and high status of teachers in the town.

The school support and middle-class professionalism of Pinedale are descriptors of the white community rather than the black community: the black middle class in this area generally lives in the neighboring town of Carver. Black children have trouble succeeding in Pinedale schools, and while the white community is aware of this and continuously aims to alter such outcomes, it finds it exceedingly difficult to enact any effective measures. In a juxtaposition that speaks volumes, just as more and more white families are moving to Pinedale to get their children into what is considered one of the better school systems in the state, many black families are moving out of Pinedale to Carver so that their children can attend schools where there is a stronger black voice and the perception of a better chance of success. I do not want to say that Pinedale is a racist town; the term connotes to me a sense of purposefulness and malice that I did not see there. I do think, however, that the sort of impenetrable underlying institutional racism that permeates this nation is evident in the difficulties Pinedale faces in serving the needs and wants of the black community.

Teacher-Centeredness and Liberal Intentions

Amid this context, Mrs. Hooper teaches kindergarten. Her style of teaching is very teacher-centered, very controlling, as is evidenced in the opening vignette, above. As a further example of her style, in controlling the way centers are enacted, she allows only two children at a time at each center and discourages small talk: the children are directed to "help their neighbor" complete assigned tasks and are admonished to "work to be smarter." The children are generally not coached to "explore," "discover," or "play" at classroom activities. All attention and direction funnels through Mrs. Hooper, who has very specific ideas about what needs to be covered and completed in a given period of time, and has no trouble in using her power to see these plans through. This teacher-centered approach, coupled with an emphasis on making products such as puppets, masks, posters, and cards, creates a focused and industrial classroom environment. Mrs. Hooper uses the language of work to describe worthwhile or important tasks and constructs rituals to simulate workplace conditions, such as a "punching-in" morning ritual upon the children's entry to the classroom.[6]

To achieve her ambitious instructional goals, Mrs. Hooper must use a strong management style. Toward this end, she dedicates the first six weeks of school to teaching the children how they are expected to be in her classroom: what rules and procedures to follow; what rules apply in which classroom spaces at which time of day; how they are to interact with each other, with her, and with classroom materials; and how they are to move from activity to activity throughout the school day. While elsewhere I have described this process of socially constructing "students" in detail,[7] it serves the purpose of this paper to explore, briefly, this process as a management issue.

Mrs. Hooper follows an organizational morality in her approach to schooling. That is, highest priority is placed on students' understanding what their role is within the organization called school, and a student's "goodness" is judged by how well he or she succeeds at contributing to organizational goals such as completing products, maintaining equipment, or enhancing efficiency. Relational goals, such as making friends, learning how to resolve conflicts, and learning how to negotiate are important and addressed, but they are prioritized below organizational goals, dropping out when conflicts between goals arise. Managing to achieve organizational goals requires that the children learn to value the organization above themselves.

This is taught in several ways. First, valuing the organization is taught through verbal coaching, such as saying, "We are going to be the best team at Green End," and, "Thank you for helping your neighbor to keep his house in order." Second, it is taught through tying student-made products (the organizational outcome) to students' identity by displaying their products on the classroom walls and continuously associating these products with the purpose of school. Third, it is taught through Mrs. Hooper's modeling a love of organization in her own behaviors as teacher. And fourth, it is taught through internalizing organizational processes by verbalizing and modeling cognitive strategies, such as introducing a new activity, modeling it, and saying, "Okay, class, now that I've finished my drawing, what do I need to do? I need to think about what I should be doing to make myself smarter."

My initial reaction to Mrs. Hooper's management and teaching styles was one of discomfort. Philosophically, I was and am more of a "progressive" or "experiential" educator.[8] I prefer a neoromantic view of education in which children are able to become "the authors of their own existence," a view sympathetic to social reconstructionism in which we move beyond socialization to "a vision of a new social order that is free of all forms of oppression, tradition, and presumably, the socialization process itself".[9] Through my lens as a progressive educator I saw

Mrs. Hooper's teacher-centeredness and product-orienta-tion as reproducing dominant and oppressive cultural codes.

However, I came to realize over the course of my fieldwork that Mrs. Hooper was teaching and managing in a way that best served the needs of her students. That is, she was teaching them the sorts of skills they needed to have in order to achieve success in Pinedale's pre-dominantly essentialist school system. I realized this by talking to parents and other teachers in the school, who almost universally acclaimed Mrs. Hooper's ability to "get kids ready for first grade." Her teacher-of-the-year awards and the level of parental lobbying for access to her classroom are also indicative of her knack for helping children attach to school. I realized by watching Mrs. Hooper practice her craft that it is far easier for a liberal academic to be a nonparticipatory critic of teacher's use of power than it is for a liberal academic to remain so while taking an active role in the instruction of children. That is, the vision of our children all being as Rousseau's *Emile*[10] falls away quickly under the realization that these same children must fight through at least twelve years of public schooling in which success necessarily equates with one's ability to navigate and accommodate bureau-cratic, organizational structures.

Disciplining Black Boys

As we moved further and further into the school year, the instructional emphasis moved from teaching life skills and adherence to organizational morality to more aca-demic tasks such as literacy, numeracy, and getting through instructional units. Mrs. Hooper expected the children to know the class rules and procedures by early October, and this is when her instructional shift occurred. Perhaps not coincidentally, this is also when the child-ren's stress level rose, when there were more instances of acting out, of resistance, of rough play at recess, and of overt use of disciplinary measures such as timing out. It was Mrs. Hooper's expressed goal to only use "positive attention" with the children. That is, she only wanted to recognize them publicly in a positive light. This entailed openly praising children when they did something right, instead of admonishing them for doing something wrong, as well as redirecting attention away from a disrupter by saying something like, "Thank you, Cam, for not letting yourself be distracted," when another child was poking him. As we moved closer toward focusing on academic goals, more and more instances of negative attention occurred, in which Mrs. Hooper publicly recognized "bad" behavior. She would get very angry with herself when this occurred because she knew that this sort of attention only served to reinforce the negative behavior by giving it the attention that it so desperately sought. The felt need to get the children ready for first grade exacts a toll on both the children and the teacher.

In my initial analysis, this toll was particularly paid by the black children, especially the black boys.[11] The black boys were the most frequently timed out and received the most negative attention, such as verbal warnings and thumbs-down signs. I saw the white boys "getting away" with more than the black boys got away with, and I saw Mrs. Hooper's management and disciplinary practices as symptomatic of the sort of institutional racism that was driving the black community out of Pinedale. I did not and do not consider Mrs. Hooper to be a racist. Indeed, she was a founding member of Pinedale's multicultural curriculum committee and had fought throughout her twenty-five year career to include black teaching materials and instructional themes wherever she taught, beginning with a battle with a principal during her first year of teaching over using black dolls in the kindergarten. However, the white middle-class values of hard work, organizational adherence, independent work, task orientation, and product orientation seemed to be stifling the black boys. They seemed to me to be prevented from expressing their blackness, their apparent creativity, collectivism, energy, and artistic aptitudes by Mrs. Hooper's teacher-centered control. There seemed to me to be some ways of knowing, à la Gardner's multiple intelligences, that were not being addressed through the curriculum.[12]

Yet despite this "stifling," Mrs. Hooper was sought out by black families to be the teacher of their children. In Pinedale, children are assigned to classrooms according to lottery. The rosters are then modified to achieve racial and gender balance. Known "hard cases" are also balanced out so that there are not too many disruptive students in one class. This grouping practice is supplemented by very active lobbying on the part of some, generally powerful, parents to place their child with the teacher of their choosing. Since Mrs. Hooper is such a well respected teacher, the principal receives a good number of phone calls concerning access to Mrs. Hooper's roster. In the last year I was in her class, we had the children of the assistant superintendent of Pinedale schools, three Green End teachers, one Green End teacher aide, and various prominent citizens in the Green End attendance zone.

Interestingly, the teacher aide who lobbied for Mrs. Hooper is black and is Michael's mother—the Michael who is always getting timed out. Mrs. Hooper had taught her daughter a few years before, with good enough success to warrant lobbying for Michael. Mrs. Hooper is also given the "really hard cases" by the principal—the children that no one else wants or is able to reach. Besides Michael, the class contained Malik, a black boy who was repeating kindergarten due to a lack of attendance and a perceived inability to learn, and Dontonio, a black boy who had been diagnosed as ADHD, among other things, at the tender age of four. These placements, along with the lobbying, indicated a level of success in teaching, disciplining, and socializing black boys that provided a stark contrary analysis to my view of her stifling and oppressing these children.

Race and Explicit Power

In attempting to reconcile these disparate elements, a reading of Delpit's "The Silenced Dialogue" and Noblit's "Power and Caring" helped me to understand better the lenses I was bringing to bear on the research as a white middle-class liberal academic.[13] Delpit was speaking to me when she wrote that:

> To provide schooling for everyone's children that reflects liberal, middle-class values and aspirations is to ensure the maintenance of the status quo, to ensure that power, the culture of power, remains in the hands of those who already have it . . . Many liberal educators hold that the primary goal for education is for children to become autonomous, to develop fully who they are in the classroom setting without having arbitrary, outside standards forced upon them. This is a very reasonable goal for people whose children are already participants in the culture of power and who have already internalized its codes . . . But parents who don't function within that culture often want something more . . . They want to ensure that the school provides their children with discourse patterns, interactional styles, and spoken and written language codes that will allow them success in the larger society.[14]

Delpit was saying that what black middle-class parents want for their children in white middle-class schools is for the teachers to be explicit in their use of their power as teachers, to overtly teach their children how to get by and succeed in the larger white society. Liberal educators are often afraid or unwilling to use their power in teaching, disciplining, and socializing children. Instead of accepting the responsibility of their position and explicitly using their power to shape the school-based identity of children, liberal educators often use their power indirectly in an effort to not oppress others, which leads to an indirect oppression of black students because they are deprived access to the cultural codes and rules of interaction that white students have access to by virtue of their membership in white middle-class culture and society. Seen this way, Mrs. Hooper is an effective teacher for black students because she accepts the responsibility and power of her position, and explicitly uses that power to teach her black students how to succeed in the white schools of Pinedale.

I found affirmation of this analysis, as well as with this struggle with liberal conceptions of good teaching, in Noblit's ethnographic study of a second grade classroom. He spent a year with Pam, a black teacher in a predominantly black school, and found in her approach to teaching the sort of teacher-centeredness and use of power that makes a white liberal academic uneasy, but that works well in helping children succeed in schools as currently constructed. Pam was firm with her students, demanding much more of them than they had been used to in other classes. She was not one to see her black students as "disadvantaged" and thus in need of a lower set of standards in order to boost their self-esteem. Instead, she boosted their self-esteem by expecting much and helping them help each other achieve it. She saw her position as being imbued with a moral responsibility to be in charge of guiding what her students could and could not do, and rather than be repelled by this, her students embraced her and her standards.[15]

Perhaps what Pam, Mrs. Hooper, and people like Michael's mother are telling us—telling me—is that what black children, especially black boys, need is not the sort of permissive and progressive management and discipline that aims to allow the child to maintain a sense of autonomy as he charts his own course and creates his own self. Perhaps the black boys, needing to understand a culture that is not their own, require a different, more overt, form of nurturance. Success for these boys may depend on these teachers showing them what they need to know and be as public citizens, in a white-dominated society represented by the arena called school.

Constructing Bad Boys

Yet even if we acknowledge that white middle-class teachers may need to use their power more explicitly in disciplining other people's children, a serious problem still remains in addressing the issue of helping black boys achieve success in white schools—that of a lack of fit, understanding, or respect between the dominant white school culture and the minority black home culture. It is a problem that neither Delpit nor Noblit directly address. For Noblit, this is not an issue since his was a study of a black teacher working predominantly with black children. Pam's use of collective-oriented rituals, such as organizing a class chant of consonants, worked with rather than against the home culture of the black boys in her class, as did her way of instilling self-respect through her instructional style. For Delpit, the issue was directed toward the idea of teaching black students the cultural codes they need to survive in white society, and to ostensibly ignore the outside or home black culture, leaving the latter as the domain of the family and community.

For Mrs. Hooper and Pinedale, the line between home and school cannot be so clearly drawn. As Gloria Ladson-Billings points out, oftentimes white teachers' "perceptions of African American students interfere with their ability to be effective teachers for them." These perceptions are derived from "mainstream society's invalidation of African American culture."[16] Television, movies, newspapers, political rhetoric, talk radio, pulpit extremists, and corner coffeeshops all contribute to this public discourse, often through code words. In my own university classrooms I know to whom people are referring when they mention "the low SES element." These perceptions are acted upon in classrooms everyday by well-intentioned people. They manifest themselves in the sort of excessive negative attention that Ladson-Billings found in her fieldwork:

> Imagine yourself in a kindergarten classroom. . . . As the [white] teacher attempts to discuss a story she has

read them, various children talk to their neighbors, hop up from their seats, and move to different areas of the room. No one particular student or group of students is participating in this kind of behavior more than any other. However, over the course of a thirty-minute period, the only children who are verbally reprimanded for their behavior are the three African Americans.[17]

Ladson-Billings attributes this inequitable disciplinary behavior to the teacher's perception that black students need to be controlled to be taught and that they are harder to control than other children. In my own work in Mrs. Hooper's classroom, I saw that she, too, felt that she needed to be extra firm with the black boys because of the perception that they were not controlled at home, which indicates a lack of respect of the home culture, but also because of the perception that black boys are marked in white society, which indicates an understanding of and real sympathy toward a media-fed reality. Mrs. Hooper was harder on the black boys in her classroom, and with good intentions—she knew that they had to work extra hard just to pull even.

The unanticipated consequence of these good intentions, however, was the construction of the black boys in her classroom as "bad."[18] By paying more attention to Michael, Malik, and Dontonio in an effort to help them understand what they needed to know to survive in the white schools of Pinedale, Mrs. Hooper inadvertently lead to Judith's asking me, "Why is Michael always getting timed out?' and to Caroline's hearing a commotion and saying, "I bet Dontonio did it." This construction inadvertently feeds the negative perceptions mainstream society holds toward black America.

Michael and Neil

To explore this construction further, I will compare Mrs. Hooper's interactions with two of the boys in her class. I have chosen two who have similar backgrounds:

they are both from middle-class families; both have two-parent families with both parents engaged in professional work; both were born in Pinedale; and both are in trouble often. The descriptions of these boys are drawn from an analysis of fieldnotes collected during my participant-observation stay in Mrs. Hooper's classroom. One of the boys is Neil, who is white, spent the year prior to kindergarten in a Montessori school, and "is bright, but somewhat headstrong; he scoffs at authority." He tends to wander while moving between activities and has a tendency toward bratty comments. The other boy is Michael, who is black, has a vivid imagination, and an inability to hold it in check, which leads to his inappropriate talkativeness and tendency to be tangential. He "knows he should cooperate and share, has a short attention span, and lots of energy." Both Neil and Michael were characterized by Mrs. Hooper as needing limits imposed on them.

Mrs. Hooper treats both boys the same in many ways—ways by which she tries to treat all her students. For example, she tries to separate the behavior from the person by admonishing "bad" behavior and quickly following with playful reinforcement of the person. Mrs. Hooper does this by taking away a card a child might be playing with at meeting, but then quickly playing an impromptu peek-a-boo game with it before putting it away. Similarly, if a child is excluded, either through her discipline or through self-exclusion, she tries to follow up as soon as possible with an inclusive gesture such as the following, which occurred during a play song activity:

> Michael had not wanted to participate in the prior song, saying "I'm scared," so Mrs. Hooper let him sit at his seat while the others played. For this next stage, she coaxed him out of his chair to join the group. We sang the song up until "hi-ho," and then Mrs. Hooper shouted "Freeze." We all stopped in our spots and she asked the students to tell her something they saw in the room. She picked Michael second and lavished

praise on him for his response, which was something fairly innocuous like "spider" (there is a spider in the science center). Her act of confirmation, however, put a big smile on Michael's face and brought him back into the class—where he had pulled himself out of membership in the group before, he now pushed himself back in and participated for the rest of the day.

The main differences lie in the types of public negative attention the two boys received. For Neil, a smart-alecky comment is either ignored or shut down quickly with a short, sharp, "Ut!" from Mrs. Hooper. When he speaks without raising a hand, Mrs. Hooper says, "I need to see a hand," rather than disciplining him. If he is poking his neighbor, she will more often redirect attention by saying, "I like the way Cam is keeping his house in order," than address Neil negatively. For Michael, on the other hand, comments, tangents, and rule-breaking are met with direct negative discipline, such as, "Michael, what is your job at centers?" or, "Michael, you know that you are supposed to raise your hand before asking a question. Next time its five minutes of play time." As indicated by a comparison of responses to speaking without the raising of a hand, the penalties for the same infraction can be quite different.

Negative Constructions

What is revealed, I believe, in an examination of Michael and Neil's interactions with Mrs. Hooper is what Ladson-Billings called the "invalidation of African American culture" that sees, among other things, black boys as being harder to control, and thus in need of more overt disciplinary measures.[19] This sort of belief is what Mrs. Hooper seems to be expressing in her interactions with Michael. Again, this is not to call Mrs. Hooper a racist in any way; instead, it is a warning to white middle-class teachers (and academics) to attend to their (our) own culturally subtle ways of responding to, and contributing to, the negative mainstream conceptions of black youth and black culture. One result of Mrs. Hooper's trying to help Michael succeed is her constructing of him as a "bad" person, someone who is to be recognized negatively and disciplined habitually.

This construction is understood by the other children in the class, not only by their questions about "Why is Michael always getting timed out?" but also by their taking on the role of disciplinarians themselves in their interactions with Michael, Malik, and Dontonio. The latter is something I contributed to myself in my own well-intentioned effort to help the students who were "not getting" the organizational procedures. I suggested to Mrs. Hooper that the children who understood the rules might be able to help teach the children who did not understand the rules, and that the creation of a sort of "buddy system" might help the children learn relational skills. Deferring to me as the "expert" from the university, she agreed and we matched up some buddies. The unanticipated consequence of this system was that those who understood the organizational procedures also quickly came to understand the construction of "good" students and "bad" and the power differential between the two. This solidified the construction of the black boys as "bad" and provided a mechanism for the children to express this new construction.

Michael and Neil are similar boys, differentiated by race and its cultural capital perhaps more than anything else. Cultural capital can be described as the interactive and communicative codes that a culture or society uses implicitly to frame how it views and understands phenomena.[20] An example of this is the understanding that people from the same culture share concerning the significance of returning a compliment or the meaning of a raised eyebrow. Shirley Brice Heath uses the example of a white student's "knowing" culturally that the question, "Is that where the scissors belong?" really means "Put the scissors on the shelf," while a black student may receive it as a question with several possible answers.[21]

While these examples are simple and direct, they convey meanings that are shared and learned within a specific cultural domain. Those who do not possess these meanings within their repertoire of cultural knowledge (their toolbox of correct responses to questions or gestures) are inherently "disadvantaged" in that what tests out as a lack of academic knowledge, and begins a cycle of labeling and tracking away from success, can more accurately be described as a lack of cultural knowledge.

For Michael and Neil, this plays out in Neil's implicitly compensating for his wandering by asking questions pertinent to Mrs. Hooper's instructional goals while Michael does not follow the organizational flow of the class and consequently receives more negative attention. For example, Neil seems to "know" that Mrs. Hooper wants to move her lesson or unit along and after pushing her a bit, he can provide answers to meeting-time questions that help her to do that in order to escape punishment. Conversely, Michael does not seem to "get" Mrs. Hooper's organizational goals, and thus has no escape mechanism when punishment draws near. Michael had not been previously "taught" those things that would help him to "play the game" of schooling in white society.

This is more clearly evident in the difference in cultural fit between Malik and Green End Elementary. Malik is a tough case. He is repeating kindergarten in part due to a very low attendance rate the prior year. Apparently, his mother, who lives alone with Malik and his two older siblings, does not consider attending school to be an important issue. Mrs. Hooper lamented Malik's deprived home life, where he was allowed to stay up late at night watching "inappropriate" movies, did not eat well, was not monitored, and was not taught any sense of responsibility for self. In one interview she related a view that corresponds to Ladson-Billings' critique: "Black children need to learn [life skills] much more quickly than white children because in their culture they act much more differently than they do here. Their environment is not that structured."

This view of some children having a "cultural deficit" plays out in how children are disciplined and taught differently. Malik, for example, was treated much more harshly than the white boys, with more negative attention, more severe language, and more instances of disciplinary action. A differential access to instruction results from this view as well. For example, in discussing some children's differential learning, Mrs. Hooper related how one white boy, Adam, was having a processing problem, so he could ask his neighbor Caroline for help with his letters. She also noted that she thought Neil was having a processing problem. I noted that these were two white boys whose parents could pay for such diagnoses and could talk such language with their child's teacher. Malik's efforts to interact with his neighbor were never viewed as possible attempts to "make himself smarter" or to seek help in processing. Instead, they were invariably seen as disruptions and addressed negatively.

Seeking a Better Fit

Once again, however, the disciplining of Malik and Michael was an effort made to provide them with the structure that was seen as necessary for them to succeed in the white schools of Pinedale, an effort that could be described as being in line with Delpit's admonitions to white middle-class teachers to teach black children what they need to know to "be successful in the white man's world."[22] If the black people she teaches and touches are any indication, Mrs. Hooper is quite successful at this. Her aide, LaShonda Maxwell, has been with her for over eight years and supports Mrs. Hooper's teaching style. While I was with her, two black boys from the prior school year came back to visit Mrs. Hooper and told her how much they missed her and how well they were doing in first grade. Also, the parent of a black boy from the prior year stopped by one day to say hello, chat, and reminisce with Mrs. Hooper. In this way she mirrors Noblit's Pam: "You love her more after you leave her."[23]

Finally, as Michael's mother bears out, black parents lobby to have their children be taught by Mrs. Hooper. Partly this is because she knows how to teach children to succeed in Pinedale's schools. Partly, too, this is because Mrs. Hooper genuinely cares about her students, even if she is hard on them at times. She desperately wants them to find success, and genuinely hurts with them when they fail, for she considers their failure to be hers as well. In the case of Malik, despite all the trouble she had with him and all the disruptions of her routines and plans he caused, she was visibly shaken and saddened when his mother pulled him out of school in December and moved to another part of the state. "I think I was really starting to get through his wall," she told me. Perhaps Mrs. Hooper's teaching represents an effort to "will" the black boys into conformity with white culture rather than an effort to teach them white cultural codes. This may indicate a difference in how overt nurturance is manifested in white teachers (e.g., Mrs. Hooper) versus black teachers (e.g., Pam from Noblit's study).

If we consider the question, "Why is Michael always getting timed out?" to be answered for now, and the answer to be intertwined with a lack of cultural understanding and respect, the remaining questions are, "What went wrong?" and "What can be done?" I see no easy answers to these questions, and indeed feel cynical about the prospects of making any real change in regard to white teachers' ability to value black students and black culture. Mrs. Hooper is a teacher whom I greatly respect and admire, an outstanding shaper of children into students, and, frankly, if she constructs black children as "bad," then I am not sure it can be avoided. Perhaps part of the answer lies in recruiting and retaining more black teachers, not just to teach black children, but to teach white children how to understand and respect black people and black culture, to teach white children what they need to know in order to teach black children how to succeed in the dominant white society. But this answer would not help Mrs. Hooper or other white liberal educators currently practicing their craft.

One thing that seems certain to me is that the answer does not lie solely in such things as multicultural curricular materials, posters for Black History Month, values education, or simply wanting to "do the right thing." Mrs. Hooper's position on her school's multicultural committee indicates that the answer lies not in the curriculum. Delpit wants white teachers to teach black children how to succeed, but to do that well they need to understand black cultural codes well enough to respect and value these codes, which is something they cannot get from posters or reading about black people alone. Similarly, values such as respect for difference cannot be chosen off a character education menu or addressed solely through curriculum.[24] Everything adults do in school—and outside of school—expresses values and must express a valuing of respect. And this is a tall order to fill, one that cannot be filled given the current state of the popular, mainstream image of black America.

There are, however, some ideas I can share about what some people think or demonstrate can be done. I will present these as a way of ending this discussion for now while hoping that it does not end. Delpit suggests that white teachers use their power, their authority, explicitly in dealing with black children. White teachers must be direct in transmitting their expectations and standards and must establish meaningful relationships with their students. Mrs. Hooper does these things in many ways, but what she does not do is teach her black students to value their native way of being, the final suggestion Delpit makes. This is in large part due to her fundamentally not respecting the native ways of being of her black students. The socially supported way of interacting with black youth, that of being stern and "staying on top of them" helps to push Mrs. Hooper's expectations to the level of oppressive disciplinary practice.

A further failure in teaching that Delpit does not point out lies in a white teacher's not transmitting the message to white students that there are differential ways of disciplining and managing black and white students. The sort of structure and explicit power use that Mrs. Hooper displays conveys the message to white children that black boys are bad, rather than conveys the message that she is working extra hard to help them learn the things that white children already know about school. Teachers can and do explicitly talk about difference with children when it concerns cognition and physical ability, but not when it concerns cultural knowledge or cultural capital. Teachers often expect that all children are able to adhere to organizational processes equally, while simultaneously expecting that they all learn at different paces and teaching their students to respect that in others. We have made great strides in accepting that some students have processing problems or recall problems, changing how we teach to address these problems, and teaching our students that it is not bad or shameful to have these problems. Yet we have done very little to accept the cultural and organizational challenges that many students face, change our teaching accordingly, or teach our students to be accepting of these challenges to others.

Noblit suggests that white teachers need to learn more from black teachers, about how black teachers teach, how they value and connect to students, and how they incorporate the concept of the collective into their teaching. Pam, the teacher in Noblit's ethnography, used collective rituals, such as class chants, recitation games, and classroom maintenance routines to help the children not only attach to school organization but to also help them attach to each other. Her goal was for everyone to help everyone else succeed, as opposed to Mrs. Hooper's goal of having no one prevent anyone else from succeeding. The latter is a goal that promotes individual advancement over collective growth. Further, Pam saw building the collective through rituals to be an end in itself, while Mrs. Hooper used rituals as a means of organizing children for the larger end of completing projects and products.

Vivian Gussin Paley, a noted white kindergarten teacher in Chicago who works with a rainbow of urban students, echoes the call for addressing social and collective concerns as an end in itself in her call for teachers to incorporate open dialogue with children into their teaching. This is a suggestion offered by Nel Noddings as well. According to Paley, children "never tire of giving you their ideas, and [through dialogue] you can manage to use them all, no matter how far off the mark."[25] Engaging in open dialogue with kindergartners poses management and disciplinary threats, as I can attest from my own efforts at doing so. However, the threats relate to fears and assumptions about teaching that may benefit from being challenged. These include the notions that classrooms require quiet independent work, that a noisy classroom is out of control, that children must stay on task rather than wander in their discussions, that any deviation from the lesson will lead to the children taking over the class. Letting go a bit requires an ability to use children's imaginations to carry a story along, to guide them through a discovery and exploration process, an effort that might help a child like Michael connect more strongly to schooling. The teacher here needs to care more about how children go about knowing and learning than being constantly concerned with what they know. This sort of exploration does not fly in the face of the idea that a teacher needs to be explicit in his or her teaching, as Ms. Martin, a black counselor at Green End, demonstrated. She came into Mrs. Hooper's class every Wednesday to discuss counseling issues with the children through the use of puppets and stories. She let the children ask many questions and often wandered with their tangents. She never, however, lost control of the class, and managed this through being intellectually nimble enough to connect the children's tangents back to her major theme for the day and through using jokes and changes in her intonation to signal to the children when they were going too far afield. Her style led to a noisy class, but it was a class in which all were engaged and in which Michael, Malik, and Dontonio were able to contribute positively.

Finally, Ladson-Billings suggests that white teachers understand themselves as political beings and act on this understanding. The sort of broad institutional racism that is perpetuated by the lack of cultural understanding and respect is something that needs to be challenged. Teachers need to "help their [black] students understand that societal expectations for them are generally low. However, they [need to] support them by demonstrating that their own expectations are exceptionally high. Thus they [can] indicate that to prove the prevailing beliefs wrong, teacher and students must work together."[26]

In order to move white middle-class teachers closer to a conception of teacher-as-political-being, of teacher as challenger of racism, structural inequality, and injustice, Ladson-Billings suggests that prospective teachers need to be led to question their own assumptions about what teaching is and led to an understanding of how schooling privileges white society. What she is talking about is what Bowers calls a relativizing of taken for granted beliefs about education; that is, a casting of doubt upon the verity of some of our bedrock beliefs.[27] This is no easy task, and certainly not one that can be completed overnight. But it is one that we must pursue, I believe, if we are ever to make any real change in our teaching, managing, disciplining, and shaping of all of our children. This chapter is intended as one move in that direction.

Notes

1. All names in this article are pseudonyms, for both confidentiality and narrativity reasons. The former protects the participants from research harm while the latter acknowledges that in representing the lives of others, researchers necessarily

fictionalize participants to some degree, since a "true" representation is unobtainable.

2. Hereafter I will refer to the teacher as Mrs. Hooper since in Green End Elementary, every adult is addressed formally as "Mr.," "Mrs.," "Ms.," or "Miss," even outside of the presence of children.

3. In my fieldwork the balance between participant and observer was weighted heavily towards participant, not through my own intentionality, but through the impossibility of spending large amounts of time in a kindergarten without being drawn in as an actor. Hence, my status as a "teacher" of sorts.

4. I am borrowing this phrase from Lisa Delpit's insightful 1988 article, "The Silenced Dialogue: Power and Pedagogy in Educating Other People's Children," *Harvard Educational Review*, 58 (August 1988): 280–298; also in Delpit, *Other People's Children: Cultural Conflict in the Classroom* (New York: New Press, 1995), pp. 21–47.

5. I have chosen to use the referent "black" instead of "African-American" because at Green End "African-American" was used by white people either when black people were "around" or as a code word to signify one's "correctness." In my conversations with black teachers, children, and parents, "black" was the preferred self-referent.

6. See Brian M. McCadden, "Becoming a Student: The Moral Significance of Entry into Kindergarten," *Educational Foundations*, 10 (Spring 1996): 23–36.

7. Brian M. McCadden, *It's Hard to be Good: Moral Complexity, Construction, and Connection in a Kindergarten Classroom* (New York: Peter Lang Publishers, Inc., forthcoming).

8. William H. Schubert, "Curriculum Reform," in G. Cawelti, ed., *Challenges and Achievements of American Education: The 1993 ASCD Yearbook* (Alexandria, VA: Association for Supervision and Curriculum Development, 1993).

9. C. A. Bowers, *The Promise of Theory: Education and the Politics of Cultural Change* (New York: Teachers College Press, 1984), p. 32.

10. Jean Jacques Rousseau, *The Emile of Jean Jacques Rousseau*, W. Boyd, ed. (New York: Teachers College Press, 1962).

11. McCadden, *It's Hard to be Good.*

12. Howard Gardner, *Frames of Mind* (New York: Basic Books, 1983).

13. Delpit, "Silenced Dialogue;" George W. Noblit, "Power and Caring," *American Educational Research Journal*, 30 (Spring 1993): 23–38.

14. Delpit, "Silenced Dialogue," p. 285.

15. Noblit, "Power and Caring."

16. Gloria Ladson-Billings, *The Dreamkeepers: Successful Teachers of African American Children* (San Francisco: Jossey-Bass, 1994), pp. 21, 22.

17. Ladson-Billings, *The Dreamkeepers*, p. 20.

18. Anthony Giddens, *Central Problems in Social Education Theory* (London: MacMillan, 1979).

19. Ladson-Billings, *The Dreamkeepers*, p. 22.

20. See Michael W. Apple, *Ideology and Curriculum* (Boston: Routledge & Kegan Paul, 1979); Bowers, *The Promise of Theory.*

21. Shirley Brice Heath, *Ways with Words: Language, Life, and Work in Communities and Classrooms* (Cambridge: Cambridge University Press, 1983), p. 280.

22. Delpit, "Silenced Dialogue," p. 285.

23. Noblit, "Power and Caring," p. 23.

24. See McCadden, *It's Hard to be Good*; cf. William Bennett, *The Book of Virtues: A Treasury of Moral Stories* (New York: Simon and Schuster, 1993); Thomas Lickona, *Educating for Character: How Schools Can Teach Respect and Responsibility* (New York: Bantam Books, 1991).

25. Vivian Gussin Paley, "On Listening to What the Children Say," *Harvard Educational Review*, 56 (2, 1986): 123; see also Nel Noddings, *The Challenge to Care in Schools: An*

Alternative Approach to Education (New York: Teachers College Press, 1992).

26. Ladson-Billings, *The Dreamkeepers*, p. 118.

27. Bowers, *The Promise of Theory*.

5

Contradiction, Paradox, and Irony:
The World of Classroom Management

❏

Barbara McEwan

I live in a curious professional world. I teach
Classroom Management and often find that, like Alice in
Wonderland, I am wandering through a paradoxical landscape. Over the past decade I have spent a considerable
amount of time exploring the many paradoxes of my field
of study as I listen to the fears and joys, despair and
elation of in-service and preservice teachers. Classroom
management is a topic I find to be fraught with more
curious contradictions in the form of moral dilemmas and
a desire to make right decisions all the time.

There are paradoxes and contradictions embedded in
the topic itself. Some people call what I teach "classroom
discipline," a title that makes the subject seem deceptively
simple. After all, most of us are enculturated with notions
that the term discipline has to do with such phrases as
"Spare the rod and spoil the child," or "Children should be
seen and not heard." There are, of course, alternative
perspectives on the subject, and I spend most of my
working hours teaching about and researching these
alternatives. I examine a variety of tools for building
classroom climates, particularly those tools that mutually
encourage all members and rely on self-management as

opposed to authoritarian controls dependent on threats, coercion, and punishment.

I find Classroom Management to be the most fascinating topic to teach and to research in large part because it is so loaded with personal memories, values, ego, fear and, at times, panic. The students in every class I teach spend a good deal of their time trying to resolve internal conflicts between their enculturated concepts of what is meant by discipline, on the one hand, and incorporating into that framework new strategies designed, on the other, to preserve dignity and inspire a sense of safety in the classroom.

Every teacher, new or experienced, enters my class with the preconceived notion, or perhaps a fervent wish, that management will be little more than a series of tricks or a simple formula that, when deliberately applied, consistently lead to classrooms filled with beaming, quiet, perpetually on-task children. They are engaged in a quest for pixie dust. One "Poof!" and all the problems students would ever present are fixed forever. I have come to believe that as implausible as the pixie dust theory is, it nevertheless lingers because classroom management has no equivalent concept in society. We all are cognizant of the reality that interpersonal relationships take time to build and nurture. But relationships with students are somehow not viewed through that same lens. Nothing else we do in life prepares us to guide a roomful of students on a learning adventure for five days of the week, nine months of the year. There are no transferable paradigms and thus there is a persistent attempt to apply old adages in an attempt to ensure survival.

That is only the first of many paradoxes in this curious world. Here is another: every teacher I speak with tells me that successful classroom management is the key to all learning; teachers who lack a developed set of skills in this area will experience classrooms that fall apart. Yet, despite its evident importance, classroom management is the topic least attended to professionally. Many teacher education programs do not include the study of management in their programs. Courses on educational law are even more rare. Researchers largely ignore it as a field of study. Many textbooks on the topic are little more than sales pitches in thin disguise.

Two tendencies dominate. Teacher education programs tend either to ignore classroom management entirely in their official curriculum, or they offer a discrete course in management or discipline. Both approaches are paradoxical to the nature of the subject matter. Classroom management is not something that "just happens," as is believed by many who place their faith in the magic of subject matter competency and imagine that management will occur because every student is enthralled by the teacher's wealth of knowledge. Conversely, teaching management as a separate topic sends the erroneous message that it exists apart from curriculum, rather like oil and water. There is the hope that if the mix is right and appropriate blending occurs, somehow curriculum and management will work together. But separating curriculum from management, I believe, sends teachers the false message that the two are something other than interwoven threads of the same cloth.

So, at this point on our journey we have explored two basic paradoxes that color our perspective of what classroom management is or is not or what it should or should not be. The inability to even clearly define what the topic is or its need to be included in teacher education protocol creates a muddle not only for preservice teachers but those who have been teaching for a long time.

In the classes I teach and the workshops I present, I encounter teachers who have been professionally engaged for years. For many of them management has become a source of constant struggle and anxiety. For some, it has become the monster who resides in their classrooms, threatening eventually to drive them into careers of selling aluminum siding. Their concern can be boiled down to one constant theme that runs through the comments they make: their fear of losing control.

I have never worked with any educators who desire to become "mean" teachers. Yet the fear of losing control while experimenting with management practices new to them causes educators to believe that in a crunch they will revert to behavioral measures that, in their words, "work" to end inappropriate conduct. And this leads to yet another paradox, even more curious. Namely, many of the adults with whom I work were far from model students when they went to school. In fact, they were often quite the opposite. And whatever the particulars of their school careers, they all have stories they relate to me of the misbehaviors in which they engaged as students and the treatments they received as a result.

I begin the course I teach on classroom management with story telling. I do not ask my students to think of the most dramatic examples of authoritarian discipline they experienced, but, in fact, that is usually what first comes to their thoughts. For some, the events occurred twenty or thirty years ago, but the fears and humiliation they experienced as students are as keenly painful to remember as they were when they first occurred.

The memories are vivid and acute. I hear stories of how they were locked in dark closets, tied into chairs, or made to sit under desks. In one instance, a teacher recalled being forced as a child to sit under the teacher's desk and smell the teacher's feet. Another student recently related the story of her third grade teacher who, on the first day of class, told the students she was a witch who would "get them" if they were not good. Then, if a child was talking out of turn or exhibiting some other behavior deemed to be inappropriate, the teacher would walk over and pluck a hair from the student's head. The hair would be stored in a jar in the teacher's cupboard.

Many of the discipline stories I hear reflect treatment that was very different between the genders. One woman recalled how being locked in a closet became the "place to be" in her fourth grade classroom. The teacher would send female students there if they were caught talking. As soon as more than one was in the dark closet they could continue their conversation unabated. Although this might seem like fun, there was the ever-present fear of being punished by being locked away in a spooky place. It was considered a more desirable place to be, though, because the students were more fearful of the teacher than of the dark closet. One of my male students recounted how a music teacher he had in the seventh grade began each class by putting on very dark, red lipstick. If a female student was caught talking, nothing happened. If a male student was caught talking, he was called to the front of the room and kissed by the teacher so that the lipstick left an imprint on his cheek.

The educators with whom I work also will tell tales, equally troubling to them, of times when their names were written on the blackboard, of being forced to wear gum on their noses and, most common, having to stand outside their classrooms and become highly visible in the hallways of their schools. As adults, they now believe the common factor in all these strategies was the desire of their teachers to control them through fear and humiliation.

And here is the paradox, the contradiction, if you will: As dramatic as such examples of intimidation are, I have yet to hear from a single adult who will testify that she or he learned to behave in appropriate and responsible ways from these experiences or are better people because of them. Further, these same teachers go to their own classrooms and seek to gain control through the model most imprinted on them. Sadly, the deepest impressions are left by the traumatic residue of fear and humiliation. When these same people feel the desperate need to enforce control over their own students, they revert to the very strategies that most controlled them.

I once witnessed a former student of mine who, after nearly a full year of discussing and reflecting on issues of fair and equitable management practices, dismissed her students for the day by reading their names aloud in the order of their spelling scores. Those with the highest scores were dismissed first, those with the lowest were forced to sit until everyone else had gone. When asked about it later, she said she believed that the tactic would motivate students to do better and that she had seen similar practices used when she went to school. Would she enjoy an equally public display of her good and bad days during her first year of teaching, I asked? She laughed, as if it were an absurd idea and said, "No."

The point is that there is not a teacher or administrator who would welcome such treatment as an adult. So the paradox of doing to students what teachers hated having done to themselves, suddenly has a second and equally devilish paradox attached. That is, the message we are sending children is that while teachers may, students may not. Children are not allowed to yell, hit, or treat others with disrespect. Teachers are allowed to do all those things, by virtue of being older and bigger, for purposes of being in charge. So the message to students becomes, "When you are big, this is how you get to act." It is a dangerous message to send our young people. While such techniques are being applied as immediate solutions to behavioral problems, none of them employ any educational process that would help students manage their behaviors into adulthood. However, those techniques ironically enculturate them quite well to reproduce humiliation and disrespect in their own efforts to gain some shred of control.

But we are only getting started. Let us move onto yet another paradox. In the current educational scene, a number of democratic curricular and pedagogical practices are finding wide acceptance in K-12 classrooms. Cooperative learning, authentic assessment, math as problem solving, and critical thinking strategies, among others, are gaining adherents and achieving good academic results. My students often express a desire to incorporate these democratic practices in their classrooms.

At the same time, though, they cling to their perceived need to manage those democratic curricular practices through authoritarian management measures, despite the contradiction between the two. Authoritarian discipline, by its very nature, works in direct opposition to the curriculum strategies intended to encourage independent learners. The paradox lies in intent. Authoritarian discipline intends that students will exhibit, on command, teacher-approved behaviors to gain promised rewards or to avoid threatened punishments. It yields dependence. In contrast, innovative curriculum intends to foster self-directed learning. It yields independence. While the teacher may want students to be in charge of their own learning, there is little belief that they can make wise choices over their own behaviors. It is an uncomfortable fit indeed between curriculum that advocates self-efficacy and management strategies that establish the teacher as sole determiner of what is and is not appropriate.

Even more ironic, most teachers will respond to questions aimed at uncovering the source of such contradictions with statements that reveal a deeply held distrust for the educational process itself. Educators often argue that teaching students appropriate behaviors is a pointless waste of time. They assume, in effect, that if students are not controlled through basic behavioral strategies, they will lie, cheat, steal, not work, and turn into thugs who cannot be managed at all. Such teachers betray a lack of faith in the efficacy of information, rationality, or inquiry to nurture responsible social behavior. Teachers and administrators mired in this assumption tell me they feel anger toward the existing educational structure and a deep despair that times have changed and classrooms are no longer filled with the apple-cheeked innocent beings who hang on the teacher's every word—assuming they ever were.

Even those who would reject such despair end up in contradiction, however. They adopt new teaching strategies designed to address various learning styles and multiple intelligences in order to provide better learning opportunities for a broad spectrum of educational needs. Yet, when putting together discipline plans, they often resort to using a "one-size-fits-all" approach, never considering that just as they design lessons which address various learning styles to make a math concept accessible, so an individualized approach to management will make the concepts of social responsibility equally understandable. Ultimately, the same mistrust of education is at work.

It is curious that teachers will adopt curricular innovations that indicate a level of trust in their students, but manage the process with strategies that indicate a high level of distrust. And the inevitable disequilibrium resulting from the mismatch of curriculum and management point the way to yet another paradox, the increased focus on action research in education. Many teachers and administrators are eager to engage in a critical examination of their own curricular and pedagogical practices. Yet I find these same educators will justify their use of behavioral management practices with statements such as, "If it works, what's wrong with it?" In other words, if a teacher is employing management practices in the classroom designed to result in obedient, on-task behaviors, those discipline strategies appear to be acceptable. It is a rare experience when I meet a teacher who wants to critically examine her own management practices.

One teacher I work with and with whom I usually find myself philosophically compatible shocked me by dismissing her students one day in the order of their scores on that day's timed math test. While the students were gathering their coats and books, she laughingly said to me, "They're so competitive." She never considered the role her dismissal practices played in the competitive spirit within that classroom. Classroom management practices are potentially rich sources for action research, yet I seldom meet educators who are willing to hold that particular "mirror up to nature."

Every discipline decision teaches lessons to students, but too often what is learned is not the lesson teachers had in mind. In fact, the phrase "I'm going to teach you a lesson," when used in conjunction with classroom management, usually means that there is a punitive response in store for the student, as opposed to any sort of worthy educational experience. I see few attempts to critically examine management practices. In fact, teachers often become angry, defensive, or distant if I suggest a joint action research project to examine management styles. Their reasons for avoiding an examination of this most important aspect of education are legion.

When educators place the focus of their decision making on controlling the overt behaviors of students while ignoring all the possible causes of the behaviors, the emotional and educational needs of young people go unattended. Educators too often choose to mire themselves in discipline responses designed to control symptoms rather than to treat the causes of the problems and effect any meaningful change in how a student might respond to difficult situations.

My observations of why this might be happening have led me to believe that the answer lies, at least in part, in the painful and personal nature regarding teachers' preferences for some sorts of students over others. Teachers who declare their comfort zone as one defined by quiet require of all students who walk into the classroom that they be quiet. There is no concern whether that paradigm works against students' ability to learn. Too often the methods employed to achieve a quiet, obedient classroom are detrimental to building a climate in which every student can learn successfully. In fact, based on my observations, I am reluctant to equate a silent classroom with a well-managed one. Constantly quiet classrooms look as they do because the students are being controlled through fear, intimidation, frequent appeals to competition, and public embarrassment. While any of the above approaches may be deemed to "work," inasmuch as they are effective tools of control, they most often work against students who already find themselves on the fringe of the school's social environment. While some students may be willing to bend to the control systems practiced by educators, particularly when those practices are consonant with the homes from which the students come, there are others who will view imposed, arbitrary rules as a call to arms.

The compelling need for classroom practices focused on student success becomes self-evident when we look at the statistics of who drops out of our schools to learn the lessons of life on the streets. There appears to be a shared idea among educators that the problems existing in schools are solved through the practices of suspension and expulsion. In fact, these "solutions" only transfer the problems elsewhere. When educators decide to exclude students from educational opportunities, young people are faced with minimum-wage jobs, the street, or prison. The problems do not go away, they only become more dangerous and more costly to a civilized nation.

The high numbers of students with disabilities and students of color who appear in the statistics of school dropouts is, I believe, no coincidence. When our media create a hero out of Joe Clark, whose fame rested on his desire to select the students who would or would not be educated in the high school he administered, the message sent to teachers was that if schools would just expel all the problem students, they would only have to teach those remaining; in other words, only the "good kids" would be left. Equity is not served by such thinking.

The difficulty is that teachers tend to define appropriate behaviors according to their own family backgrounds and values. In a classroom made up of twenty-seven students representing twenty-seven diverse economic, ethnic, family, or religious backgrounds, some deliberate instruction must occur if all its members are to function together as a community of learners. The educators who express the desire to rid their classroom of the undesirables, leaving only those who seem truly deserving of an education, typically hold a preconceived notion of who is worthy of membership in the community. In most cases it is those students who look like, act like, and share the same values as, the teachers.

How we manage students in our classrooms is an issue that reflects many of our struggles in this country to come to terms with demographics that are increasingly multicultural. Given the fact that the vast number of licensed teachers in the United States belong to the majority culture, typically students considered to be potential trouble makers are students of color, students who belong to a minority culture, students who are of a different economic class as the teacher, and students who learn best in ways that are different from the way the teacher acquires knowledge.

If we accept the premise that solving educational problems can be done through mass expulsions, then the students who would be left in the classroom once the "less desirable" ones were gone would typically hold middle-class values, share mainstream religious values, and be native English speakers. Certainly becoming knowledgeable about and sensitive to the needs of many students from a variety of cultures and family structures is challenging. Nevertheless, they are equally deserving of consideration within an educational setting.

When teachers directly address this issue with me, often the question they ask is, "When is it okay for me to just give up on a student?" My answer to that question is the one I believe most teachers least want to hear, and that is "Never." And while that answer might seem impossibly naive, I argue it is not an answer resulting from being ill-informed, but rather the answer of someone who has seen where young people go when society gives up on them. When I offer that response to teachers, they typically counter by telling me that the other students in their classrooms need attention and they cannot spend time with one student at the expense of the rest of the class.

Teachers who express this view seem to believe that their classrooms can only be the way they are now. There are no alternative paradigms that they can imagine, often because they have been presented with no alternatives in their training or subsequent professional development. As a result, they are perpetually seeking quick solutions to the negative behaviors they see in their students. They lack a framework for understanding the potential impact of deliberately creating expectations that establish and maintain a democratic classroom environment based on mutual respect and equitable decision making, and the effect such strategies can have on mediating the anger and frustration existing in so many classrooms.

I have found, however, that when teachers make the commitment to employ specific ideas that encourage appropriate behavior while not demeaning students, they typically report back to me that their discipline decisions are resulting in more positive outcomes in terms of classroom atmosphere and a higher level of trust established with and among students. I have also found that until most educators have been presented with some level of "cookbook" strategies, they have difficulty imagining alternative approaches.

Thoughtful decision making takes time, tricks do not. Adopting management strategies that admittedly take time is the toughest sell in the world of education. However, if educators truly desire to create classroom climates that are supportive of all learners, there must be an investment of time to discuss expectations, set up rights and responsibilities, and follow up on disruptions in ways that will help and not harm students. Building a democratic classroom climate requires an effective integration of pedagogical knowledge, educational psychology, patience, hard work, an unwavering dedication to equal educational opportunity for all students, and a passionate belief that everyone, including the teacher, can learn from mistakes.

The contradiction between this view of management and what is happening in most classrooms is that the statement above indicates the attributes educators are least likely to consider when they are deciding how their schools or classrooms will function. It has been my experience that most educators want quick remedies that will work all the time with every student in all situations, even though logic tells them that the nature of human interactions means no such solutions exist. The payoff for management strategies requiring an investment of time at the beginning of the school year is that classrooms tend to hold together into April and May, thus saving time at the end of the year.

I see in many classrooms a proliferation of teacher-proof approaches to discipline. The subtle but very real message embedded in such management models is that educators cannot be trusted to make their own good decisions, so the model excludes them from the loop. As educators adopt materials that do not require their own creative thinking and professional skill, they are being duped into accepting the underlying premise that their decisions are not worthy. And, ultimately, if their own decisions cannot be trusted, how can the decisions of young people be?

I find myself walking a tightrope between promoting the use of democratic management with some practical, how-to strategies while trying to avoid the trap of reducing those strategies to step-by-step procedures reminiscent of the very teacher-proof approaches I distrust. Yet, in working with teachers, I have found that there is a greater likelihood of trying democratic manage-ment strategies if there is some conversation about what to do in the classroom on Monday morning. As a result, I have come to believe that when assisting educators in the process of abandoning the behavioral discipline practices that rely on extrinsic rewards and punishment, and adopting instead those strategies designed to encourage self-esteem and personal responsibility, it is necessary to present teachers with both the rationale for change as well as some ideas to make it happen.

One compelling rationale for change is the ethical dilemma presented by a reliance on rewards and punish-ment as a means for establishing discipline. Not only should educators be concerned with the lack of self-efficacy involved in behaving in a proscribed fashion in hope of a reward or out of fear of punishment, but there is also the issue of whether or not the behaviors that are rewarded will in any way serve the needs of democracy when students grow to adulthood. If only the most quiet, docile, dependent behaviors are seen as worthy of reward, what behaviors then can we reasonably expect students to exhibit when they reach the age of majority? Even more alarming is that classrooms that depend on extrinsic methods of behavioral control typically spawn peer rejection and distrust as a natural outcome of some students being punished more often, others being rewarded more often.

Once an educator makes a commitment to employ discipline techniques that will inform rather than punish and are more compatible with democratic curricular models, the next step is to explore what pieces of information are needed for educators and students in order to have everyone modeling and practicing better self-management skills. If educators agree that their teaching practices should be focused on encouraging students to become responsible, independent learners, there are a number of approaches to democratic management upon which they might draw. Although many teachers may long for one prescribed approach to discipline, applicable to every circumstance with no variations, my own experience as a teacher, and the narratives I collect from current classroom teachers, indicates that no one model successfully meets every student's needs in every situation. Rather than depending on one approach to be the answer to all management or curriculum issues, the most effective teachers I see are those who comfortably synthesize ideas from a number of cognitive models.

There are those who suggest that to use ideas from various discipline models only creates confusion in the minds of students. I argue, though, that the more ideas educators carry with them into the classroom, the more prepared they will be to handle the diverse range of problems encountered on a daily basis. Therefore, if teachers are to master skills that will enable them to create positive and stimulating learning environments, it is most important to assist them in learning about the assortment of discipline techniques aimed at preserving self-esteem and fostering personal responsibility. However, a synthesized approach to management can only have meaning if it arises from a well-grounded philosophical foundation.

When deciding what management models would best serve a democratic classroom environment, it is sensible to begin with a foundation that reflects the precepts our society holds as fundamental. It seems logical to me to begin with a consideration of those elements that are common to our democratic system. If this is the point of departure, then the foundation for a democratic class-room begins with the concept that individual rights are sacred yet always balanced against the equally compelling needs of society. There is a dignity that naturally accom-panies affording students the recognition of their human rights. There is mutual respect interwoven into an edu-cated perspective of the ways in which our actions have an impact on those around us. Educators who begin with this premise are helping to ensure that all students who enter their classrooms do so on an equal footing.

This leads to a further paradox, one related to the skepticism about educating toward appropriate behaviors rather than relying on unreflective behavioral control. I receive one consistent bit of feedback on the contents of the course I teach, a nearly universal sense of surprise that the concepts which I encourage my students to consider are actually effective. As one intern said to me, "I thought those ideas you were teaching were crap that would never work. But now that I am teaching, I can't believe how well they work." The paradox lies in trying to imagine why I would spend my time teaching ideas that have no practical application. I am dismayed that the significant role democratic decision making plays in the construction of equitable learning opportunities is too often dismissed as being "touchy-feely" and certain to result in chaotic classrooms.

The skepticism with which the ideas presented in my class are viewed and the difficulty my students have in understanding their practical applications rests, in part, with the fact that, however hellion-like they might have been as children, as adults they are typically highly motivated students. Teaching democratic classroom management to adult learners does not provide many opportunities to model the concepts except during role-playing. The interns and teachers with whom I work are not likely to be discipline problems at this point in their development. Occasionally those enrolled in my class engage in side conversations, but more typically they are on-task individuals not given to seriously disrupting the educational environment. Although we do a good deal of role-playing, the truth is that the course is removed from direct classroom contact and teaching the content equates to teaching a sport without access to a playing field or the appropriate equipment. The students enrolled in my course often learn the material by *imagining* what it would be like to throw, catch, and run, rather than by throwing, catching, and running.

Unfortunately, when the preservice teachers in my class do enter the classrooms to which they have been assigned, they are more likely to see modeled the very strategies that are least likely to promote classroom equity. It is too easy to dismiss the ideas discussed in class once the interns and teachers return to their schools and are told by their colleagues that such strategies just are not effective. I have found that many of the practicing educators who are most quick to disparage the content of the course have not actually tried any of the strategies, or they have tried them as they would have tried some behaviorist "trick"—they applied the strategy in isolation from its philosophical foundation. Educators who fall into either of the above categories express the conviction that democratic management practices are worthless notions presented by a professor who has breathed the air of the ivory tower a little too long.

As I respond to the myriad of issues raised in the course I teach, I consistently try to assist my students in developing responses to behavioral problems that will vary depending on the needs of the individuals as well as the group. I present to them the idea that all human relationships are built with time, patience, and hard work;

there is no reason to expect classroom relationships to be any different. There simply is no magic pixie dust that can be sprinkled over our educational environments resolving all problems and curing all ills as it slowly settles on our shoulders.

One of the recurrent issues students bring to me is a suggestion for a way to keep all students on-task with a minimum investment of time. This is an issue that my students as well as workshop participants repeatedly will raise with me. I find it to be reflective of my earlier statement that educators seem to view time limitations universally as their greatest barrier to implementing democratic management practices. It frustrates them to hear that any student-centered management strategy must be, by its very nature, "time consuming," just as are the interpersonal relations they have outside the classroom.

Time can be viewed as a tyrant that leaves no opportunity to engage in humane interactions or it can be viewed as a commodity that educators can choose to invest in ways that will best serve the needs of all classroom members. Time can be spent working with students to reach a mutually acceptable solution to problems or it can be spent engaged in power struggles with students that lead to stress and result in students who drop out and teachers who burn out. Any problem will take some time to resolve; the issue is how to best spend that time.

Time can either be spent after problems have occurred, trying to come up with perfect punishments in an attempt to ensure it will never happen again, or time can be spent before problems have occurred, at the beginning of the school year, engaging students in discussions concerning behaviors that sustain a safe and encouraging learning environment. And, thereafter, time can be invested in patient communications that reflect the commitment educators must assume to keep students in an educational environment. During our class discussions, I find that my students are consumed with worry about how they will handle the student who is in a state of outright rebellion. What they have trouble imagining is the difference in classroom climate that occurs when every class member understands and has had some voice in the common expectations.

Educators can learn to empower themselves to resolve the behavioral issues that occur in schools. They have the training and ability to move beyond prescribed models of discipline and into the realm of decision making based on democratic principles. Time is not the enemy. It can be an ally depending on how it is used. To take advantage of available time, educators might ask themselves some of these suggested questions:

• What expectations have been discussed that will lead to a classroom climate that supports the needs of all its members?

• If I did not hold the discussion at the beginning of the year, what expectations are most important to focus on now?

• Will all students have some input into how the expectations are established?

• Will the expectations be presented in ways that are accessible to all learning styles, not just auditory learners?

• Are the expectations too high for some students?

• Are the expectations too low for some students?

• If so, what adjustments need to be made to be equitable?

Spending time setting mutual expectations is a proactive approach to building a democratic learning environment that will address the special needs of all students and reduce the sense that problems are so overwhelming there are no solutions. The time spent on establishing a democratic classroom climate will also help educators shift their focus from the subject matter to learners who need to acquire knowledge of the subject matter. The hard work comes with the decisions teachers make from minute to minute and from one day to the next in order to sustain a democratic classroom. The words selected when speaking with students, the phrasing used when developing a syllabus, the amount, color, and type of displays present in any given class-room, even the physical arrangement of the classroom, will all serve to support or destroy the attempts of educators to maintain the democratic climate.

If expectations are stated in the form of rules, the rules should be posted in order to provide students with notice, and posted in the languages the students speak. Cross-cultural communication can be enhanced by having students share expectations in their own native languages. Educators can ask themselves if the expec-tations are understood and consistent. Did the expecta-tions evolve out of a solid theoretical and philosophical base, or were they made up as time and circumstance seemed to demand? So much to think about, and yet these questions are so crucial to whether or not the playing field students walk on will have any even ground.

Working toward a democratic classroom requires an integration of all decisions, with the definitive goals being the security and self-esteem of every student. While teachers will always be concerned with issues of control, a sense of confidence can evolve from being well prepared with a variety of ideas that assist in responding equitably, appropriately, and professionally to difficult situations in the classroom. The concerns teachers express about democratic management are very real and not to be taken lightly. I have come to believe that preservice and in-service teachers are best served when they are pro-vided with information designed help them incorporate democratic strategies into their teaching as they also learn to confront their anxieties concerning practices which enhance self-esteem and enable their students to feel like valued members of the school community.

And so we look out at this convoluted landscape where little is what it seems to be. Contradictions abound and success is often measured in terms of a day gone well and a year without too much disruption. And what sense can be made of it? Perhaps the answer is that no sense can be made of it because paradox, contradiction, and irony is the logical outcome when paradigms of linear management strategies are imposed on the natural messiness that results from compelling representatives of all the world to attend public school classroom.

Another way to examine this issue and, perhaps, bring sense to it might be through incorporating Chaos Theory into our understandings of the daily give-and-take in school. One premise of Chaos Theory is the recognition of independently arising patterns as well as the misfit of trying to impose structure on that which cannot be structured. If recurring patterns are evidence of Chaos Theory, then the recurring patterns of student behaviors that arise consistently in direct opposition to authoritarian rules make a great deal of sense. If we can accept this premise, then it would also explain the fact that in the years I have worked in this field, I rarely hear a new question from teachers or administrators. And when I talk to my international colleagues, they tell me they are always faced with responding to the same issues as I am. Time and control consistently are the universal threads found in the concerns about management expressed by teachers everywhere.

Perhaps understanding effective classroom management is the same as accepting paradox as endemic to the topic and the resulting chaos might be the natural outcome of what happens when we work to create climates in which diverse groups of people can come together to seek knowledge. It might be that learning to celebrate the differences and enjoy the nature of all students will bring educators closer to the goal of a calm environment than will the authoritarian constraints that sound so good in theory and so often let down the practitioner.

Bibliography

Barr, Robert D. and William H. Parrett. *Hope At Last for At-Risk Youth* (Needham Heights, MA: Allyn and Bacon, 1995.

Data Volume for the National Education Goals Report. Vol. 1 (National Data, 1994).

Gathercoal, Forrest. *Judicious Discipline.* 3rd ed. (San Francisco: Caddo Gap Press, 1993).

McEwan, Barbara. *Practicing Judicious Discipline: An Educator's Guide to a Democratic Classroom.* 2nd ed. (San Francisco: Caddo Gap Press, 1993).

Nelsen, Jane. *Positive Discipline* (New York, NY: Ballantine Books, 1987).

Pocket Condition of Education (Washington, D.C.: National Center for Education Statistics, Office of Educational Research and Improvement, U.S. Department of Education, 1995).

Purkey, William W. and David B. Strahan. *Positive Discipline: A Pocketful of Ideas* (Columbus, Ohio: National Middle School Association, 1989).

6

Interpreting Glasser's Control Theory: Problems that Emerge from Innate Needs and Predetermined Ends

❏

Sue Ellen Henry and Kathleen Knight Abowitz

A really efficient totalitarian state would be one in which the all-powerful executive of political bosses and their army of managers control a population of slaves who do not have to be coerced, because they love their servitude. To make them love it is the task assigned, in present-day totalitarian states, to ministries of propaganda, newspaper editors and schoolteachers.[1]

Introduction

William Glasser has been advancing control theory in the educational literature since 1969, when his *Schools without Failure* was published.[2] However, the 1970s was not to be Glasser's decade, as Lee Canter's *Assertive Discipline*, promising "A Take-Charge Approach for Today's Educator," enticed legions of teachers who were desperate to find ways of coping with an era of conflict produced by shifting social mores and power relations between teachers and students.[3] In a field already vulnerable to the novelty and appeal of "the latest thing," the topic of classroom management remains an especially fertile terrain for any technique or plan which promises effective ways to make the classroom a peaceful, productive place. As Assertive Discipline waned in popularity, Glasser's publication of *Control Theory* in 1986 would position him to ride the waves of constructivism,[4] community, and quality in education during the 1990s.[5]

Glasser's control theory fits contemporary schools in several ways. In the spirit of constructivism, he writes of school as a place where students make meaning in the process of meeting their basic human needs. Well-suited to the trend of schools as learning communities are Glasser's ideas on cooperative learning, team approaches, and school as a friendly, comfortable environment. In an era in which Edwards Deming[6] revolutionized industrial management, Glasser's application of the Quality principles to school and student management holds a common-sense appeal for many American educators.

Glasser's Quality Schools are beginning to appear on the educational landscape. Indigo Elementary School,[7] the school profiled in this chapter, resembles schools in Glasser's growing Quality School Consortium which use control theory and the ideas in *Quality Schools* and *Control Theory in the Classroom* as guides to restructuring. While not a member of the consortium, Indigo's recent reorganization is the result of school leaders' exposure to and enthusiasm for the ideas that Glasser presents in his work. Through an examination of Indigo Elementary School, we paint a picture of Glasser's ideas in action. Not unlike other accounts of Glasser applications,[8] we seemed to witness an important, yet not completely successful, step toward democratic transformation of students and teachers at Indigo.

In contrast to external stimulus-response theory so prevalent in the classroom discipline literature, and especially in Canter's work, control theory is based on the assumption that all motivation starts from within the individual: "Basic to control theory is the belief that *all* of our behavior is our constant attempt to satisfy one or more of the five basic 'needs' that are written into our genetic structure. *None* of what we do is caused by any situation or person outside of ourselves."[9] The five "needs" that motivate individuals are the need to survive and reproduce, to belong and to love, "*to gain power*," to be free, and to have fun.[10] Power is the central need in this theory; Glasser holds that "the way we continually struggle for power" is evident in every aspect of our lives.[11] Students fulfill their need for power when they are able to make choices in the classroom. So central is this need for power that "if students do not feel that they have power in their academic classes, they will not work in school. . . . There is no greater work incentive than to be able to see that your effort has a power payoff."[12] As we will see, making choices—an element of power—is an important part of the Indigo day. Consequently for Glasser, the good school is defined as "*a place where almost all students believe that if they do some work, they will be able to satisfy their needs enough so that it makes sense to keep working.*"[13] Doing work that meets one's internal "needs" while satisfying course and teacher requirements is quality work.

Quality work is successful work in Glasser's theory. Quality work is done by students who are workers, guided by teachers who are non-coercive lead-managers rather than boss-managers. Students work on subjects until mastery is achieved, rather than being failed for not learning in a designated period of time. The curriculum reflects relevance, and students are tested on essential information: "The purpose of a history test in a Quality School would not be the parroting of briefly remembered nonessential knowledge; it would be to think 'sensibly' about the past and put some of this sense down on paper."[14] Success in a Quality School, put simply, means students are working at doing their best and meeting their individual "needs" in a warm, friendly environment.

Yet defining success in American education is, of course, tricky business. In an educational system which has only haltingly moved away from its origins as a factory-like system of behavioral control, it is not surprising that success might mean satisfied and productive students and teachers. For teachers who struggle each day to educate large numbers of diverse students, happy productivity is no mean feat; the pressing question of how a successful Glasser classroom contributes to society as a whole is left uninspected, however. As a democratic nation with no shortage of conflict, injustices, and national as well as international crises, it is pertinent that we analyze Glasser's ideal of "success" in light of our pressing social context. The larger question for control theory and Quality Schools, therefore, is not simply "successful or unsuccessful?", but must focus upon the ability of control theory and the Quality School to foster the maintenance and improvement of democratic life.

In fact, Glasser's theory and practice hides a manipulative, individualistic pedagogy behind a concern for school spirit, cooperative learning, and a humane workplace. Framed in a post-industrial model of management, Glasser's Quality School aims to prepare students for their place in the contemporary work world. Like many school reforms in this century, Glasser's Quality School equates the good worker with the good citizen.[15] Our critique of Glasser, using the works of John Dewey, will focus on this false equation. Dewey saw democracy as a form of social life, and placed his ideas regarding democratic life and citizenship at the heart of his philosophy of education. Central to our argument, following Dewey, is that schools should not just prepare students for some faraway end called "citizenship," or "work," but should help students experience school as a democratic society. By both practicing the skills required for associated living, and living in an associated way with others at school, the means of democratic living are made indistinguishable from their evolving end: the constantly fluctuating life in a democratic society. When means and ends are separated, the likelihood for a counterfeit form of education occurs; a student may be given "control" over certain aspects of school life, but if this control is inauthentic, the democratic project is weakened.

Our critique on the work of Glasser spotlights the weaknesses of control theory as an educational guide, showing how the means of Glasser's theory—an individually-based "needs" curriculum—generates fixed ends which are insufficiently communal for a democratic society.

Control Theory and Quality Schools

Glasser draws a parallel between American education and the once-failing American automobile industry, presumably rescued by the quality principles of Deming. He asserts that, "Probably fewer than 15 percent of those who attend [school] do quality academic work in school, and even many of these do far less than they are capable of doing."[16] His goal is to use control theory in order to help all students do quality work, just as Deming used Total Quality Management to revolutionize the assembly lines in Detroit to increase the quality of production of factory workers.

Unable to meet students' individual "needs," schools become dismal places that hold little positive energy or good feelings, either for teachers or students. Glasser metaphorically describes feelings about school as "pictures in the student's head."[17] He states that these images of ourselves at school can be positive or negative, based upon our experiences at school. Students who do not succeed at school have a higher likelihood of having negative pictures of themselves at school, thereby making school a place of pain. Using a "needs"-based model, Glasser explains why some students are not motivated to come to school or work once they arrive.

Because "needs" form the basis for control theory, failing to meet these "needs" marks the genesis of problems for both students and teachers. Given that all these "needs" are constantly present and signaling us to meet them at various times, Glasser asserts that students who choose not to do work in school do so because doing the work assigned does not meet their "needs." Therefore, the role of the teacher is to create an environment that offers students opportunities to meet their "needs," so that successful learning experiences—pictures—are amassed in their memories. The result is a desire to attend and perform quality work at school.

These "learning pictures" are crucial for Glasser. He states that we can diagnose a child who does not work at school as a child who pictures learning as an unsatisfying activity. Further, before a child rids himself of a positive learning picture of school, "he usually has some idea that [working] can be replaced by another satisfying picture even though this new picture may be self-destructive."[18] Turning to drugs, sexual activities, or rock music are the ways that children usually get their "needs" met, Glasser concludes. This deficit of positive pictures is a vicious cycle: students who have negative pictures of school in their heads don't do work, fail, and reinforce their negative pictures of school. Glasser firmly informs the teacher in this situation: "No teacher will successfully teach anyone who does not have a picture of learning and those who try are doomed to failure."[19] If teachers experience too much failure, they too become discouraged and alter their own pictures of school and of students.

Consistent with his business framework, Glasser recasts the teacher as a manager, and draws a contrast between boss-managers and lead-managers. Boss-managers use coercion to motivate workers to do quality work. Conversely, lead-managers have management responsibilities in the classroom. "Teachers are people managers," he asserts, and are responsible for maintaining consistent experiences across lessons, structuring the class so that "needs" can be met, and developing means by which students can obtain a voice in the classroom environment.[20] The teacher as lead-manager is a crucial element in the successful implementation of control theory in the classroom, because taking the suggestions of students seriously and helping them develop a voice increases their sense of power without undermining the teachers' influence in the classroom. Glasser maintains that this role-switching is difficult for most teachers because historically they have not defined themselves as managers, but in fact perceived themselves as workers. Glasser's view of the teacher as manager means that the teacher works on a system, and the students are workers in that system.

What about grading and evaluation in this model? Glasser contends that in a quality school, the record should show what a student knows, not what he does not know, and that grades should never be on a "curve." In striving for competency and quality, students should be involved in self-evaluation. Through this process they become familiar with what quality work looks and feels like, creating a self-generative cycle that is mutually rewarding. The emphasis on self-evaluation is suggestive of a method to increase responsibility and personal accountability for work in the classroom, rather than an externally-driven system of motivations and rewards.[21]

Glasser is essentially an individualist whose theory of education expects an aggregate of individuals in a class-room to form a community within which individual "needs" are met through the activities of the day. Glasser supports cooperative learning methods that get students working together, because in this process they are mutually meeting their instinctual need to belong while accomplishing their work. He states that educators ought to harness all that is educational and communal about co-curricular activities (athletics, band, clubs, etc.) and create this same atmosphere in the classroom. "Not only do the team members fulfill their own 'needs,' but good teams add both power and belonging to the whole school. We call this school spirit." Individual "needs", when ful-filled, drive the system.[22]

We now turn to see one such system in motion, a school where Glasser was interpreted methodically by teachers who found his control theory appealing and applicable to their work. Led by a teacher who had studied Glasser and experimented with his theory in her classroom, the third and fourth grades of Indigo Elementary enthusiastically constructed classrooms based on the "needs"-based theory. Incorporating teaching strategies that encourage feelings of belonging, power, freedom, and fun, these teachers integrated Glasser into their pedagogy in unique ways, illustrating the potential implications of control theory.

Indigo Elementary School

A chance to observe a theory "in action," as it is interpreted and unfolded by practitioners, is a unique opportunity. As the third and fourth grades of Indigo Elementary implemented control theory in their classrooms, qualitative fieldwork helped us understand how Glasser makes the transition from theory to practice. The fieldwork, performed in 1993, focused mostly on the third grade of Indigo Elementary. We conducted twenty-one hours of observations and interviews; we also analyzed school literature, a parent-produced orientation video, and classroom handouts.[23]

Indigo Elementary School (K-6) is located in a large county in the southeastern United States, dotted with suburban neighborhoods as well as rural farmlands. When this fieldwork was conducted, Indigo enrolled approximately 280 students. Over ninety percent of the students were of European-American descent, with African- and Asian-American students scattered throughout the grades. This racial mix was particularly evident in the third and fourth grades, the only grades using the Glasser model. The entire third grade class, for example, had one African-American student among its ranks. Teachers said that the greatest form of diversity was the socioeconomic range among students.

The fifty-member third grade was split in half, with twenty-five members spending part of their day with Janet, the language arts teacher, and the other half of the day with Ron, the science and mathematics teacher. Students also worked in the Learning Center for "pull out" enrichment activities with Lucy, the Learning Center Coordinator and the supervising teacher for this restructuring project. The school, and these grades in particular, did not group students on the basis of ability. To cope with the range of abilities evident in the third and fourth grades, the teachers developed special strategies for assisting children with varying competencies, such as clubs, mentioned later in this chapter. Each day started with a class meeting, and each Friday the entire grade gathered for a community meeting. Consistent with the Glasser model, "evaluation meetings" between teachers, parents, and students substituted for grades. Students brought home written evaluations from their teachers, and evaluation meetings to discuss the material followed.

Changes such as these in the third and fourth grades at Indigo required leadership both within the classroom and within the school. For this leadership, Ron and Janet turned to Lucy, their supervisor in this process, and to their principal. Lucy was an especially important person in this undertaking. She was the theoretical and practical sounding board for the program; she did not teach in a regular classroom, but helped the teachers interpret and integrate control theory into everyday practice. The principal's primary role was to support the creative changes Lucy and these teachers were trying to make, and to explain and promote this model to members of the school board, the superintendent, and parents.

Set in a forested area, the school had ample fields and playing areas surrounding the building. As we entered the school parking lot, school buses dropped off students. The principal, a smiling woman, stood at the front of the building and greeted the children and their parents. As we entered the foyer, we saw paper maché fish hanging from the ceiling, and posters on every wall. Along nearly every wall were displays of student artwork. Thematic posters, where children had collectively designed murals on different emphases (recycling, "What I'm thankful for . . .") were present throughout the school. Some of the titles of the works were in languages other than English, usually with a definition of the word relevant to the artwork displayed. Coat hooks and spaces for lunch boxes and other school supplies lined each hallway.

In Ron's classroom, we noticed that there were no desks. Like his teaching partner Janet, who teaches in a similarly-arranged classroom, his classroom was arranged so that children sat at round tables of four students each with enough space for twenty-five children total. Belongings were strewn about; supply bags, pencils, pens, paper, and toys were on the floor surrounding each chair. Like the hallways, the classrooms were cluttered with students' belongings and necessary materials for schoolwork. Above the supply closet in the back of the room was a class slogan in large letters: "When I am courteous I: cooperate, listen, help, share, 'lift others up.'" A detailed script used in conflict resolution rested against the chalkboard. The mediation process began with each person describing his or her feelings to the other and the behaviors that created these feelings. Complete with paraphrasing and asking, "How can I help?", the chart was used by students, generally with the help of a teacher, in settling both large and small disputes. On the chalkboard was the written schedule for the day. A math lesson, reading aloud, physical education, study of plants and lunch were interspersed with time for clubs, a class meeting which opened the day, and "choice" time.

Walking into the Learning Center, it was evident that this was not a typical classroom; there were no desks and only a few tables scattered about with chairs for about fifteen people. Beanbag chairs filled the corners of the room. There were three computers and a laser printer in the back. Plants thrived in this sunny room, along with a spider, bird, and gerbil. Multiple copies of books for group reading packed a small reading nook in one corner of the room. Student-made painted book covers for a book-making project hung from a string that ran along the wall of windows. A chalkboard covered one entire wall. As in the other classrooms, Lucy's desk was not apparent when one entered the room; one had to search for it. The "courtesy" banner and conflict resolution script were also present here, in addition to three other banners, each on a different wall: "School is a home for our minds"; "It's not how smart you are, it's how you are smart"; "Some people see things as they are and ask why; I dream of things that never were and ask why not?" The room was characterized by the plainness of a conference room, but with the bright colors and engaging nature of elementary school decor.

"Kid-Centered Classrooms"

In school, much of what students are asked to do does not feel good right away. Because of this, a lead-teacher always tries to manage in a way that the students put the teacher into their quality worlds as a need-satisfying picture. To get into the students' quality worlds, the teacher must have a track record of asking the students to do what feels good in the long run and of asking them to do it in a way that feels good right away. This means that lead-teachers add kindness, courtesy, and humor to whatever they ask students to do.[24]

A "kid-centered classroom" was the label used by the Indigo adults to refer to elements of the class that are under students' choice. Students exercised their power in the classroom primarily in the realm of choosing activities when given deliberate alternatives by the teacher. An example of choice-making by students was the choice to study for an upcoming test offered to students by one of the fourth grade teachers. A student teacher in the class-room seemed troubled by the "choice" of studying for the test; instead she thought it should have been mandatory.

Lucy explained to the student teacher the importance of framing appropriate choices:

> you could have stood up there and turned blue in the face to try to review, if they weren't interested in and didn't see value in it, they weren't going to learn it. So you've got to make some choices. . . . you also give them choices whereby you're probably going to end up winning; your choice isn't to come study with me or play checkers.

In addition to choice in academic time, students were also given choices during break times and discipline situations. After students had finished their work in a certain segment of the day, they were able to choose other activities such as playing checkers or chess, drawing, writing in their notebooks, or reading. Ron remarked that at the beginning of the year he did not have the chessboards out because he felt they would be a distraction, and that he and the class had not negotiated their use during academic time. After a discussion with the students concerning the purposes of "choices" (the label given this time of day on the schedule), Ron felt he could put the chessboards out in a permanent location in the classroom, believing that the children were more prepared to make wise decisions about how to use their discretionary time.

Giving students choice involves giving them genuine power to make decisions. That was occasionally problematic at Indigo. A confrontation between Lucy and a student during a community meeting illustrates how choices were occasionally inauthentic. The discussion, following a group dialogue regarding the placement of snack-time in the daily schedule, centered around whether candy bars were appropriate for snack-time. A student had raised this question. Lucy asked the group, "How many people think candy bars are a healthy snack?" A few children raised their hands. Lucy concluded by explaining why the school did not want children to have candy during snack-time and continued onto the next topic. One male student asked her why she had asked them if they thought candy was okay if she was not going to give them a vote regarding whether or not they wanted it. She responded that she trusted him to make an intelligent decision, and that bringing candy was not an intelligent decision. Lucy later suggested that,

> If it had been a smaller group, if there was more control, I would have stopped and talked about that. And say "Let's step back and take a look at that". . . . I really feel like in this whole process, in order to do it successfully, you have to be willing to admit that you made a mistake to the kids. You have to be willing to step back and say, "Whoa, you know, you're right." I felt in that particular instance that I was being perfectly honest with him, and that, you're right, you didn't make a choice, but I trusted you to be smarter than that.

Trusting students is a difficult undertaking for many adults, and the teachers at Indigo struggled at times with allowing students to make genuine choices. The adults in this system attempted to trust that children would make the best decisions—those which correlated with the decision teachers would make if teachers had control—and commonly referred to the ability of children to "rise to the occasion." Lucy reminded us of the essential nature of trust when commenting on the process of small groups of students training a new group to take care of the animals in the classrooms (referred to as Zoo Club). A teacher must believe that students are basically "intelligent beings," she said, and if they are not behaving as such, "then they don't have a right to belong in the process." A teacher must make expectations clear, and then "trust the kids that they're going to do the right thing."

This element of trust was evident in the physical environment at the school. As noted earlier, personal belongings and valuables were left in the hallways, not behind locked doors but open to the public. In our time at Indigo, no problems were suggested by this arrangement and children seemed comfortable with sharing and trusting their classmates with their personal effects.

Besides trust between all members of the learning environment, Lucy also characterized the classroom and the school structure as one where information flowed freely between students and teachers about student behavior; open dialogue was encouraged. This second important element of the "kid-centered classroom" employed a collaborative approach to students and their parents. When talking about impending parent-teacher conferences, Lucy told us of an interaction she had with a student whose mother was coming in soon for a conference. "I was going to talk to his mother about getting him tested for special education services because I think he's definitely LD, and I talked to him about that because I didn't want that to come to a surprise when his mom came in. . . ." The student, Lucy reported, seemed "okay with that." Lucy was not uncomfortable about offering this information to the student, but instead felt it was her responsibility as the teacher to converse with the student about her evaluation of his work. She reinforced this responsibility during evaluation time when she asked each child to fill out a Learning Behaviors Checklist on themselves "and then I try to set aside time to talk about what I'm going to tell their parents and what I see, and we try to set a goal for the next nine weeks on what they're going to do." Open dialogue, as modeled by Lucy, attempted to draw the student into the process of evaluation; the student was not the mere object of evaluation, but was a subject within his own evaluation.

Another unique aspect of Indigo's third and fourth grade classrooms were student clubs. While most schools have some sort of ability grouping that is rather obvious in the classroom setting, Indigo created a system that resisted the labeling associated with gifted and slower programs by developing what they call "clubs." The clubs were small groups of students who came together by teacher invitation, either to pursue a specific area of interest or to enrich a particular competency area in which they were lacking. The clubs met weekly in the Learning Center or at the appropriate site (for example, in the garden for the Green Club) for approximately one hour. Lucy instituted this idea two years ago in her classroom as a teacher for the fourth grade, and then the following year, with the help of her teaching partner, expanded the program to include more types of clubs and gave them names, for example, Men's Cursive Club, Tuesday Book Club, Herb Specialists. Lucy noted that she had not seen the students label any of the clubs as "slow" or "retarded," and explained that much of this was due to the fact that not all the clubs were based upon additional needs in an area. Because the groups were fun and social, the focus was taken off the fact that some of the students were doing remedial work to improve particular abilities. At the end of the second year of clubs, Lucy surveyed the children for their feedback. She stated that, across the board, students said they liked the clubs and wanted learning to remain fun. Because of this feedback and the positive response that Lucy had found in using the program in her classroom, it was incorporated into both the third and the fourth grades.

A number of "needs," as Glasser envisions them, were met by reorganizing the classroom toward a "kid-centered" approach. Clubs combined an interest in power and fun with the team-approach that Glasser espouses. Clubs placed student "needs" at the pedagogical center. However, clubs were not necessarily open-ended time for students to come together around a common interest; in some cases, they were vehicles that teachers used to engage students in remedial work—to make such work more "fun" and appealing. Yet, by Glasser's standards, the "needs" for power and fun were still met by the club activity.

The need for choice was met not only through explicit time within the day for students to choose their own activities, but, as we will see later, in conflict resolution scenarios, choice was offered to students in a variety of implicit ways through their informal interactions with teachers. Choice did not mean complete freedom to choose, however; choices were limited by the teacher's assessment of which choices were desirable and which were not. The need for belonging was also satisfied by the club activities, as well as through community and class meetings. The need for power and freedom was satisfied in students' participation in open dialogue, yet students may have lacked genuine power to challenge a teacher's decision, as we saw in the discussion regarding candy as a healthy snack. "Kid-centered classrooms" at Indigo attempted to put student "needs" at the center, but at Indigo "needs" were sometimes determined by teachers for students, instead of by the students themselves in their own contexts.

The focus on community, as we describe in the next section, was another extension of individual need. Just as we need power, we also need, in Glasser's theory, to belong. Indigo's community and classroom meetings were an interesting and unique aspect of the Indigo curriculum.

Emphasis on Community

Good lead-managers recognize that when they can promote and support worker cooperation, they have laid the foundation for quality work.[25]

Prior to the start of school, a sense of grade-wide community was initiated with a field trip taken by the entire grade, community meetings held every day for the first week of school, and grade-wide projects completed, such as the making of each students' supply bag and journey book (a writing notebook for language arts). To maintain this bonding between members of the grade, who were divided into different classrooms, community meetings were conducted weekly and class meetings were held daily in each classroom.

Community Meetings

Each Friday the third and fourth grades met for approximately forty-five minutes to discuss issues of importance to students and teachers such as playground behavior, snack-time, clubs, reasons to be thankful, and "I feel" statements. The children sat on the floor and formed a large circle, while the teachers, less conspicuous in their casual clothing, sat among the students. Lucy took a place within the circle and welcomed the students to their community meeting. The meetings opened with a fun, rhyming song requiring animated movement, which engaged the students as they enjoyed the singing and dancing. After they took their seats again, the adults in the circle remained attentive to the children who were not being active listeners—those who were lying down, leaning against cabinets, or talking to neighbors. If the teachers felt that students were not yet attentive, they verbally thanked the group for being "attentive learners," and went on to describe what such behavior looked like. "Attentive learner" was a label that the students and the teachers co-constructed in the beginning of the year to mean sitting up, with eyes on the speaker, participating in the activity.

Lucy asked for suggestions for the agenda, and hands shot into the air. As items were generated by the students, they were written on the board by a teacher, and then prioritized by Lucy's suggestion. For example, one day a student suggested that the community discuss membership in clubs. She reported that some students were in them and some were not, and a teacher wondered aloud how the club system was going. A student seconded this by saying she also thought they should talk about the clubs. Another student followed up this comment by asserting that "all students should be in a club before some get a second club." A fourth student suggested that students who were already in a club could invite others to a club meeting and they could stay if they liked it. Another student criticized this idea, stated that clubs might become too large, and illustrated her point: "If each student brought one friend, a club of seven people would become fourteen, which is seven plus seven—and that would be too big." More students entered into the dialogue and offered a multitude of comments and opinions. A teacher stated that everyone would be in a club eventually, but students pressed on in their discussion, and new students entered the conversation. In the end, the community decided to create a suggestion box to address club issues as they arose, and Lucy announced two new clubs, open to everyone, that would be starting soon.

Discussion in the meeting moved from topic to topic according to the agenda, and students trailed each other's comments or, when necessary (during a large debate), students called on each other to speak. When they had discussed everything on the agenda, they concluded the meeting with either "I feel" or "Thank you" statements. The meeting ended with everyone in the circle rising to their feet and joining hands. Lucy led them in the following responsorial dialogue:

> I am who I am, I am special, I am important, I am important to the third grade community, the only time I look down (*all in the circle crouch down*) on a person is when I lift them up (*all stand one by one, each pulling the next up until everyone is standing*). Peace (*all make peace sign out in front of themselves*), Love (*all hug themselves*), Respect for everybody (*all touch index and third finger of both hands to forehead then extend out in front of body*).

Students were extremely attentive to one another during these meetings. They seem truly invested in the conversations taking place, as evidenced by their numerous contributions to the dialogue. One day the topic for discussion was snack-time, and the children and teachers worked out a decision concerning the placement of snacktime in the daily schedule. During this dialogue, the teachers made their own wishes known without stifling the student's voices. The teachers' role during the community meeting was to facilitate discussion, serve as moderators, offer factual information to clarify inconsistencies, and to provide conclusion to topics. The teachers were considered part of the entire group, and as such were part of the "everyone" who needed to agree on what the group decided.

While attention in these meetings was paid to reaching consensus, ultimately the teachers had the ability to veto any decision that they "could not live with." Students, on the other hand, did not have this ability. In the discussion on snack-time, the teachers indicated they did not feel comfortable with having snack-time occur whenever a student felt like eating. When that statement was made, two other opinions were offered by students, both of whom said that they believed that if they were going to have snack-time, they wanted a real time for it. Before the vote was taken, all the alternatives that did not specify a certain time were taken off the board, with discussion about why the teachers "couldn't live with" that decision. A question was posed to determine whether everyone could live with any of the remaining alternatives. All indicated yes by raising their hands, and a vote was taken.

Class Meetings

Each day, both sections of the third grade began the day with a class meeting, immediately following the lunch count, attendance, moment of silence, and the Pledge of Allegiance. Students moved to the front of the room and sat in a circle with the teacher. The agenda for this meeting started with the teacher writing a few items on the board that he wanted to discuss, and then children suggested issues important to them. The students showed items they had brought from home, discussed how class assignments from the previous day went, and talked about school-wide projects such as recycling and book fairs.

Similar to the community meetings on Fridays, class meetings addressed specific classroom issues, some of which were student-centered and some of which were teacher-centered. One day during the class meeting, a student announced that he would not be going to school anymore after Christmas. The teacher asked him a few clarifying questions, and the child responded that he would be moving to Louisiana in December to live with his mother. Discussion continued for a few minutes, as students offered their stories about moving and changing schools.

Sometimes the "needs" of the teacher were met during the class meeting. An example was a conversation about homework that occurred during a class meeting. Some parents, and a few students, too, mentioned that they wanted to see more homework. Ron began the meeting by saying that he was willing to offer more homework, but since it would take quite a bit of extra effort, he wanted to make certain that the students were interested. Ron negotiated the commitment with the students by asking a number of successive questions, started by finding out who was willing and interested in doing extra homework, and finished with who would be willing to have the homework checked and signed by their parents each night. In the end, the entire class, save one child, agreed to do more homework each night under the conditions Ron supplied along the way. Ron concluded the negotiation by reminding them, in a slow, calm tone, of two things: "It's not required; it's voluntary and up to you," and if they made the commitment they would need to follow through on it.

Negotiation, dialogue, and building commitment characterized the Indigo approach to community building. Community meetings were forums for a range of topics of importance to students and teachers, from snack-time to clubs to homework to feelings of fear, excitement, or happiness. Indigo teachers also developed a ritualistic performance that was most unusual in a public school setting. The weekly closing to the community meeting involving a mantra as well as bodily movement where all members were holding hands, which linked students and teachers together in a symbolic union. The need for belonging and power was satiated in these meetings where, through ritual and participation, students made meaning of the third grade community and the issues that were important to them.

Discipline

> When disruption occurs in school, it is usually with students who have had great difficulty satisfying their needs in school. . . . In the quality school, lead-teachers must learn how to handle a disruptive student in a way that is not punitive yet gets the situation under control and, at the same time, opens the student's mind to the option of beginning to work in class.[26]

When disciplinary conflicts arose, the staff instilled a sense of ownership into the resolution. Those involved in the conflict had responsibility to find solutions and to live with the consequences of the choices they made. Because students' problems could not be given to the teacher to be solved, a sense of accountability was created for those involved in a conflict. Misbehavior was a shared learning opportunity for the students and teachers. During our visits we identified two chief areas of conflict: teacher/student conflict, and student/student conflict.

Teacher/Student Conflict

When teacher-to-student conflict ensued, Ron generally used the Glasser "needs" language approach. During a math lesson, Ron moved around the classroom while most students were seated or took turns writing solutions to a problem on the board. He observed Troy leaning on the back two legs of his chair against some cabinets. Ron approached Troy, and while still engaging the class, placed both his hands on Troy's shoulders, leaned over him and said quietly, during a students' explanation of a math equation to the class, "That feels unsafe to me, Troy." Troy acknowledged this by putting his seat on the ground and pulling it closer to the table. Rather than announcing Troy's activity to the class, Ron privately and personally let him know that he had a "need" for Troy to engage in safe chair use.

On another occasion, Ron made use of the "observation chair" and its procedures that the staff at Indigo had created. When a student misbehaved, three choices were available: the student could sit in the observation chair (which gave a bird's eye view of the classroom) and observe what his or her behavior was supposed to look like; the student could choose to speak to Lucy in the Learning Center; or the student could elect to go to the principal's office.

We observed Ron use this discipline process when two students, Denise and Jimmy, approached him after a class meeting during which they had a conflict. After hearing about the nature of the conflict, Ron told Jimmy his behavior was "unacceptable," and proceeded to tell Jimmy that he "had choices." As Denise started to move away from the scene, Ron tried to persuade Jimmy into choosing one of the three options he had in this situation. Ron asked Jimmy if he would like to talk with Lucy, and Jimmy nodded his head affirmatively. As Ron went to the phone to call Lucy, Jimmy edged toward the observation chair. By the time Lucy was located, Jimmy chose, through unspoken gestures, to sit in the observation chair. Ron pulled up a chair beside the observation chair and after a short conversation, Jimmy returned to the classroom after approximately twenty minutes. Ron followed the Glasser model in this instance: he remained calm, was persistent in offering choices to the student, and eventually reached his goal of having the student make choices regarding the consequences of his actions. Discipline was provided but not in a punitive sense of the term.

Student/Student Conflict

Student-to-student conflict generally made use of the conflict resolution model mentioned previously. The teachers hoped that, with adult assistance, students would begin using the model themselves to solve difficulties prior to asking a teacher for help. Use of the conflict resolution model (or at least a portion of it) was frequent, especially in Ron's classroom. For instance, a table of four was having a conflict and chose to see Lucy to resolve it. Lucy later described the process she used to mediate their dispute over pencils:

> I said before we start, we need to find out if you guys are willing to work it out. I said "working out" means that each person gets to go around the circle and tell how this situation makes them [sic] feel, and everyone else will listen to them. Are you willing to work it out? So I went to the first boy, [he said] yes, and the second boy, [he said] yes, and I got to Sarah and, [Sarah said] no. [So I turned to Sarah and stated,] "Sarah, you're no longer a part of the group. That's alright [sic]. You need to be sure you understand what this means: this means that if you're not willing to work it out with the group that you're by yourself in the classroom. That you are saying you don't want to be part of the classroom". . . . So we went around and then what it came down to was that...sharing pencils was an issue and the wiggling of the table came up. And Sarah said, "I'm not doing that," and there again I say, "The message you're sending is that you're doing that, that's obviously not what you mean to be doing, and you may not be, but whatever you're doing it's sending the message that you're wiggling the table." And that way nobody ever has to lose; no one ever has to admit they're guilty. And that's very important. . . . So we finally came up to the plan that they would put a container in the middle of the table that each of them would donate a pencil to that can, so if you [sic] broke your pencil . . . you could take a pencil from the can and you would . . . bring another pencil the next day.

Lucy went on to mention that it was important to find out what was important to the children: "It's not like, oh my god, it's just pencils. . . . [These are] really big issues [for the students]." Glasser's model helped Lucy to take seriously the genuine conflicts that arose between these students, and in this scenario, Lucy followed Glasser's prescription for education that feels good. Sarah was not made to feel guilty, as Lucy pointed out. Glasser's theory of individual "needs" also compelled Lucy to ask each student if he or she agreed to engage in the process before it began, thereby implying choice. When Sarah stated that she was not willing to work out the conflict, Lucy stated that this was acceptable, yet continued by saying that Sarah was no longer a part of the group, which, as Lucy probably knew, was not an acceptable outcome for a third grader. It was unclear whether Sarah made a genuine choice in this case, because Lucy conducted the conflict resolution process with Sarah present and involved.

We can see Glasser's influence throughout the Indigo school day. Community meetings bring a sense of power and belonging to the students' and teachers' lives. Discipline involves choices. Conflict requires open dialogue and ownership of problems and solutions. Clubs bring a sense of fun, belonging, and power to learning. As Glasser recommends, the teachers attempt to meet students' "needs" in their management of the classroom. Indigo teachers have become lead-managers, and the word "community" is infused in their school. Yet what sort of community are they constructing? What are the consequences for public life?

Individualistic, Fabricated Means to Pre-determined Ends

> [W]hen men act, they act in a common and public world. This is the problem to which the theory of isolated and independent conscious minds gave rise: Given feelings, ideas, desires, which have nothing to do with one another, how can actions proceeding from them be controlled in a social or public interest?[27]

While there are many seemingly worthwhile components of Indigo's interpretation of Glasser's theory, there remain three fatal flaws in the theory that inhibit the creation of an authentic democratic environment. All three of these flaws flow from the individualistic nature of the theory, yet each have different, dramatic outcomes. Our first concern is that the use of community to achieve individual fulfillment undermines democratic hopes for genuine community-building. Second, by confounding the good worker with the good citizen, Glasser undercuts the importance of public spheres of life where children live not as individual workers, but as citizens with other students. Third, due to the lack of genuine democratic principles upon which to base the theory, and Glasser's focus on meeting individual rather than social "needs," Glasser's theory promotes the manipulation of students and settings in place of legitimate democratic choice. Taken together, these are heavy blows to the development of democratic classrooms. At Indigo we saw teachers attempting to change the classroom environment toward a more humane atmosphere, a change which in itself is valuable. However, because of these critical problems, we are unconvinced that Glasser's theory results in democratic education or democratic citizens.

Practitioners at Indigo Elementary School show us how Glasser's theories lead to the development of caring classrooms which foster peaceful conflict negotiation, personal accountability, learning without coercion, and open classroom dialogue. Indigo's community meetings engage students in collaborative problem-solving, and attempt to construct a spirit of solidarity between students and teachers.

Using Indigo as an example, one might even align Glasser's educational philosophy with Dewey's democratic classroom. Such an alignment is the basis for The John Dewey Academy, a prep school which Glasser describes as providing therapeutic assistance to self-destructive adolescents in an atmosphere which encourages them to "participate actively in developing their . . .

potentialities." Teens who are experiencing severe substance abuse problems work with instructors to take part in school governance and operations. The principal of the Academy states that older students have special responsibilities in supervising younger students and "assuming managerial roles. . . . In so doing, seniors internalize Judeo-Christian values by recognizing personal payoffs of earned achievement."[28] While The John Dewey Academy obviously claims a Deweyan pedagogy and thereby a balanced emphasis on individual and community "needs," the suggestion of "internalizing" predetermined values due to the "personal payoffs" provided is a highly individualistic expectation of education, lacking any recognition of a communal sense of school or society. We can also see these same individualistic tendencies in the Indigo School, which characterizes community as a mere setting for personal fulfillment. While consistent with Glasser's simplistic biological "needs"-based theory, the use of community for the purpose of individual fulfillment negates the possibility that classrooms and school communities are more than an aggregate of individuals. Glasser's solely individualistic understanding of students makes the development of community a tactic rather than a necessary element for democratic relations in the classroom.

This underlying individualism in Glasser's theory also problematizes the goals of this educational theory. Glasser's writings equate the good worker with the good citizen. At Indigo, students learn skills that will enable them to succeed in the world of work—they will know how to be accountable for their own work, how to interact successfully with a team, how to solve conflicts, and how to treat others with respect and dignity. On first glance, these are unobjectionable goals for an educational theory. But these goals lack the power for explaining reasons for or sustaining interest in participation in the educational enterprise beyond a sense of self-fulfillment. Alone, these goals are necessary but not sufficient for a fully developed sense of education in a democratic society, which must include a commitment to the public sphere. Glasser's model serves the public interest only in the sense of a narrow definition of the public; indeed, Glasser focuses explicitly on the private, if we think of employment as a largely private pursuit of individual goals and interests.

Moving from Glasser's educational ends, the third breach of democratic philosophy centers around the issue of manipulation in the class day and the impact this factor has on the creation of a genuine democratic society in the classroom. Students, both in Glasser's theory and at Indigo Elementary, are offered choices throughout their interactions with teachers and students. The ability to choose supports Glasser's conception of the "needs" for power and freedom. Yet, how legitimate these choices really are should be questioned if the goal of a democratic education is to be fostered. A commitment to a democratic classroom suggests that students share control of various aspects of classroom life with other teachers and students, and that the decisions they make through democratic processes be authentic. However, an adherence to Glasser's use of choices to fulfill certain individual "needs" undercuts the power of shared classroom governance because it diminishes the reason for such behavior. Rather than sharing power in a classroom so that students can practice democratic processes, Glasser's theory advocates a utilitarian, individualistic reason for incorporating such components into the classroom setting. By so doing, Glasser strips the classroom of its potential to be a genuine forum for democratic participation and creates an aversive climate for the pursuit of a full public life at school.

To see how Glasser comes to such a limited view of public life, let us review the assumptions of Glasser's "needs"-based curriculum that serve as the means to the Quality student product. Glasser writes that we have "needs" built into our genetic structure, and all five "needs" (survival, belonging, power, fun, freedom) "must be reasonably satisfied if we are to fulfill our biological destiny." In addition, we cannot help but "feel a continual urge to behave when any need is unsatisfied and we can no more deny this urge than we can deny the color of our eyes."[29] Problematic in this account is the rigid distinction between internal and external motivations, the classic nature versus nurture question. If one's public actions are seen solely as extensions of her private "needs," the public is stripped of its value as a legitimate sphere of human life. An enlarged sense of the public can drive the educator's continual search to bring individual and social "needs" together, as opposed to undermining the importance of the public by exclusively promoting the individual. Yet to place individual and social "needs" in synergy, Glasser's troubling elevation of individual "needs" as genetic, inherent, and omnipotent must be recast.

Human "needs," as described by Glasser, are described as human interests by Dewey. Children have interests (also called impulses) which serve as the "natural resources . . . upon the exercise of which depends the active growth of the child."[30] These interests—conversation or communication, inquiry or finding things out, construction or making things, and artistic expression—are what students bring to school. The role of the school is to harness students' interests in the direction of growth, which we can define as both individual and public expansion of potential. The distinction between "needs" as defined by Glasser and "interests" as characterized by Dewey is not merely semantic. Both Glasser and Dewey view the child as bringing to school a set of internal drives, yet while Glasser organizes school around meeting these internal, inherent biological urges, Dewey views school as the place where these impulses become transformed and directed toward a public sphere.

Let us take two examples from Indigo to illustrate the distinction and its implications. First, the language Ron used to address conflict in the classroom relied heavily on Glasser's basic "needs." Ron had a "need" for Troy to engage in safe chair use, and told him so with that language during their conflict. This resolution was typical of how other such conflicts were handled. Secondly, in the conflict resolution scenario with Jimmy, Ron offered a range of choices to Jimmy, the "problem" student. Denise is removed from the scene; the problem that was present in a public domain was instantly privatized into Jimmy's problem, and choices were organized to meet his "needs" alone. Jimmy's "needs" are psychologized, instead of kept in and solved through their originating public domain. An alternate solution would attempt to bring Jimmy and Denise together, to work out their problem in the context of the problem. Both individual and public ends can be met if they are considered inseparable from one another, rather than two distinct spheres of life between which one jumps back and forth.

Reconceptualizing individual "needs" in view of a public context requires a vision of educational ends beyond those that Glasser identifies. Glasser's Quality School seeks to enable all students to do quality work through the satisfaction of individual biological "needs." What ends of education could be sensitive to both individual and communal needs? One answer is Dewey's notion of education as growth. While Glasser's educational ends focus solely on the creation of the student as quality worker, Dewey sees individual and social transformation—or growth—as the only appropriate educational outcome. Education should use the interests of the child to expand the child's horizons beyond herself. Satisfying these interests is not the desired goal of education; instead, education is the process whereby we transform these interests into habits of associated living. "The natural . . . impulses of the young do not agree with the life-customs of the group into which they are born. Consequently they have to be directed or guided."[31] Turning individual citizens away from egocentric tendencies is the goal of education in a democracy. Our critique of Glasser's individualistic means challenges the strict and unwavering dualism between internal "needs" and external conditions found in control theory; instead, the context of democracy requires that educators understand students' "needs" and constantly work to align them in public problem-solving.

Individual and community growth cannot take place in a system in which outcomes are pre-determined and ends are static. The system that Glasser suggests has an inorganic quality not suitable to the growth of students, teachers, or evolving democratic life. Glasser's system is closed because the ends are determined by our unalterable biological "needs." This viewpoint of education cannot be democratic because it is fixed and undercuts a "thick" view of public life which is constantly under construction. Dewey states that "Fixed . . . ends, mark fixed limits to change. Hence, they make futile all human efforts to produce and regulate change except within narrow and unimportant limits. They paralyze constructive human inventions by a theory which condemns them in advance to failure."[32] Reconstructing our public life is the activity of democratic living; through public problem-solving we continue to reshape our public life. We do this not separate from our individual "needs," but rather in concert with them. Further, fixed ends that promote "narrow and unimportant limits" could accurately describe current fixations with test scores and a national, standardized curriculum, obsessions which can transform vital teachers and interested students into workers caught in a desperately incoherent system.

Fixed ends not only inhibit growth of a vital public sphere; they can also contribute to social reproduction. Glasser's model is highly susceptible to promoting social reproduction; schools teach children how to be obedient, faithful workers to their company by fostering these same relationships with teachers and authority figures at school. By focusing solely on education as work, students as products, and teachers as lead-managers, Glasser's business terminology suggests that the ultimate product of his educational scheme is a good worker: someone who knows how to manipulate the work environment to meet his or her individual "needs." Yet society—including various social inequities in realms of race, class, and gender—

remains unchanged by a process of schooling which mimics rather than revolutionizes our social context.

Public life is filled with situations where ends are in flux. An example might be when a community must decide how to zone a certain segment of property; the larger question which must be addressed is, what do we care about as a community? What are our present "needs" as a whole? What are our interests? "We" in this situation is not a collection of "I's", individuals who get their "needs" met in a group. The "we" in such a situation are people who are all directly or indirectly affected by the situation at hand, and who hold interests in the decision that are as informed by their individual impulses as their status as citizens. As Dewey conceives of education, schools would direct individual interests outward toward public life. Interests are not mere biological drives that must be fed. Interests inform citizens in associated intelligent activity.

The Zoo Club at Indigo Elementary provides an example of uniting individual and public "needs" in the educational ends of growth. Zoo Club is organized so that students rotate membership at regular intervals, bringing in new students to the pre-existing club. Students train other students in the details of feeding, cleaning cages, and handling the animals. Not only are these children learning to teach one another, they are learning to coordinate a part of their public life that they find valuable: the presence of animals in their classroom. It is true that they meet their own "needs" for belonging and fun, but they do so not to the detriment of their public "needs" but in accordance with their public concerns. Ultimately, children take care of the animals not because the teacher has forced them to do so, but because they are interested in having animals in their class and doing so meets some of their individual "needs" as well.

Education that transforms individual impulses into public activity can be found in other school activities like band, athletics, or clubs, the elements of schools which Glasser finds instructional because they fulfill individual "needs" for fun, belonging, and power. A marching band takes individual interests and pulls them into a public domain; as a collective, the band must work on individual performances as well as integration of those performances. The band has a genuine problem to solve, together. In addition, the knowledge of music is valued by society; it is not knowledge for the sake of knowledge, but relevant to social enhancement (not simply because the teacher has told students that it will be important later in life, as Glasser advocates[33]). Similarly, a newspaper club takes individual interests for communication and expression into a public sphere, where students solve a shared problem every time they pull together all the elements of a successful publication. The publication is not a mere instrument to fulfill one's "needs" as teacher or as student—it has a life of its own in the public sphere, and is thereby valued by students as an authentic contribution to their school community.

The notion of genuine contributions made by students is important when considered in the context of the choices students make at Indigo. Recall the student who asked why Lucy had allowed the class to discuss the worthiness of candy as a snack; why did she ask how many students thought candy was an acceptable snack when she had already decided against it? The student asks a legitimate question that highlights the problem of offering choices to fulfill innate, biological, individual "needs." Satisfying individual "needs" is the purpose behind giving individuals choices in the Glasser model. If candy would satisfy one's "needs," why could it not be a sanctioned snack? There are no replies to this available to one following Glasser, if "needs" are fulfilled; therefore, the teacher remains the one to "give" the alternatives, and she usually frames the options from which the students choose. "Giving students choices" as practiced at Indigo inherently reclaims and maintains an undemocratic system of power allocation in the classroom. By "giving" choices the teacher manipulates the classroom environment so her agenda can be met. Lucy pointed to this element of choice when she remarked that "you also give them choices whereby you're probably going to end up winning." Unless power is shared, a democratic atmosphere cannot be sustained. Glasser's theory of individual "needs" as rationale for inauthentic choices seriously abates the democratic potential of the classroom because central control of the classroom remains with the teacher.

The Quality School seeks to bring the fun, belonging, and empowerment of the band and the newspaper into the classroom, but absent here is the consideration of larger pedagogical issues. For Glasser, cooperative learning produces quality work because it fulfills individual need. For Dewey, collaborative learning involves solving genuine problems, and constructing knowledge as habits of inquiry and work are formed. Inquiry can only proceed outward from the individual, toward a public problem, if authentic work is done and if genuine questions and problems are resolved, and this can only be done when ends are not pre-determined.

Students engage in such work when they discuss, in their weekly community meetings, the placement of snack-time in their day. Where is it best placed in the day? How can we satisfy "needs" and meet the goal of the group, which is to engage in a day of learning together? The problem is real, the solution undetermined except through public participation. Similarly, in the conflict resolution scenario involving shared pencils, the teacher left the resolution up to the students; because the ends were not predetermined, students could become involved in a genuine problem that needed resolution.

In visiting Indigo we saw how at least two teachers interpret Glasser's theory. In some situations the individualism of Glasser's theory was tempered with a healthy dose of a communitarian ethic and public problem-solving. In this process, students were indeed granted much more power over their lives than they would be in traditional classrooms. Students had the opportunity to evaluate themselves, to engage in discussions regarding how to spend their time at school, and to resolve their own conflicts with one another. There is much to be celebrated in the education students receive at Indigo. In some classroom situations, however, Glasser's fixed innate "needs" led to predetermined ends. What is comforting about the Indigo example is that it is a thoughtful introduction of Glasser's theory into a real classroom situation. What remains problematic about the Indigo example is that if, as Glasser suggests, the teachers truly assume that these fifty children are ruled by biological "needs," the likelihood is that the communal pieces of their school experience will continue to be add-ons to what is primarily an individualized education. As Purpel and Shapiro note, discipline is not a private problem; it is "a key element in acting with responsibility to and for others."[34] Glasser's entire theory negates the social dimensions of the educational experience.

The critique of Glasser positions the students as subjects rather than objects of their own education. In *Brave New World*, the citizens are the objects of the decisions made by the superior Alphas. In Glasser's scheme, students are objects because they simply react to their innate "needs," and their behavior is a testament to these required drives; they are captives of their biological destiny and the teacher's direction of this destiny. The teacher steers the students' destiny by offering choices to students, yet maintains authority because she frames the choices, rather than the choices being generated through a democratic process. Students remain the objects of teacher discretion as opposed to subjects participating with teachers to create an individually and communally rich classroom atmosphere.

We have described a number of concerns with this framework. The biological, individual drives that undergird this theory create a fixed, pre-determined set of educational ends that are not subject to the process of democratic decision making in the public sphere. These circumstances create the perfect avenue for the reproduction of some of society's most pressing problems. Not only does this theory discount the weight and value of the public sphere, by definition it separates students from one another, except in cases when to co-mingle helps an individual meet his personal "needs." In opposition to Glasser's scheme, we suggest a fundamentally democratic pedagogy, one which holds that students are subjects in their education, participating members in the making of meaning and solving public problems. Taking from Dewey, the classroom environment would not be constructed on preconceived ends but toward the growth of both individuals and the public life of the classroom. Genuine public problem-solving transforms both individuals and their social connection through the habits of inquiry and intelligence. Unlike Glasser, this construction of education is sensitive to the growth of society as well as the growth of the individual. The classroom we envision here would utilize some of the techniques and methods used at Indigo Elementary, but the pedagogy framing the technique would be dramatically different from the control theory that is essential to Glasser's plan for Quality Schools.

But a plan is exactly what Glasser offers teachers that Dewey does not, and herein lies the problem. In a confusing era in which schools are besieged by internal and external problems and pressures, the immediately useful recipe that Glasser offers is very attractive. After reading *Quality Schools* or *Control Theory in the Classroom*, a teacher could put into motion the techniques Glasser advocates: collaborative learning activities, class meetings, and a focus on meeting students' individual "needs" in disciplinary situations. Just as Lucy and her colleagues did at Indigo, teachers can read Glasser and easily understand how his theory might translate into their current classrooms. Dewey does not make the conversion from theory to practice so simple. His viewpoint calls on teachers to be critical about their classroom environments, the role of teacher and school in a democracy, and the goals of education.

Yet, that which is most attractive about Glasser, the ease with which one puts his theory into play, is a critical downfall in the theory. Glasser lacks respect for the teacher as a professional, reflective practitioner with a mind and constructive thoughts about the broader pedagogical, public aims of schooling. In a culture with a pervasive mythology of individual potential, rights, and choices, using a theory that understands classrooms as collections of individuals may seem to follow common sense. Unfortunately, Glasser's individualistic foundation and fixed educational ends ultimately leave his theory with very little to enhance individual growth in a communal, democratic context.

Notes

1. Aldous Huxley, *Brave New World* (New York: Harper and Row, 1946), p. xv.

2. William Glasser, *Schools without Failure* (New York: Harper and Row, 1969).

3. Lee Canter, *Assertive Discipline: A Take Charge Approach for Today's Educator* (Santa Monica: Canter and Associates, 1976).

4. Constructivism holds as a basic premise that all knowledge is constructed; meaning is made by the learner, not simply transferred from knower to learner in a passive manner. The roots of social constructivism can be traced to Piaget. Constructivism currently dominates math and science education, and is also a basic tenet of cognitive psychology. Dewey and Vygotsky are also labeled constructivists, but emphasize the social dimension of meaning-making.

5. William Glasser, *Control Theory in the Classroom* (New York: Harper and Row, 1986).

6. See W. Edwards Deming, *Out of the Crisis* (Cambridge: Massachusetts Institute of Technology, Center for Advanced Engineering Study, 1982). Deming's influence in education, as evidenced by the TQM movement, is most recently documented in *Contemporary Education* 67 (2, 1996): 60–113.

7. A pseudonym, as are all names of persons described in the Indigo case study.

8. Melanie Fox-Harris and R. Carl Harris, "Glasser Comes to a Rural School," *Educational Leadership* 50 (3, 1992): 18–21; Glasser, "The John Dewey Academy: A Residential College Preparatory Therapeutic High School. A Dialogue with Tom Bratter," *Journal of Counseling and Development* 68 (5, 1990): 582–585.

9. Glasser, *Control Theory*, p. 17, italics in original.

10. Glasser, *Control Theory*, p. 23, italics in original.

11. Glasser, *Control Theory*, p. 23.

12. Ibid., *Control Theory*, p. 27.

13. Ibid., *Control Theory*, p. 15, italics in original.

14. William Glasser, *The Quality School: Managing Students Without Coercion* (New York: Harper Perennial, 1990), p. 219.

15. Bowles and Gintis' work is probably the best known social reproduction theory to emphasize the "correspondence" between schools and workplaces; see Samuel Bowles and Herbert Gintis, *Schooling in Capitalist America* (New York: Basic Books, 1976); see also Jay MacLeod, *Ain't No Makin' It: Leveled Aspirations in a Low-Income Neighborhood* (Boulder, CO: Westview Press, 1995).

16. Glasser, *The Quality School*, p. 5.

17. Glasser, *Control Theory*, p. 32.

18. Ibid., p. 36.

19. Ibid., p. 38.

20. Glasser, *The Quality School*, p. 16.

21. Glasser, *The Quality School*.

22. Ibid., p. 70.

23. Sue Ellen Henry and Julie Martin observed the entire grade functioning as a community during "community meeting" on four separate occasions. In addition, we observed classroom interactions, and conducted individual interviews with the Learning Center Coordinator and the Math/Social

Science teacher. After each visit, we wrote extensive field notes and transcribed all taped interviews. We collected and analyzed all relevant school literature, promotional videos and footage of earlier community meetings, and took photographs of the school grounds.

24. Glasser, *The Quality School*, p. 75.

25. Glasser, *The Quality School*, p. 48.

26. Ibid., p. 135.

27. John Dewey, *Democracy and Education* (New York: Free Press, 1916), p. 297.

28. Glasser, "The John Dewey Academy," p. 583.

29. Glasser, *Control Theory*, p. 23.

30. John Dewey, "The School and Society," in *Dewey on Education*, Martin S. Dworkin, ed. (New York: Teachers College Press, 1957), p. 61.

31. Dewey, *Democracy and Education*, p. 39.

32. John Dewey, *Reconstruction in Philosophy* (Boston: Beacon Press, 1957), p. 70.

33. Glasser says that the "real-world value of the material to be learned would have been emphasized in lectures, in class discussions, in cooperative learning groups, and even in homework assignments that ask students to discuss with parents or other adults how what they learn in school might be useful outside of school." Teachers, rather than designing curriculum around genuine problems that students know to be relevant in their world, are to convince students of the relevance throughout the lesson. William Glasser, "The Quality School Curriculum," *Phi Delta Kappan* 73 (9, 1992): 690–94.

34. David E. Purpel and Svi Shapiro, *Beyond Liberation and Excellence: Reconstructing the Public Discourse on Education* (Westport: Bergin and Garvey, 1995), p. 193.

Part III

Toward a Curriculum of Democratic Civility:
Exploring the Possibilities of
Critical Constructivist Discipline

Contemporary mainstream classroom discipline and management fails teachers and students daily. It promises short-term orderliness, and orderliness is, without a doubt, an absolute prerequisite to learning. But the long-term consequences, and the immediate ethical and political contradictions, sully its effectiveness. Just as seriously, contemporary discipline and management fails our society. It encourages habits of the mind and of the heart antithetical to the sorts of reflective, intelligent, grounded understandings that are prerequisite to democratic political, social, and economic life.

Part III begins to explore alternatives to contemporary classroom practices. As argued in the Introduction, critical constructivist alternatives will best respond to the critique we are sketching in this volume. While the past must inform the search for those alternatives, there is nothing in our past that provides a ready-made alternative. We must, instead, look to what we know of constructivism, adding a critical perspective, to begin to build alternatives.

We are not left without any models, however. We offer one framework here, Judicious Discipline. Judicious Discipline does not end our search. Rather, it provides one of many beginning points. We offer, as well, a critique of Judicious Discipline that serves as a model of the sort of critical perspective that must inform a revitalized discourse around classroom discipline.

We need more frameworks and models built on a deep respect for the minds and capabilities of teachers and of children, rigorously tested in classrooms, answerable not to the ethic of efficiency but to the morality of care, democracy, and community.

7

Judicious Discipline

❏

Forrest Gathercoal

judicious . . . *1: having or exercising sound judgment . . . , 2: directed or governed by sound and dispassionate judgment; characterized by discretion . . . syn. see wise.* Webster's Third New International Dictionary

discipline . . . *2. training that develops self-control, character, or orderliness and efficiency . . . , 3. self-control or orderly conduct . . . , 4. a system of rules . . . , 5. treatment that corrects* . . . Webster's New World Dictionary

An uncomplicated yet workable rule has been evolving in the classrooms of successful teachers throughout our country which simply states, "You may do what you want in this classroom until it interferes with the rights of others." This premise provides a means by which teachers can acknowledge individual differences among students while at the same time protecting the need for an educational environment free from disruptive forces. Application of this philosophy in an evenhanded manner teaches students that they have individual rights as well as the expectations for their roles as responsible members of the learning community.

A school community that practices democracy is one where educators deliberately teach and model principles of civility as the foundation for personal growth and interactions among its members. It is a school in which individual differences are respected and students feel they have permanent value as citizens and students. The constitutional framework ensures an atmosphere of civil morality that cuts across the many cultural, ethnic, and religious traditions represented by the diversity of family values children bring with them to school.

The scaffolding for this principled level of social interaction is embedded in the constitutional tenets upon which all our nation's laws have been founded; freedom, justice, and equality balanced against the welfare needs and interests of society. These time-tested concepts, which have sustained our country for over two centuries, are equally effective as a basis for establishing expectations of learning and behavior in school.

A Constitutional Perspective for School Rules

To create a school culture where students' human rights are respected, students and educators need to experience a common language of civility. The first step is to learn about our nation's democratic principles and how they can be integrated into the school environment.

Students often confront educators with a statement like, "You can't do that to me, I've got my rights." Asked to explain what they mean by their "rights," most respond by saying something like, "I don't know, but I've got my rights." Although many students and parents talk about having rights, few understand what that statement actually means.

The Bill of Rights was written to protect three basic human values: freedom, justice, and equality. These three basic values have their antecedents in the United States Constitution and are fundamental to understanding the meaning of human rights. The controversy over the question of how, when, and where to limit individual freedoms is never-ending and often tests the mettle of the most ardent supporter of our liberties. To live in a free society, however, does not mean we have license to do as we please. It means we have freedom to think and act on behalf of our own self-interests while always balancing our actions with the welfare needs of the larger community. The difficulty, of course, lies in the fact that there is no precise formula to constitutional decisions; rather there is a reasoned set of guidelines that serve to indicate when freedoms have exceeded rightful bounds.

Justice is concerned primarily with due process and deals with basic governmental fairness. In America we share the substantive right to be governed by fair and reasonable laws. Justice also provides for the procedural right of adequate notice, a fair hearing, and the right to appeal the laws and decisions which take away life, liberty, and property. The safeguards provided by our nation's justice system are well-conceived, but as with most systems in our culture, the forces of economics, politics, and the "human factor" cause it, on occasion, to fall short of its intended purpose.

Finally, equality presents us with the problem of how to distribute burdens and benefits. The proposition that "all people are created equal" has never meant that we all possess the same abilities, interests, or talents. Although all students may not be achieving or performing at the same level in their schooling, it is the opportunity to succeed in public education that is the constitutional right which must be equal to all. In other words, equality is interpreted as meaning an equal opportunity for everyone.

Rights in School

Freedom, justice, and equality are goals of our society. The particulars of how we achieve those goals are set out through the rights and responsibilities embedded

in our constitutional framework. Individual rights are protected by the Bill of Rights, the first ten amendments to the
Constitution. Although other amendments and legislative
laws are occasionally applied to learning and behavior
issues, students and educators knowledgeable about the
First, Fourth, and Fourteenth amendments have a solid
foundation when talking about student rights.

Until 1969, court decisions historically supported the
concept of *in loco parentis*, but today the situation is
much different. Courts rarely use the concept of *in loco
parentis* when writing opinions on student disciplinary
issues. This concept has been replaced by language that
addresses the constitutional rights and responsibilities of
students. Although there have been prior questions
considered, the United States Supreme Court in *Tinker v.
Des Moines Independent School District*[1] for the first time
held that students in public schools have constitutional
rights in the area of student discipline.

The Tinker case involved high school students suspended by their principal for wearing black arm bands
to school in protest against the United States' involvement in Vietnam. The students won the right to express
their political beliefs when the court stated for the first
time, ". . . First Amendment rights, applied in light of
the special characteristics of the school environment,
are available to teachers and students. It can hardly be
argued that either students or teachers shed their
constitutional rights to freedom of speech or expression
at the schoolhouse gate. . . ."

It is apparent that times have changed from the days
when school rules were arbitrary and resembled those
used in most families. Today, the rules school authorities
use must take into consideration the constitutional rights
of students. A graphic illustration of student rights might
be to imagine students dressing each morning in attire
selected from their wardrobe of liberties. By the time they
have donned their mail of "freedom," buckled on a sword
of "justice," and grasped the shield of "equality," they
might be reminiscent of knights of King Arthur's Round

Table clad in full battle dress, as they walk the hallways of our public schools.

This may be seen as a formidable image and in many cases very intimidating to educators who come face to face with student discipline problems every day. To complicate matters, frustrated educators are frequently heard to say, "Students have more rights than we have." This, in fact, happens to be true. Educators have no constitutional rights in the student-educator relationship. Their rights exist only through the employer-employee relationship.

We are now at the core, the very heart of the question facing disciplinary issues in public schools today. Is there a way to establish and maintain an effective learning environment in our schools, while at the same time respecting student rights of freedom, justice, and equality?

Compelling State Interests

As foreboding as respecting students' constitutional rights appears at first blush, there is another very important side to the scale of justice. There are, in fact, four time-tested public interest arguments crafted in the courts and construed for the precise purpose of limiting constitutionally protected freedoms in the interests of the general welfare and the common good. These arguments are as well-grounded in legal principle and history as the line of reasoning that allows for individual rights.

These public interest arguments are commonly referred to as compelling state interests. They simply mean that in some cases the welfare and interests of the majority are more compelling than those of an individual. This general welfare principle, used in conjunction with our government's responsibility, gives educators all the legal authority they need to create and carry out fair and equitable school rules. Compelling state interests may deny individual rights when the exercise of those rights involve:

1. Property loss or damage,

2. Legitimate educational purpose,

3. Threat to health and safety,

4. Serious disruption of the educational process.

School rules and decisions intended to protect these four compelling state interest arguments will, in all probability, withstand the test of today's court rulings despite the fact that they deny students their individual rights. Educators not only have a legal authority to deny student constitutional rights, but a professional responsibility to prohibit student behaviors when their exercise of those rights seriously affects the welfare of the school.

In dysfunctional situations where personal and societal boundaries are not respected, students have the feeling they are not "whole." When personal identity is blurred by co-dependency and disempowerment, students will seek to gain power in ways that appear to be dysfunctional but make sense given that they are trying to function in a system that seeks to control rather than understand them. Trying to remember "all the rules" is much more difficult than accepting and abiding by a moral and ethical code of relatively few principles from which all interactions flow.

The real issue is how a democratic management style influences students to understand that they have a valued place in the school community. In a school environment in which students do not have to continually prove their worth or live in fear of punishment, they experience real feelings of belonging. Regardless of their background, abilities, and behavior, they are accepted and made to feel they have permanent value. Their insecurities are then replaced with concern for others, feelings of self-worth and confidence, a sense of belonging, and a cooperative attitude.

Ultimately, practicing democratic principles guides students toward understanding and accepting a social contract with others. In democratic classrooms, responsibility flows from a principled level of thinking where students learn to balance individual freedoms with the welfare interests of the school community. On the other hand, autocratic classrooms often equate responsibility with obedience. There is something anomalous about the phrase "student rights and obedience," but that is a typical phrase used by autocratic educators when they give lip service to student rights. Educators who teach students about our nation's civil morality and provide them an opportunity to experience individual liberties are giving new meaning and substance to the phrase, "student rights and responsibilities." This is not only a legally defensible position, but an ethical one as well.

The Democratic School Community

Educators who want to create a democratic environment must approach rules and consequences as a way of building community and keeping students in school, rather than using them as a means for pushing students out. This judicious mindset views rules as guidelines as opposed to restrictions, and uses consequences for diagnostic purposes instead of for punishing students.

The problem lies in one of our educational system's more glaring contradictions—autocratic schools are the vehicles we presumably use to teach students to be responsible citizens in a democratic society. Ironically, the first experience most students have with government is when their state's compulsory education laws require them to attend school. They are forced into a system of rules, decisions, and authority which rewards obedience, punishes offenses, and needs no justification other than, "I am in charge here."

If the management system in our public schools creates an autocratic environment, it follows that educators are preparing graduates who are unlikely to understand or function well in a participatory society. In the long run, the benefits of enabling students to think and act as responsible citizens far outweigh the disciplinary expediency of teaching blind obedience.

Most educators fear losing control over their students and so they are reluctant to relinquish autocratic methods. It is very important, therefore, that students and educators both understand from the beginning that a democratic classroom does not mean there is a permissive environment or that every decision is decided by a majority vote. The principles of a democracy offer considerable structure for government to prescribe proper civil behavior and place a great deal of authority in the hands of governmental officials.

If democratic principles are applied to a classroom, teachers then become analogous to government officials and have the same authority to enforce rules and resolve disputes among its members. In every democracy there is a critical need for good leadership in order to keep its principles strong and viable. The same is true of educators in a democratic school community. How much more effective our schools could be if we would teach the rationale for society's boundaries and the intrinsic value of informed compliance. Until students are allowed to have some control over their actions and begin to feel an ownership in their learning community, their desire and ability to function responsibly will always be at risk.

In a democracy, human rights can be limited by government to a reasonable time, place, and manner. For example, freedom of speech in a classroom does not mean students can speak up at any time or in any manner they choose. Students need to know that the responsibility that comes along with their constitutional right of free speech can be reasonably regulated by their teacher to the learning environment needs of the classroom.

The concept of time, place, and manner is a good organizer for groups to use as they learn to process the balancing of power. It also reminds students of the need for regulation and the educator's authority in the balancing process. But the best part about empowering students is that when they disrupt class by talking too loudly, there is much less stress created by asking them, "Is this a reasonable time, place, or manner for talking?" than to open up the possibility of a power struggle with the usual demand, "Stop the talking!"

Democratic and autocratic classrooms approach rules from two entirely different directions. In democratic classrooms, rules are based largely on the concept that students are free, but their freedoms are limited through the school's welfare responsibilities. In autocratic classrooms, rules begin with student responsibilities, and freedoms are earned through good behavior. The question is one of emphasis. Should educators place more importance on students' individual freedoms and the responsibilities that accompany them, or on rules that leave behaviors not covered by predetermined restrictions as being acceptable?

The approach chosen usually makes a significant difference in how students react to authority. For example, to err in an atmosphere of freedom, justice, and equality results in learning experiences, allowing students to experience cognitive growth. In such classrooms students act in ways that indicate they are more motivated, capable, respectful, and independent than was previously evident. Conversely, to err in a classroom that emphasizes personal limitations results in perceptions of unfairness, humiliation, and indignity. This creates a debilitating environment that causes students to be more unresponsive, defiant, insecure, and co-dependent. The philosophy adopted by educators directly affects the attitude and behavior of students.

The Professional Relationship Model

Rules serve the purpose of providing boundaries and are effective only until they are broken. When students waiver from judiciously imposed boundaries, they need a mentor or advisor nearby who is able to guide and support their recovery.

A mentor helps students discover their best selves, not by making them dependent, but by deepening their confidence in their own abilities to resolve the problems facing them. When a behavior problem does occur, it is a dedicated mentor-educator who pauses to think, "What needs to be learned here?" Every student's problem then becomes an educational opportunity. For example, when students make academic mistakes, good teachers use these mistakes for diagnostic purposes and employ effective educational strategies to help them overcome their learning difficulties. Professional educators are usually patient and understanding with students and know that academic accomplishments take some time to develop. It would only follow then, that the same professional approach toward behavior problems would be equally as effective. And just as we would approach an academic quandary with students by first asking what the matter is, so we would also begin to resolve a conflict by trying to discern the nature of the problem.

Developing the Question

In every other professional relationship, the professionals ask questions and their clients do most of the talking. Physicians, for example, would not prescribe automatically two aspirin tablets to every patient who complains of feeling ill. Rather, physicians respond to medical problems with, "Where does it hurt?" "How long has it been that way?" and "Is it worse when I do this?" Before a lawyer agrees to represent anyone, considerable time is taken pursuing the facts and interests of the client. Without gathering appropriate and relevant information, professionals simply cannot act in the best interests of the people they are employed to serve. Just as with other professional fields, educators must learn to approach discipline problems by asking the same professional questions.

Behavioral problems should be approached by asking general questions of inquiry and concern in an effort to encourage students to talk about what they perceive happened. "Coming to the point" does not mean beginning with an accusatory statement. It means approaching the problem from the perspective of the student with the intent of getting to the heart of the problem. Asking, "What happened?" or "Is there something I can do to help?" or offering a descriptive statement like, "It looks like you might be having a bad day. Would you like to talk about it?" usually prompts students to open up and discuss the problem.

The focus of the conversation must be away from students defending who they are and toward encouraging them to talk about what they have done. Therefore, as a general rule, always avoid asking students, "Why did you do it?" Students who are in trouble usually know the rules and are aware that they have messed up. Given the opportunity to speak with an educator they trust, students will usually bring up the infraction and be willing to talk about it without coercion.

Asking a question, rather than delivering a lecture, preserves due process and shows respect for students by hearing their side of the story rather than leaping to conclusions about the situation. Questions also move educators away from sounding threatening or accusatory. For example, a teacher who says, "You really messed up!" will probably get a defensive response from a student. But a teacher who asks students if they are having a tough day empowers students to take a participatory role in finding a solution to the problem.

By asking leading questions and listening carefully, the underlying issues of any conflict begin to emerge. Professionals in every field get very adept at asking leading questions based on their expertise and intuition. "Professional probing" can take many forms, such as personal reactions, interested inquiries, or even a shared opinion on the subject. For example, students caught cheating on a test do not need a lecture on morality, but an opening response such as, "Could it be that you did not have adequate time to prepare for the test?"

In summary, asking leading questions and listening carefully to the answers are strategies which can be used over and over again with powerful results. The more authority students have over their lives, the more they become accountable for their own thoughts and actions. Once they are ready to assume responsibility for their actions, judicious consequences that are focused on restitution naturally follow.

Judicious Consequences

When approaching consequences, educators usually begin thinking in one of two completely different directions: (1) how do I confront this student and what would be the most appropriate punishment; or, (2) what more do I need to know about this situation and which educational strategies will be most effective for bringing about a reasonable resolution? Each of the two mindsets conjures up various scenarios, at times mutually exclusive, and eventually become the basis of new expectations as consequences are played out.

To many educators, the first may appear to be the more reasonable approach; violating rules followed by "an eye for an eye" type of punishment would represent a logical extension of the justice model. After all, justice seems to be what Judicious Discipline is all about. Contradictory as it may seem, judicious consequences for misbehavior are exactly where the justice model must be abandoned and a completely different approach must be used—that of a professional relationship.

Although the principles of justice work well in the development of fair and just rules, the justice model carried over to consequences may work as a detriment to educators working to change attitudes of misbehaving students. Within the criminal justice system, for example, offenders are punished by sending them to jail. In the case of students, that equates to sending them to detention. Being treated as criminals and isolated from others is exactly what students in trouble do not need. The criminal-justice system is traditionally society's last resort to resolving community problems and is used by our government only after everything else fails. It does not make sense for educators to use the criminal-justice model as the first resort, before employing what they were professionally prepared to use—educational and mentoring approaches.

There are two important aspects to consider when developing judicious consequences. First, the consequences should be commensurate with the rule itself, and second, the consequences should be compatible with the self-esteem and personal development needs of students balanced with the welfare of the school community.

"Commensurate consequences" mean that the consequence applied to resolve a problem is consistent with, and flows logically from, the student's misbehavior. A "compatible consequence" addresses issues ranging from the student's need for personal self-worth to her academic achievement.

Using these two aspects together, a commensurate consequence might logically have a despoiling student scrub marks from a wall. But to also be compatible with the student's self-esteem, academic, and personal development needs, the cleaning should be mutually agreed upon and done at a reasonable time. A reasonable time, for example, might be when the student did not have a class or a sports event she had planned to attend or some special activity with her family. Also important to a student's self-esteem would be a time when others were not around, ensuring freedom from the ridicule of peers.

Compatible also means educators must avoid the tendency to want to extract a "pound of flesh" from troublesome students. In the example of the soiled wall, it is hard for most of us to get past the feeling of wanting to force students to clean up their messes at a time when they would miss something they had planned to do. But the importance of allowing students to feel they have some control in their acts of restitution cannot be overstated.

This ability to focus on the compatible nature of the consequences is the essence of helping students make positive changes and become accountable for their own behavior.

A judicious style, therefore, would be exemplified as wisdom blended with authority to make decisions and act upon them, but only after pivotal questions have been considered and the real issues have emerged. The move away from "autocratic talk" to communicating respect and dignity flows logically from asking "judicious questions." Engaging students in discourse is a strategy that ultimately empowers both students and educators through the role each plays in the school community.

Shaping Consequences

Students should know that when rules have been broken, their discussion with educators will center around two important future aspects: (1) What needs to be done and (2) What needs to be learned? "What needs to be done" usually involves two concepts, restitution and an apology. Both are designed to make things right by making the situation whole again. For example, when a student is caught taking something from another student, the leading questions center around restitution of the property and a discussion of an appropriate apology. By focusing on restoring property and feelings, educators can avoid the negative effects of punishment and focus on empowering strategies to make things whole. Students and educators will not get mired down in superficial arguments of right and wrong which are not constructive to successfully resolving the problem.

While "what needs to be done" is meant to take care of the past, "what needs to be learned" is directly related to changing future goals and attitudes of students. An educator's ability to enhance students' feelings of self-worth following a negative experience is truly an art form. Therefore an underlying philosophy for shaping judicious consequences must be carefully weighed and practiced until, like second nature, it becomes spontaneous.

Effective communication occurs when both parties believe they have some control in the conversation. While working toward equitable solutions, students must believe their feelings and opinions are a valued part of the process. The secret to shaping consequences, therefore, is to work with students on solutions that are volitional. In the long run, this sense of accountability feels much better to students than being "let off the hook" with a lecture from an authority figure.

Individualizing Consequences

There are two important aspects in determining consequences for each student's misbehavior. The first is to understand the real nature of the problem and the second is to account for individual differences among students. For example, if two culpable students were asked to clean up a vandalized wall and one student replies, "Okay, I have the time right after school," and the other belligerently responds, "That's not my job, that's janitor's work and you can't make me do it," the under-lying problem is different for both students. As a result, a different approach and consequence would be needed to get to the heart of each student's individual problem.

In the case of the first student, the wall would be cleaned willingly and, in all likelihood, this would not be perceived as punishment but rather as a reasonable act of recovery for someone ready to make amends and get it over with right away. As for the other student, a more serious problem has surfaced and scrubbing the wall becomes secondary to getting to the cause of a defiant attitude which is now apparent as an underlying problem.

This process of working toward a mutual resolution often requires time for student attitudes to change. When this change does eventually occur, however, it may be too late for the second student to help clean the wall. But with a change in attitude, it is likely the second student could decide to rectify his or her past indiscretion by participating in cleanup activities at school as well as apologizing and thanking those who did clean it up. On the other hand, if both students feel they were forced to do the cleaning, the first student who did not need to be coerced could resent it as punishment, and the second student's indignant attitude would not only go unattended, but could lead to bitter reprisal and an escalation of the problem.

Consequences should not be designed to punish students. By definition Judicious Consequences are designed to take into account individual differences among students in order to meet the emotional and learning needs of each involved. Students who misbehave simply may have different ways of learning from their mistakes and, as a result, different consequences are necessary.

For example, two students experiencing difficulty reading would not necessarily both improve their reading if given the same learning strategies by their teacher. It only makes sense then for educators to employ different educational consequences as they work with the many different individual needs and attitudes students bring to behavioral problems.

But when that window of opportunity presents itself, educators can little afford not to take the time necessary to help students process and grow from their misconduct. In the long run, educators spend much more time scolding, reminding, coaxing, confronting, demanding, lecturing, lamenting, conjecturing, and cajoling, than they ever would if they invested the time and effort needed to develop attitudes of respect and responsibility.

Professional Ethics

Professional ethics is the conscience of a school community and constitutes the acceptable standards of moral and proper conduct. Ethics are considered to begin where the law stops. For example, there is no law against a teacher confronting a student with, "Why can't you be as good as your sister was in this class?" But the professional ethics of comparing students is considered poor educational practice, often precipitating attitudinal problems which affect the success of student achievement.

The foundation of professional ethics lies in the manifestation of educators always acting in the best interests of their students. For example, misbehaving students sitting alone in hallways can seldom see the logic of how isolating them is helping them resolve their problem. Students rarely believe the educators who take these kinds of actions are really on their side. Rather, students perceive them to be adversaries who are trying to push them away from the school community. As a result, educators must avoid saying and doing things that cause students to feel alienated and instead establish a professional relationship that welcomes and serves. The lifeblood of an ethical relationship lies in students believing that their best interests are foremost in the minds of their educators.

There is often a difference between what one says is the ethical thing to do and what one actually does when a problem presents itself. When an ethical dilemma actually occurs it is often complicated by time constraints, unforeseen situational factors, and emotions which are not present when a person reasons abstractly about a hypothetical course of moral action. As a result, until educators are put under pressure to act, they are never really sure how they will behave. The ethics educators espouse, therefore, must be practiced over and over before students will feel secure knowing what they can expect. Over a period of time, though, this wariness will abate as students gain confidence that educators are acting in their best interests.

With practice, educators can develop a mindset of professional responsibility where behavior problems are viewed as secondary to the educational and developmental needs of students. If the thoughts and acts of educators consistently play off the importance of maintaining the trust and care indispensable to a strong professional relationship, the question asked again and again becomes: how would a student-centered educator act upon this matter?

An example of this would be when a teacher asks the whereabouts of a homework assignment and the student answers, "The dog ate it." There are two very different approaches that can be taken. "Yeah, right. I've heard that one a thousand times. Can't you think of something more original?" is the response of a teacher-centered educator focusing on the wrong issue, in this case, the veracity of the student's excuse.

However, a response such as, "So when do you think you can get it done?" is that of a student-centered educator who believes that the possibility of a lie is less important than is the greater professional responsibility of helping students complete assignments. It is also a powerful message to students that they do not have to lie to educators who are primarily interested in their learning. The issue of truthfulness is always an important one, but in this case it becomes secondary to the students' trust that their educators are making every effort to help them succeed in school.

Gradually the nuts and bolts of ethical responses are mastered, technique is transcended, and a professional and judicious relationship becomes a natural form of interaction. In the end the Personal Self is suppressed and a Professional Self emerges. As this Professional Self develops, educators will experience a sense of being in a "zone of professional consciousness" which becomes the sustaining force behind every student interaction. Only through enlightenment and effort can educators learn how to focus on the needs of students as they lose their Personal Self in the communication and activities of an ethical professional relationship.

The ethics of any profession are at best fragile and difficult to manage when put into practice. Initially, educators must exhibit a general concern for ethical behavior due to the fact that morality is, generally speaking, a matter of personal character. For ethics to be viable, there must be a continuing, ongoing moral and ethical inquiry. When educators wear well the mantle of their responsibility, biases and personalities take a secondary status to the needs students have to be guided.

To our students we appear larger than life and, therefore, must personify a model worthy of emulation. It is imperative that we keep alive our students' belief that we are acting in their best interests through a strong and viable student-educator relationship of trust and care. In its final analysis, a teacher's classroom is a student's world.

Implementation

Judicious Discipline is not intended to be used independently, but as a foundation upon which to build other cognitive strategies and ideas. Because it is designed as a framework, other cognitive management techniques must also be employed in order to meet the needs of all students. Cooperative learning and whole language, for example, will easily integrate with Judicious Discipline's philosophy and language. The real world practicality of cooperation in a learning environment and the democratic nature of whole language fit logically with what students are experiencing through Judicious Discipline.

In addition to academic strategies, educators who have been employing William Glasser's Control Theory or Rudolph Dreikurs' Social Discipline have been using strategies designed to take over exactly where Judicious Discipline leaves off. After one of my speeches on this subject, a very excited teacher came up to talk to me. She said to me, "This is great! I have finally found something that makes my classroom management complete. I have been using Glasser's Control Theory for two years and now you have given me the democratic foundation I needed to go with it." I reinforced her discovery by telling her that was exactly how Judicious Discipline should be used.

There is a healing nature inherent in the principles of our nation's Constitution from which "good vibes" and mutual respect seem to emanate. As a result, Judicious Discipline works to minimize classroom stress and anxiety for both students and teachers because of the environmental emphasis on human rights and individual dignity.

In summary, Judicious Discipline is a management style based on the synthesis of professional ethics, good educational practice, and student constitutional rights. It is a philosophy that uses rules and consequences to build an educational community designed to keep students in school, rather than push them out. Educators have always believed students should take responsibility for their actions and that teaching citizenship is an important part of any curriculum. Judicious Discipline, however, takes that belief one step further—it asks educators to create an environment which respects the citizenship rights of students. As a result, students will be learning and experiencing a model of discipline that emphasizes personal responsibility.

Students who are consistently treated as if they are significant will eventually begin looking at themselves that way. If students are going to develop feelings of self-efficacy, they need an environment where they can practice the responsibility that comes with being themselves. Creating this democratic school setting is clearly the purpose of Judicious Discipline.

Notes

1. 393 U.S. 503.

8

But Will it Work? The Practice of Judicious Discipline in Southern Minnesota Schools

❑

Virginia L. Nimmo

When I was trained as a school psychologist, over fifteen years ago, my training was grounded in educational principles, cognitive development, and social-emotional development. I was taught how to assess a child and set up the appropriate plans to help a child be successful in school. I was involved in helping many teachers set up behavioral programs, most of which established baselines of target behaviors, followed by reward systems to reinforce the desired behaviors. Some of these systems were so successful that some teachers set up entire classroom reward economies. One teacher determined a "banking" system was effective with her students, complete with "savings accounts" and "checking accounts." She wanted rewards available to all her students, not just the ones who were in need of a contract.

Although these behaviorist approaches to handling student behavior were well received by the teachers involved, both they and I began to question why each year we needed to set up more and more of these plans. The sheer number began to overwhelm us. Which plan was Billy on, which step, which reinforcers? The paperwork became a burden. Staff and parents would lose track of when to reinforce, at what level of reinforcement.

I experienced mounting frustration. In each school I served, my mailbox filled daily with notes regarding various students' behavior. I spent much of my day consulting with staff regarding what a particular child had done, and what "plan" we needed to set up. Staff were confronted by foul language directed at adults by even the youngest of students. I was getting the message from many teachers that they felt personally responsible for the behaviors they were seeing, and in retrospect I was experiencing that feeling as well. I felt a great deal of stress, and some days I questioned whether I had the energy to deal with all the requests for assistance that were coming in my direction.

At the peak of this frustration, I began to review data that was accumulating in the schools where I worked. In my first year as a school psychologist (1980–81), I had assessed or consulted on 97 children. Only six of those student requests were related to behavioral issues, or 6.2% of the total evaluations. Eight years later, I had assessed 112 students, 17.5% of which were referrals for behavioral concerns. During the 1993–94 school year, there were 125 evaluations completed, 37.0% which were behavioral referrals. I began to wonder why the number of behavioral referrals were increasing and if there might be a more proactive approach to discipline we could be using.

Many of the teachers in our district were familiar with the components of "Assertive Discipline" and had used it for a number of years, yet they were not getting the results they expected.[1] They felt uncomfortable putting students' names on the board for everyone to see. Students reported to me, "I get my name on the board every day—they expect me to." I realized that it was a discipline program rooted in the lowest level of moral development, punishment and reward. It did not help our students to learn to make decisions about handling their own behavior. We wanted to be able to "teach" our children, not be "police officers." We agreed we wanted our schools to be places where children could feel safe, responsible, and respected.

As adults we wanted the same things. It was not happening. As educators, we felt we were failing to provide what our students needed in order to help them become responsible citizens.

Our Schools Today

Across southern Minnesota, a small but growing group of educators have begun to make changes in how they deal with student discipline. I have witnessed these changes in many of the buildings in which I work. I have also been a part of the transformation of several other districts in the southern Minnesota area. By adopting and implementing a new philosophy, these schools have altered the experience of school for students and for teachers, improving the classroom climate, student learning, and teacher satisfaction.

Walking into one of our schools today, a visitor will be struck by the mutual respect among staff and students. She will see students comfortably visiting with staff and peers, finding ways to help one another. One morning, just after parking my car, two students asked if they could help me carry in my belongings. "You always look like you have a bunch of stuff to bring in each week; can we help you?" they asked. These were sixth graders, both diagnosed emotionally/behaviorally disordered in their previous schools. They were constantly in fights, angry, and disrespectful to peers and adults. Currently, they are earning A and B grades. Most days they handle their behavior well in the environment we have created.

Visitors see rights and responsibilities posted in corridors and classrooms, with pictures and examples of judicious behavior offered by the students. They occasionally hear an adult or peer reminding another of a responsibility that needs to be followed. Substitute teachers comment on how they enjoy working at the school. Parents remark about how much their children enjoy attending that school. Moreover, they talk about how much they appreciate that their child's individual needs are being addressed by educational professionals.

In the schools where this transformation has occurred, one will not see names on the board or lists of student posted for detention. Staff members do not fear meetings with parents to discuss behavioral issues. They do not demean students, publicly compare students to each other, or seek revenge in the name of justice. Rather, student issues are heard by staff and peers.

How did this dramatic change occur? It required a fundamental change in the ways we view students and their behavior, a change inspired by the work of Forrest Gathercoal.[2] *Judicious Discipline* combines the principles of the U.S. Constitution, notions of moral development drawn from Lawrence Kohlberg, and an understanding of the reasons for misbehavior as developed by Rudolph Dreikurs.[3]

Judicious Discipline is much like the frame around a picture. It is not a "program" or a set of step-by-step procedures. Rather, it is a frame by which we can examine our stated philosophy and the techniques we use when dealing with issues of student discipline challenges. We might ask, "Does this fit in the frame? Is this a judicious way to handle this particular situation?" Many cognitive techniques "fit in the frame," but punitive measures do not.

In two of our schools where Judicious Discipline has been in place at least two years, surveys show that the staff is finding it important to instruct students regarding rights and responsibilities in order to self-manage behavior and become responsible citizens. In addition, staff reports feeling more "professional" and being a part of a team in the process of change.

Since Judicious Discipline was introduced in one of our middle schools three years ago, fights occurring on school grounds have dropped from a fight occurring nearly every week, to zero. After students were trained regarding their constitutional rights and responsibilities as citizens of the United States, there was a 100 percent drop in school ground fights. In this same school, students previously had been assigned to in-school suspension at the rate of two or three per day. Out-of-school suspensions were as high as one every other week. After the use of Judicious Discipline, a suspension was a rare event, used only with three students during the last school year. The concept of an in-school suspension was eliminated, and in its place was a problem-solving session with the principal, counselor, or teacher of the study center.

A special education teacher for emotionally/ behaviorally disordered students in one middle school setting, the only staff member in her building using Judicious Discipline, reported, "This is the best year I have ever had. The students respect me more, and they understand the concepts easily. The power struggles are minimal, because the rules make sense. Other staff members are beginning to ask me what I am doing!" A classroom teacher saw the growth in her students with the use of Judicious Discipline. After she became a school counselor, she became even more impressed with its value. She reports using it every day in her inter-actions with students, staff, and parents. "The language is legal, ethical, educational, and respectful. I use it even more now than I did as a classroom teacher. I am really amazed at how valuable it is for counselors."

One supportive judicious administrator who often finds opportunities to work with staff who need to look more closely inside their "frames" has been criticized for not adopting a more punitive philosophy. He has often been heard to comment, "If ever we see a need to change our philosophy from Judicious Discipline, it had better be something incredibly good! What could be better than following the Constitution of the United States?" Another commented that Judicious Discipline "has taken the mon-key off my back. I'm not forced to carry out a punishment I find inappropriate for the individual, or one that is useless in helping him learn a better choice."

Does Judicious Discipline always work perfectly? No. We all make mistakes, both staff and students. However, assuming responsibility for mistakes is easier because of the Judicious Discipline framework.

What I have learned while working with Judicious Discipline is that administrators like the legal and ethical components of the philosophy, while teachers like the educational aspects. As a school psychologist and former elementary counselor, I appreciate the proactive, developmental, cognitive approach to helping students examine their behavior and how it affects the society in which they function.

The Process of Change or Where do We Begin?

Joel Barker has observed that "It is still a great risk in our society to offer new rules for the game."[4] Our school management practices need to change, but how do schools begin to move from a programmed approach toward classroom management to a truly student-centered philosophy? Many school districts have already become involved in peer tutoring, peer mediation, conflict resolution techniques, cooperative learning, etc. Such approaches, along with many others, are well suited to the concept of a democratic classroom. Many schools have sought "programs" that will provide a structure for a classroom democracy. Principles for democratic classroom management can be found in the work of Dreikurs, Glasser, Albert, and others.[5]

Part of the initial change for us involved a committee to study the effectiveness of the current school discipline policy. The committee included the principal, psychologist, counselor, teaching staff, a support staff member, and, when possible, a parent. The committee sought members who were not supportive of a need to change, as well as those who felt a strong need to change. Initial committee action included surveys of staff members, parents, and students regarding the discipline management needs of the building. Such action develops a base of support as to how discipline is currently perceived by these groups of people. In addition to exposing ineffective discipline procedures, the study revealed effective techniques. The findings of the committee were then reported to the staff with recommendations for needed change. We identified student respect and responsibility as areas in need of change. As we began our search for a new philosophy, we sought answers to the following questions:

1. Is this philosophy student-centered?

2. Does this philosophy allow adults to model the responsibility and respect that they wish to see in student behavior?

3. Does this philosophy create a democratic environment in the classroom rather than an autocratic or permissive environment?

4. Can the philosophy be clearly understood by all students and adults in the school?

5. Does the philosophy allow all individuals to feel safe (physically, emotionally, and legally) when dealing with issues of discipline?

Following this initial process, our committee searched for philosophies and materials that were currently employed in other school districts. After considering educational, cognitive, legal, and ethical issues, we were drawn to Judicious Discipline. A powerful element in this approach is in the interpersonal respect among students, improved school-home communication, enhanced self-respect among educators, and the development of a democratic classroom.

In the process of change, those involved in the shift must be trained. Typically the amount of training time varies with each school or individual. My experience involved attending a one-week workshop during the summer to learn the basic concepts of Judicious Discipline, returning in the fall to train the staff. Subsequent inservices provided were as short as two hours in some buildings, or as long as two days in others. No matter what time is given to initial inservice training, it must be viewed as an introduction. The real training occurs "on the job," applying the concepts to behavioral dilemmas encountered every day by educators.

In our district, the school buildings where I have found Judicious Discipline has been most effective are those where regularly scheduled "support" groups have been formed. Although group attendance at such meetings is optional, all staff members are encouraged to become involved. In such settings we discuss discipline challenges and appropriate "judicious" responses. For Judicious Discipline to be effectively employed, dialogue among staff members is critical.

Moreover, if parents are to understand the philosophy of Judicious Discipline, they, like the staff, must be trained. We remind parents that they are their children's first teacher, and that in order for any discipline policy to be effective, they must reinforce the concepts with their children. In order to give parents a brief overview of the philosophy, we scheduled informational meetings at the beginning of the school year. During the year, monthly newsletter articles outlined specific parts of the philosophy, as well as ideas as to how these concepts could be used at home. In addition, parents were also informed that the author of *Judicious Discipline* has also written *Judicious Parenting*.[6] It was helpful to make this book available to parents for loan from the school library.

Student training is an integral part of implementing any disciplinary philosophy. In implementing Judicious Discipline in our schools, the school principal and school psychologist, counselor or social worker were involved in the initial training. This involved a twenty- to thirty-minute presentation in a classroom setting, outlining the philosophy. At the secondary level, one school developed a videotape for use in each homeroom or social studies class of the principal and counselor discussing the philosophy. One school found it helpful to have a video presentation available in order that new students and parents could view it at any point during the year. The methodology of delivery is not as important as involving the person who holds a responsibility to provide a safe environment. All students must receive the same information. As the school year progressed various lessons were taught by our staff to help the students understand their rights and responsibilities as they related to the school community, and ultimately the community outside the school doors.

In classes employing Judicious Discipline, teachers commonly post student rights and responsibilities. They find that students use the language of constitutional rights as a means of solving their conflicts, and that offending students understand and respect those rights. For example, when a student has forgotten her responsibilities and has broached another student's rights, such as one student using a pen or book that belongs to another, a common student response is, "That's my property, you do not have permission to use it." Or, "Read number three—you are harming my safety." One day, a second grade student taking a reading test was heard to say to another student, "Would you please stop tapping your pencil? It is disrupting my thinking!" Students begin to use the language of constitutional rights and responsibilities in ways that resolve issues without teacher involvement. In most cases, the offending student stops the behavior, due to an assertive yet respectful response by her peer. The real difference between these encounters and those we saw previously when we relied upon Assertive Discipline is that students understand the mutuality of rights and responsibilities. They are empowered to handle many of their conflicts themselves in a respectful manner. Before employing Judicious Discipline, students would become upset and go to the adult to resolve the situation and dole out the punishment.

Students respond favorably to the philosophy of Judicious Discipline. We surveyed our middle school students, who responded with comments such as these:

"If you aren't being a responsible learner, you aren't giving yourself a fair chance at an education."

"Now I know my boundaries and I can resolve the problem without anyone getting hurt."

"When I get mad, because someone is violating my rights, I can go up to them and calmly tell them. It's not me saying that, it is the Constitution."

"Now I can handle things differently, without fighting and screaming."

"Everyone is equal. I'm more responsible this year than I have ever been before. I don't blame others, and make excuses that much anymore."

In schools where Judicious Discipline is used, every adult in the school building becomes, by definition, a resource with special expertise to assist students. As educators, we must ask, "Have we used all our resources to help this student?" Considering our resources requires us to look beyond punishment to find a consequence that helps the student learn how to make the situation right. It also helps the adults focus on the cause of the student's misbehavior, not simply the act. Students, staff, and parents need to understand that when dealing with behavior there are a number of resources available to them. In many cases, student behavior may arise from unmet needs. In such circumstances, resources for help may include school nurses, counselors, school psychologists, social workers, special education teachers, the principal, cooks, custodians, or the school secretary.

Occasionally, all resources seem to have been exhausted in trying to help a student, with little success. Under such conditions it may be helpful to schedule a meeting with the parents (and student, if appropriate) in an effort to demonstrate genuine concern for the student.

In the case of one high school student, the principal and school psychologist outlined the many resources that had been tried throughout the student's school experience, albeit with limited success. Three pages of resources were noted. When meeting with the parent and student, the principal and school psychologist read the list and described the resources currently in use. At that point the psychologist said, "We have run out of school resources to help your son. We need help from you, and from other community resources." It should be noted that this was a parent who, in previous years, had been very defensive about her son, having refused to seek outside help. It was not the intent of school authorities to avoid helping the student; indeed they wanted him to get the help they could not provide. For the first time, the parent agreed to get help for her son, and the rest of the family.

Judicious Consequences

Teaching the basics of Judicious Discipline is quite a natural process. Because we were trained to teach, educating students regarding rights and responsibilities can be a natural part of our professional work. Students who have learned Judicious Discipline make appropriate choices more consistently than students trained to respond to rewards or punishment. There are, of course, circumstances when inappropriate behavior will occur— learning, after all, requires both successes and failures along the road to competence. When that occurs, "judicious consequences" must follow. Judicious consequences must be logical, must enhance the child's self-esteem, and must promote the academic success of the student.[7] The educator must ask, "What does this student need to learn, and what needs to be done in order to provide restitution— how can the student 'right' the 'wrong?'" Judicious consequences are not intended to be punitive, but rather to provide a chance to recover, learn from the mistake, and restore the child to the group. The concept of restitution, or making things right again—restorative justice—indicate what action a teacher will take.

As one might imagine, judicious consequences are not as simple as "If you do this, then this will happen."

Many schools have policy manuals outlining lists of infractions and specific consequences for each infraction. Schools employing Judicious Discipline find such policy manuals inappropriate. Our schools began to realize we could never list every infraction possible—there was always something left out. We also found that certain circumstances did not make a specific consequence appropriate in every situation.

Since the conditions surrounding each infraction are likely to be different, the consequence for student "A" may need to be different from student "B." An often employed and effective technique in clarifying an appropriate consequence involves the offending student in identifying what needs to be learned to arrive at the action that should be taken. When an educator understands this process, he or she usually finds it becomes more genuinely educational than punitive approaches. I find it interesting that we have learned that all students have different learning styles; we vary our approach to each child when teaching them how to read or to do math. Yet in the area of discipline we cling to programs that treat all children exactly the same. We would not consider teaching reading, writing or math without allowing for individual differences; we should similarly view consequences by what the individual needs to learn. That is true fairness.

Parents and school staff often ask, "What are some 'judicious consequences'?" Because the consequence will vary, depending on the situation and the student, prescribed examples are inappropriate. For the purposes of this chapter, I will discuss the compelling state interests as they relate to examples of behavioral dilemmas, and the associated judicious consequences which were used in the individual situations.

Property Loss and Damage

This concept is fairly easy for most students to comprehend. School property and the property of others must be protected. Early in the school year, immediately following a presentation on Judicious Discipline by the principal and school psychologist, a student chose to use the soles of his black shoes to scuff a black mark from the classroom and down the hall. His homeroom teacher happened to observe the incident. She followed him to the lunchroom, and asked to speak with him in private. After reporting that she had observed him make the marks, she reminded him that the custodial staff had worked very hard to clean all the property during the summer in preparation for the start of school. She asked him to think about what might need to be done to make this right again, and then asked him to visit with her after he had eaten lunch.

After lunch, the teacher and student decided that in order to make the situation right again, the marks would need to be cleaned. To avoid his absence from class, and to avoid embarrassing him, they agreed that he would clean off the marks after school. At the end of the day, while in search of the custodian, they noticed the marks had already been cleaned. After the student told the custodian what had happened, the teacher asked the custodian for the amount of time that was used to clean the marks. The student offered to help the custodian for an equal amount of time after school, completing other jobs the custodian had to put aside. The next day, the student and teacher talked over what had been learned; there was much work to be completed in a school building every day and the custodian's time was too valuable to be used restoring property that had been thoughtlessly marred. The big difference in this solution was that the student was a part of determining the consequence—he was able to find a way to "right" the "wrong." The student never again repeated a behavior related to a property issue.

In another instance, a second grader was very angry with his teacher. As he left the school building at the end of the day, his anger was such that he smashed a school door window and left the scene immediately. Because the family had no phone, the parent could not be contacted. Upon arriving at school the next day, the student was called to the office, where the teacher and principal were waiting to discuss his previous day's behavior. The student reported that his teacher had asked him to redo an assignment, and he was very angry about having homework. When the principal asked the student for other choices he could have made to deal with his anger, she realized he was lacking the skills needed to control his anger. Subsequently, arrangements were made for the student to have counseling in anger management. The student also agreed that in order to make the window "right" again, he would work before and after school until he had logged enough time to pay for the window. The student was made a part of the solution. After the discussion with the student, the principal visited his mother, related the incident, the discussion, and the consequence. After the mother shared concerns related to the boy's anger management at home, the principal offered to have the school social worker make a home visit to support the parent.

Legitimate Educational Purpose

Schools exist to educate children. The school-related tasks we do each day are described as having legitimate educational purpose. Educators promise to provide children opportunities which allow them to learn; they are expected to be responsible learners. To assist students in this manner, issues regarding responsible learning are discussed daily in schools adhering to Judicious Discipline principles.

One day I was in fifth grade classroom, reviewing the concepts of Judicious Discipline. It was the spring of the year, and both the principal and I felt the need to review the students' rights and responsibilities. We were most concerned with being proactive in reminding students of safe playground behavior. I asked the students, "What responsibility might be most difficult to remember as we are entering the last few weeks of school?" Several children raised their hands to offer examples. The principal and I were both surprised that many of them felt that the most difficult task would be to continue to be responsible learners. When I asked them why, they responded that they found themselves daydreaming about recess, or the things they could do outside after school. Concentrating on schoolwork seemed an impossible task. As a class we brainstormed how they could help each other remain focused during class time. They also came up with ways of getting homework done. Several weeks later their teacher reported that it was the first year she could remember that she was not constantly reminding the students to get late work in, or to pay attention in class. She said the students often reminded each other, especially during small groups, to be "responsible learners" and to stay focused.

Health and Safety

Because of their common sense applications, issues of health and safety are easily understood by students of all ages. Since we want our schools to be safe and healthy environments, we establish guidelines in this area. It is important to understand that such rules involve both physical and emotional health and safety.

On one occasion a middle school student with an emotional/behavioral disorder went outside after lunch for some fresh air. As he passed through the door a popular female student walked out behind him. The male student turned around, and struck the girl on the arm, an event which was witnessed by an adult who sent both students inside to the office. The principal discussed the situation with the girl, who was crying. Subsequently, the boy admitted to hitting the girl, but indicated there was more information to the story which could be corroborated by witnesses. The boy related how the girl had been sitting across from him at the lunch table, insulting him throughout the lunch period. He had asked her to stop several times—she did not. His witnesses agreed that his description of events was accurate. She had continued her verbal harassment of him outside, and he struck her. The girl was asked to return to the principal's office for further discussion. After she admitted to the role she had played in the encounter, issues of physical and emotional safety were discussed with both students. What needed to be done? In some schools, detention or suspension would have been the result for the behavioral disordered student, and his version of the story might never have been investigated. In this case, both students discussed what they had learned, and in the end apologized to each other. There was no further confrontation between them the rest of the academic year.

A related and integral issue falling under the area of health and safety is that of harassment in any form. By law, in most states, there is a reporting mechanism for these complaints, and this is all part of due process. In a school employing Judicious Discipline, the student is helped to understand that the process of law is followed. Harassment must be taken seriously if students are to come to school feeling emotionally and physically safe.

Serious Disruption of the Educational Process

When defining a "serious disruption," it is critical for all involved to understand the definition of "serious." Examples of serious disruption in the classroom might include the use of profane or vulgar language, or physical violence directed toward others. Although these events might also be issues of health and safety, clearly both would cause a serious disruption of the class. As with the other compelling state interests, the issue is how educators respond to the problem.

In a particular high school, an English class was about to begin, with a student teacher giving the lesson.

She had asked the class to come to order, when a student very loudly responded, "F— you!" The student stood and walked out of the room. Following this, the student teacher left the room in tears, and the supervising teacher came in to take the class. What neither of the teachers knew was that the student had walked directly to the office, and was explaining the incident to the dean of students. The student had been harassed by other students all day about a date he had the night before. False statements had been directed at him throughout the day. He had just been passed a note in class from a student with additional negative comments regarding his date. Because the student was angry at the note writer, he had exploded verbally and left the class. His outburst had nothing to do with the class or the teacher. His consequence was to apologize to the teacher, and the next day to the class. He did not need suspension to learn a valuable lesson from this event. It was also a valuable lesson for the student teacher. As professionals, we cannot afford to take students' comments personally; it is much more important to find the circumstances motivating such comments.

Another serious disruption involved an elementary student who attempted to gain attention in various ways. One day, when the attention he felt he needed was not being given, he picked up his chair and threw it across the back of the room. His teacher quickly removed the other students to the hallway and called for the "crisis team." While she waited for the team to arrive, she walked over to the disruptive student and quietly said, "I can see you are angry, and you need to take a break from here right now. When you are calm, and I can get a chance to talk to you, we will work this out." The crisis team arrived, and in a few minutes the student walked with them out of the classroom to the "break" room. The teacher asked the other students to return to the room and then resumed instruction. This entire event lasted fewer than five minutes. Sometime later the teacher had an opportunity to speak with the student. They discussed the events, and agreed that the student could use a "cue" when he required attention. In addition, the teacher scheduled a regular time each day to "touch base" with the student. Parents were informed of the events and the school's action, and were asked to reinforce the school concerns at home. No further serious disruption occurred that year. Although many caring teachers might handle this situation in a similar manner, the "judicious" teacher is trying to help the child recover from the situation, and provide a means to get at the real problem. Previous to the shift to this philosophy, this same teacher would have had to send the child to the office, and the school policy manual would have directed the principal to suspend the child. That might have handled the immediate situation, but the child's need would have been ignored.

Conclusion

On one particular day, as a colleague and I were preparing an inservice for staff on proactive techniques, the question arose, "How do we get our staff to see a need to change the methods they have been using for years? Some are so angry about how students are behaving, I wonder if they can get past their frustration." I began to realize that what we had neglected was to help them grieve. As educators deal with the many circumstances experienced on a daily basis in their classrooms, their frustrations with the contrast between classroom management today versus ten or twenty years ago, may be very similar to a process of grieving. Kubler-Ross originally shared her concepts of grieving as experienced by those who were dying. Later work by Kubler-Ross, and others, suggested that these same stages could apply to other traumas in one's life.[8]

Realizing that the traditional methods of handling discipline are not working is much like moving through the stages of grieving. Educators need to recognize the point in the process at which they have become "stuck." At times one can feel shocked by students' comments or actions. Some educators may be in denial, "Oh, it's not that bad." Others may feel angry with students, their parents, or an unsupportive administration. I know staff who have created ways to "bargain" with an administrator in order to have certain classes or students transferred from their class lists. Many staff members have shared feelings of guilt with how a particular issue of student behavior has been handled. Others wonder whether they want to continue in the profession of teaching, expressing feelings of sadness, often citing "burnout" over the many student needs that are presented.

After giving a presentation on how the grieving process might be adapted to one's view regarding student behavior, one teacher remarked to me, "You know, I have been feeling guilty, and at times angry. I think I have been 'grieving' for the last five years. I have been thinking of getting out of education, but maybe I just need to move on and adapt my skills to what is ahead of me." When teachers can begin to accept the reality that change is needed, they move on to the adaptation stage. Once we understand that change is needed, change is possible. Such teachers are ready to reinvest themselves in a process in order to create a democratic environment in their classrooms and school buildings.

Notes

1. Lee Canter, *Assertive Discipline for Parents* (New York: Harper and Row, 1985).

2. Forrest Gathercoal, *Judicious Discipline*, 3rd ed. (San Francisco: Caddo Gap Press, 1993); see also Barbara McEwan, ed., *Practicing Judicious Discipline: An Educator's Guide to a Democratic Classroom*, 2nd ed. (San Francisco: Caddo Gap Press, 1994).

3. Lawrence Kohlberg, *Philosophy of Moral Development: Moral Stages and the Idea of Justice* (San Francisco: Harper and Row, 1981); Rudolf Dreikurs, Bernice B. Grunwald, and Floy C. Pepper, *Maintaining Sanity in the Classroom* (1971,

1990); Dreikurs, *Logical Consequences: The New Approach to Discipline* (1974).

4. Joel Arthur Barker, *Paradigms: The Business of Discovering the Future* (New York: Harper Collins Publishers, Inc., 1992), p. 206.

5. Rudolf Dreikurs, *Maintaining Sanity in the Classroom: Illustrated Teaching Techniques* (New York: Harper and Row, 1971), pp. 172–185; William Glasser, *The Quality School: Managing Student without Coercion* (New York: Harper Collins Publishers, Inc., 1992), pp. 134–148; Linda Albert, *Cooperative Discipline: How to Manage Your Classroom and Promote Self-Esteem* (Circle Pines: American Guidance Service, 1989), pp. 1–6.

6. Forrest Gathercoal, *Judicious Parenting* (San Francisco: Caddo Gap Press, 1992).

7. Gathercoal, *Judicious Discipline*, pp. 117–126.

8. Elisabeth Kubler-Ross, *On Death and Dying* (New York: Macmillan Publishing Co., 1969); Kubler-Ross, *Working it Through: An Elisabeth Kubler-Ross Workshop on Life, Death and Transition* (New York: Macmillan Publishing Co., 1982).

9

Empathic Caring in Classroom Management and Discipline

❑

Sharon A. Stanley

Introduction

When John shuffled into the counseling office for his first appointment with me, he kept his eyes on the floor. His file revealed that he was extremely bright. However, I was troubled by his long history of abuse and neglect. John's teacher had referred him to the counseling office because he "just sat at his desk and refused to do his assignments." After a long silence and several questions on my part, John told me he was tired. Too tired to talk or to walk around school or to do any work. During our interview, we made eye contact just once. I was in a quandary about how to proceed with my first client as a counseling intern, this quiet, weary ten-year-old.

The following Monday, my internship supervisor called to tell me John had died over the weekend. The autopsy indicated that his appendix had ruptured ten days before his death. John's classmates remembered that he had complained of a stomachache.

The teachers, staff, and students of this elementary school on a military base were shocked. A child's suffering had gone unnoticed. John's reaction to his academic assignments had been interpreted as obstinate behavior and his subtle requests for help were unheard. I know that I felt a profound sense of loss and failure and consciously chose to remember what I learned in reflecting on John's death.

The story of John continues to draw my attention to the complex struggles of children today. Current changes in the social, political, and cultural fabric of our society have radically affected the world of childhood. Schools and children today face intense pressures. Colvin, Kanieenuf, and Sugai cite demographic data that illustrates the magnitude of change in ethnic diversity, poverty, and psychological and behavioral difficulties. "By the year 2010, 12 states will have a 'majority minority' population," they write.[1] Diversity is increasing in social class and economic status. In 1993, nearly one-quarter of all children in America lived below the poverty level in both urban and rural areas, and the percentage is increasing.

In this atmosphere, problem behaviors rooted in psychological distress are threatening the safety of both students and staff. The ancient question re-emerges: How can we best manage pedagogy in order to contribute to the discipline of learning? We must return to the challenge Dewey provided nearly one hundred years ago: to attend to the whole child and resist the divisive forces of poverty and cultural alienation.

The crisis is larger than an educational challenge. It "cuts across the boundaries of the helping profession," according to Susan Phillips.[2] Caregivers are rewarded for technological efficiency and measurable outcomes, while concern, attentiveness, and human engagement are unnoticed. Practices that encourage depersonalization and disengagement contradict the life meaning and purpose of those who maintain a vocation to care for people.

Recently my daughter was hospitalized for a period of time with a high risk pregnancy, delivery, and surgery. Just as she was discharged, a snowstorm hit our region. A compassionate doctor made arrangements for her to occupy an abandoned room in the hospital for one night.

The doctor understood the young mother's distress in leaving her baby who was to remain in the special care nursery. In the night, two security guards noticed the abandoned room occupied, mistook her for a street person, and escorted her to the street in her pajamas. Although the medical care was compassionate and technologically advanced, the system failed to recognize human suffering.

The Failure to Care for the Human Dimension

A careful study of current societal responses to human suffering leads to the conclusion that our culture is manifesting a serious failure to care for people. Visible throughout the United States is the decline of family support services, an increase in violence, and rising rates of prison populations. The lack of adequate care for children is reflected in rising teen pregnancy rates, a dramatic increase in youth suicide, use of alcohol and drugs by preteen children, children with guns, and a "disgraceful number of children living in poverty."[3] The loss of caring is linked to current economic and social trends where relationships are superseded by "depersonalizing procedures of justice, distribution, technological problem-solving, and the techniques and relations of the marketplace."[4]

The challenge to care is a call to intervene in these trends in complex, personal and contextual ways. It requires that we attend to and care for complicated human problems, and that we resist a reliance on easy judicial and technological solutions.[5]

As a career counselor, I have witnessed a breakdown in trust and stability as hundreds of thousands of people face cutbacks, layoffs, and economic insecurity. Workers are expected to move beyond the trauma and learn new skills and abilities. Little attention is given to the breach of interpersonal connection and community bonds that is ripping the fabric of our culture as the workplace shifts into the "new economy." The emerging "new economy" is technologically based. Individuals with specialized knowledge and skills are in demand. Capital machinery replaces human labor. Where human labor is still needed, companies can now choose from a growing world labor force as trade restrictions are eliminated and capital becomes increasingly mobile. In order to assure profitability, companies increasingly value productivity, technology, and procedural justice. In a business based on procedural justice, the street person, or a vulnerable woman mistaken for a street person, has no right to shelter on a freezing night.[6]

In a society with claims to decency and dignity, providing good care cannot be dependent on the mechanical calculations of procedural justice. The calculus of rights that flow from procedural justice "cultivates polarity rather than engagement," within care systems as surely as within the civic polity as a whole.[7] Caring practices must go beyond procedural rights; they must be based on the value of people and interpersonal relationships. To expect less is to risk demeaning and degrading the essence of humanity.

Rapid changes in economic, political, and social arenas seriously affect children and the ability of adults to give them adequate care. My intention here is to challenge educators to move beyond technical and judicious approaches to classroom management and discipline in order to develop new and more effective strategies to work with children in the context of the chaos of family, educational, community, and global change.

Children need caring pedagogy and guidance if they are to become whole and knowledgeable adults. A number of researchers are urging teachers to move beyond technically efficient classrooms. They call for environments of care and relatedness. Noddings argues that relatedness and emotional connection, the foundation of human morality, must be reintegrated into our educational communities.[8]

Children at Risk: A Psychological Perspective

In a variety of educational settings, teachers are finding that emotionally distressed young people are now the norm in an average classroom. Like driftwood tossed in a storm, children are extremely vulnerable to shifting economic and social forces. A high proportion of young people are struggling to reconcile themselves with the many losses caused by divorce, blended families, highly transient life styles, poverty, disabilities, discrimination, uncertain cultural values, and confusing relationships with adults. Research indicates that a multitude of our nation's youth are at-risk of dangers from substance abuse, depression, and delinquency.[9] Slaby and Garfinkle remark:

> Today, depression is better understood than ever before. It is a biological vulnerability that surfaces when sufficiently disturbing life experiences occur. It lies dormant in some individuals only to occur or recur when negative events come to bear on the vulnerable person. Depression alters the individual's functioning, creating additional problems. For instance, lacking the energy or desire to do constructive activities, the depressed teen frequently shows a deterioration in school and social functioning.[10]

Depressed children like John often struggle silently with hidden pain, perceiving life in distorted and hopeless ways. They are apt to lose interest in academic work, have difficulty with friendships, and become vulnerable to suicide.[11] Most adults have little comprehension of the darkness of childhood depression:

> There is no understanding or recognition of the rage, the fear, and the insurmountable pain that are so much a part of depression . . . The mental pain of depression is so all-consuming that it becomes impossible to derive any pleasure or satisfaction from life. . . . Everything is bleak and gray.[12]

Serious depression is thought to affect at least ten percent of all children and is usually unnoticed. Even when diagnosed it is very difficult to access adequate treatment.[13]

Young people are also at risk of trauma. Many have witnessed the violence in families and the community or been a victim of sexual, physical, and emotional abuse. Trauma—non-normative and highly distressing events such as violence, abuse, abandonment and neglect—can result in emotional suffering and painful disruptions of a child's social and psychological development. The impact of traumatic events and depression is visible in a child's school performance. Trauma disturbs behavior, attention, memory, learning, and social development.[14]

Some young people express in disruptive behavior the intense unresolved emotions of fear, anger, and powerlessness generated by trauma. In other children, the emotional memories may go underground into unconscious disassociation and disconnection. In disassociation, a child "forgets" an event, but the emotional residue continues and may emerge in isolation or disruptive behavior. Children who have disassociated may give the impression that they have little or no affect, and adults and peers find it very difficult to connect with them.[15]

Emotional disconnection from family, friends, and peers results in feelings of isolation and alienation for a child. These feelings cause the child to resist social involvement and create further problems. Over time, if an effective intervention is not made, the pattern repeats itself and children's problems escalate and become overwhelming.[16]

The most serious manifestations of the psychological pain of children in the schools are often referred to as "problem behaviors." These behaviors include physical assault, gang violence, and substance abuse, and result in a dropout rate of 42% for students with behavior disorders. After leaving school, half of the students with behavior disorders are incarcerated or on probation while employment rates are significantly lower for students with behavior disorders. As Colvin points out, these students "serve as a compelling barometer of how effectively school goals are being achieved and students are being served."[17]

Yet children with problem behavior are merely the tip of the iceberg. All children are more vulnerable today. Educators can use the knowledge about vulnerable children when restructuring. This knowledge can direct a clear focus to the task of understanding the individual needs of young people and creating environments that are "safe havens" for learning. As teachers witness daily, the "normal" young person faces complex and confusing struggles in the psychological quest to belong, to feel accepted, and to become confident and prepared for an uncertain future.

Impersonal Classroom Management

Mainstream theories of classroom management advocate practices that tend to ignore the emotional and psychological needs of children and argue that a teacher's role is to be an effective manager. Importantly, however, becoming an effective classroom manager does not involve understanding the "sources behind student management problems." Instead, teachers are expected to maintain effective control as managers and to "promote cognitive growth of their students."[18]

Yet cognitions are laden with emotions; feelings are a critical dimension of cognition that indicates value and meaning for the learner. Value and meaning are at the heart of attention and motivation. In short, contemporary modes of classroom discipline are inherently contradictory. Operating in a climate of increasing psychological risk, when the central need is for increased care, empathy, and relatedness, the disciplinary literature increasingly relies on behavior modification and other classroom practices that manipulate and cajole.

Research in the psychobiology of emotions suggest significant educational application. As a complex biological system involving the endocrine and immune systems, emotional responses can override rational thought. Cognitive psychologists previously believed that all responses are routed through the neocortex, the thinking part of the brain. Revolutionary research has found, however, that neural pathways for feelings often bypass the neocortex, the rational brain, and take a direct route to the amygdala. The amygdala, which houses emotional memories, dictates emotional reactions far more quickly than the neocortex can formulate rational responses. Those emotional memories are deeply coded into the amygdala by stress and trauma; the more stress and trauma in the society as the youthful mind is constructing itself, the more likely it is that the amygdala will be overriding rational thought with emotional reactions.

In a classroom situation, if a child experiences disturbing and painful memories that have not come to full consciousness, the amygdala may take over and determine the behavior despite the best intentions of the child. Many more neural fibers emerge from the emotional brain into the neocortex than run in the opposite direction, so that emotion is often a more powerful motivator of behavior than logical thinking.[19]

Irrational fears, biases, and prejudices are rooted in the emotional brain center without full awareness and thus are in control of unconscious behavior. Only through a growing awareness of vaguely hidden emotional shadows can individuals become more morally responsible. Treating a child who has difficulty in controlling emotional behavior with criticism or manipulation gives rise to defensiveness or the passive resistance of feeling unfairly treated. A child needs to have an internal vision of appropriate behavior and needs to experience adult support in creating alternative actions to reach the goal of greater emotional maturity. Rather than describing or punishing a failure, teachers must encourage in young people a hope of doing better and a realistic plan to do so. Such action on the part of teachers nurtures emotional intelligence.

Describing emotional intelligence, Goleman insists upon the moral imperative of teaching children self-control, zeal, persistence, and the ability to motivate oneself. In order to respond to a society experiencing the disintegration of civility and safety, Goleman identifies two moral stances that are needed: self-restraint and compassion. In order to educate children to bring their intelligence to emotion, Goleman advocates teaching emotional literacy skills from a developmental perspective. Emotional literacy involves emotional self-awareness, management of emotions, harnessing emotions productively, and empathy. Both children and adults in the educational community need to develop emotional awareness in order to control impulsivity in themselves and others.[20]

Lessons in emotional awareness are taught each moment in the classroom by teachers. Those lessons are damaging when teachers model the management of emotions through manipulation and domination. Many commonly accepted strategies for classroom management and discipline advocate using children's fear of failure or shame to create desired effects without consideration of the emotional and moral issues involved.

Only with conscious awareness of their own feelings and the emotions of students, can educators make thoughtful pedagogical decisions regarding "misbehavior." Emotions are crucial to the clarity of cognitive thought. They guide ongoing decision making. The emotions of individuals struggling with unresolved issues can easily surge out of control and disrupt the capacity for attention and thought.[21]

Synthesizing a number of studies in the neurophysiology of emotions, Goleman explains the neural circuitry between thoughts and feelings and claims that cognitive scientists, from their "coldly cognitive view," have ignored emotions and the "higher values of the human heart—faith, hope, devotion, love." A wider view of intelligence includes the interpersonal aspects of being sensitive to the feelings of self and others.[22]

Emotions are connected with many of the difficulties that children experience in learning, including withdrawal, anxiety, attention deficits, lack of concentration, and aggression. No children are exempt from these problems. We are living in times of intense external and internal stresses. Little training is offered to either preservice or inservice teachers to support their own emotional growth and development, and very little attention is paid to children's emotions. Beginning teachers are told that efforts to deal with student's individual issues "are so time consuming that it can drain the energies of the teacher and divert him or her from the central task of classroom learning." This reaction to children's emotional difficulties reflects contemporary social values.[23]

When emotional stresses are attended to and children are taught to cope effectively with a flood of complicated feelings, they are far more able to access creativity and learning. Creativity is commonly misunderstood to be a rare moment of insight when one sees the world, a problem or an idea in a new way. The truth is that creativity is a basic human endowment. Empowering students to think and act creatively in their educational efforts is an essential skill in a world of rapidly changing reality.

With creativity, a student can go beyond available alternatives to construct new options for their lives. When we encourage children to imagine, to dream and fantasize and take liberty with reality, we teach them essential skills in adapting to intense change. In an atmosphere of isolation, anxiety and fear creativity is stifled.

If, then, classroom climate matters, for both intellectual and emotional well-being, it is necessary to identify those practices that result in impersonalization, distrust, humiliation, fear, and discouragement for both teachers and students. Conversely, it is worthwhile to identify those styles that create an atmosphere for emotional and intellectual health and creativity. Four major styles of management and discipline streams worthy of analysis include the dominator-behaviorist, the cognitive-prescriptive, the cognitive-judicious, and the empathic-caring.

Dominator-behaviorist styles of management

Riane Eisler, a cultural anthropologist, argues that dominator styles of leadership are "maladaptive," given our present level of technological development, and subtly encourage violence in an effort to establish and enforce. When a child feels dominated, a natural and healthy psychological reaction is to resist and protect personal autonomy. Yet that healthy reaction can quickly become unhealthy when it yields to withdrawal into isolation and alienation.[24]

Once a pattern of domination-resistance has been introduced into an environment, there is a contagion effect. Unless skillfully defused, negativity, anger, resistance, and blame escalate and permeate the environment, creating a non-productive, stressful atmosphere. In a dominator-resistant atmosphere, emotionally vulnerable children experience painful feelings of powerlessness and helplessness unless they can find a way to exercise some control. Without a sense of control over one's environment, it is difficult for these learners to discover, remember, and learn.

Schools that are highly evaluative and authoritarian tend to support traditional behavior management models that emphasize restrictive and reactive approaches to children's actions. Educational relationships in these schools, based on reward and punishment, are unhealthy, co-dependent and destructive of trust.[25]

Dominator-behaviorist systems depend on manipulating children's emotions of pleasure, pain, or fear for compliance with the goals of those in control. These practices have serious psychological consequences for both students and teachers. Young people trained in reward systems may obey at the moment. However, in the long run, they risk losing the intrinsic delight in learning as well as personal responsibility and accountability for their own lives. With dominator-behaviorist styles of management, a teacher is deprived of the harmony and pleasure that come with cooperative classrooms. The delight of trust and connection with children is diminished. Authoritarian relationships and the resistance they inevitably engender can escalate into more punitive measures.[26]

Punitive reactions can include reprimands, penalties, detention, loss of privileges, corporal punishment and expulsion, as well as a more subtle infliction of disrespect, blame, and accusation. Punishment instigates adversarial relationships between educators and students. As Good and Brophy remark,

> Punishment does not change students' underlying desire to misbehave or the reasons why those desires exists; it does not provide guidance to students by indicating what they should do instead; and it causes problems of its own by engendering resentment.[27]

From a dominator-behaviorist perspective, punishment appears to be the result of logical consequences—a favorite phrase in the lexicon of contemporary management theory—and immediately effective. From the perspective of the child, however, punishment is embarrassing, painful, and demeaning. Methods of management and discipline that stimulate fear or pain do not teach children what they need to know in order to behave in socially responsible ways; they serve to reinforce lessons of impersonal aggression. Emotions of fear and pain flow unchecked through the amygdala, bypassing the neocortex and short-circuiting the struggle for emotional intelligence.

A teacher may habitually use systems of reward and punishment without conscious awareness of the effect on children. Often the source of a teacher's reactive, dominator style of discipline lies in inner personal feelings of powerlessness. Autocratic environments give tacit permission to teachers to act out unconscious and unresolved personal emotions of anger and rage. Noddings points out that through our own anger and fear we espouse self-righteous principles that permit us to differentiate in our respect for another and devalue others. Domination-behaviorism serves the immature emotional needs of the dominator; it may even secure short-term order. It never serves the emotional or intellectual needs of children.[28]

The moral issues of classroom domination

Domination in the classroom is distinct from the caring use of legitimate authority. Efforts to dominate through the manipulation of children's emotions is unfair power over children. Examples of emotional manipulation can include the disappointment from the loss of a reward, fear from possible aversive consequences, and anger from a teacher who has lost self-control. Deliberately arousing painful emotions of children for the convenience of a manager can create further trauma for a child who may be already suffering from distressing events. Without awareness or intention, teachers can become part of the re-traumatization of children when feelings are ignored.

In order to learn to the capacity of one's potential, a student needs to trust the teacher. In a relationship laced with domination, trust is depleted. As a professional, the teacher bears the moral responsibility for the quality of the relationship and the educational environment. In all the helping professions, doctors, lawyers, psychotherapists, clergy and teachers, the moral responsibility for a professional relationship lies in the subtle ways a professional uses authority. Moral responsibility demands that the professional must always be conscious and oriented toward the well-being and empowerment of the client. To achieve these ethical standards, the professional educator must become reflective and emotionally mature, engage empathically with students individually and as a group and be prepared to challenge current trends of depersonalization.[29]

Strategies that focus on domination through reward and punishment have little chance of teaching a child to handle intense emotions and behavior in a healthy way. If a child's misbehavior is rooted in a reaction to earlier neglect, trauma, or disassociation, the attention to the behavior alone may result in misinterpretation of the needs of the child. "Misbehavior" can be a "teachable moment" for a distressed child, a rich opportunity to teach a child to handle difficult emotions in a healthy and productive manner.

Cognitive-prescriptive styles of management and discipline

Advocates of cognitive systems of classroom management and discipline challenge educational systems that use physical and psychological domination through reward and punishment. However, they are distinct in whether they prescribe and control certain thought processes as with William Glasser, or if they rely on a model of inherent rights and responsibilities as argued by Forrest Gathercoal.

Glasser's fundamental theory of management and discipline affirms that human beings are moved by inside forces, and while outside forces may affect what we choose to do, they do not cause us to behave in any consistent way. Our dissatisfactions with life come because, as human beings, we "want so much" and are not "satisfied with what we have." We want to belong, to be thought of as important by others, to love, to have fun, and to be free. In Glasser's schema, internal conflicts emerge from conflicting "wants"—we want to belong yet we want to be free. Emotions for Glasser emerge with the frustration or satisfaction of these wants.[30]

In his explanation of human behavior, Glasser contrasts the "new brain" (the cerebral cortex) and the "old brain" (the amygdala, though he does not use that term). The "old brain" controls the physiology of the body keeping it at a homeostatic level. The "new brain," or cerebral cortex, Glasser theorizes, is the source of our needs to belong, to have importance, to love, to have fun, and to seek freedom. What Glasser was not privy to in his foundational construct is recent developments in neural research describing the connection between the amygdala, the "old brain," and the neocortex, the "new brain." A misconception of the function of the "old brain" leads Glasser to argue that human suffering originates in our "new brain" when we are unable to satisfy the complex needs that drive it. As Goleman explains, however, painful and overwhelming emotions reside in the "old brain," the amygdala, and can overwhelm the neocortex or "new brain" when those emotions are out of reach of conscious awareness.[31]

In the belief that the neocortex creates human suffering, Glasser has created a system of managing conflicting needs to solve emotional difficulties and behavior problems. "Very few of us realize how much we choose the misery in our lives," he writes. "Even when we do, we still go ahead with the disastrous choice because we are convinced that we don't have the strength to choose better."[32] The lack of strength to make choices to end our own misery is seen as a weakness for Glasser, one that he attempts to overcome in his cognitive-prescriptive system of human management and discipline.

Glasser largely ignores the profound impact of traumatic events, poverty, abuse, and oppressive relationships with adults. His theory offers little compassion or empathy for the person who is living in misery; in fact, Glasser casts such a person as weak if she continues to live in misery. Recent neuropsychological findings contradicts beliefs supporting Glasser's theory and leave his techniques and strategies floating without accurate theory.

Cognitive-Judicious

A third model of management and discipline, cognitive-judicious, is represented by the work of Gathercoal. Of concern to Gathercoal are teachers who remain isolated in the "Personal Self," meeting immature ego needs for power and control through domination over young people. These teachers are locked within a shell of self-centeredness, unable to consider the needs of children separate from personal ambitions and desires.[33]

Gathercoal advocates the development of teacher-student relationships, carefully constructed through "enlightenment," and "an awareness of how educators' prideful and selfish motive blur the critical needs of students." Little is offered, however, by Gathercoal that might help teachers accomplish this inner developmental task. While challenging dominator-behaviorist styles of educational leadership, Gathercoal encourages educators to build a foundation for the development of justice and human rights in the classroom. He bases his practices squarely on cognitive principles, calling for teaching children to manage themselves and their relationships through constitutional principles.[34]

The movement toward a cognitive-judicious basis for discipline and management is essential to insure the protection of children from oppressive and abusive practices and the absence of compassion and empathy. Cognitive forms of discipline such as Judicious Discipline provide resources for teachers that encourage meaningful relationships with students and that promote practices that avoid manipulating or ignoring tender emotions. With logical and reasonable systems of management, children can begin to trust that painful manipulation and punishment will not randomly occur. Students are free to discover the delight of intrinsic curiosity for diligent learning. With the safety net of cognitive discipline, children can come to believe that the teacher is truly an advocate for their growth and development.

A cognitive-judicious approach to discipline allows educators to engage the minds and thoughts of students in ways that model respect for other individuals and community rights. With a cognitive-judicious emphasis. child's higher thinking processes are elicited, offering the student opportunities to use the mind to control difficult emotions and behavior. Educators who practice cognitive-judicious styles of classroom management and discipline are expected to be fair, objective, and concerned with a clear foundation in rules. They must carefully balance the rights of an individual with the interests of the group.

While cognitive-judicious approaches to discipline offer a logical, reasoned and respectful response to "misbehavior," an emphasis on rights and justice may result in sterile, depersonalized relationships and environments without a clear focus on the ethics and practice of caring. Children need and deserve an educational environment that supports human connection, empathy, and care in addition to an environment managed under an ethic of justice. However, unless the young person has been specifically taught how to achieve awareness and manage these feelings in a healthy manner, the opportunity for mastery of emotions may be fumbled.

As Phillips argues, good care is supported by the protection of rights.[35] Justice can be the container or boundaries that protect the development of relationships of care and trust. Systems of classroom management and discipline that rely on cognitive-judicious reasoning offer concrete and realistic support to the teacher in the effort to maintain an atmosphere for learning. However, it is urgent that children enter into caring, nurturing relationships with adults and learn to experience empathy for others if they are to function as caring members of society.

The caring-relational style of management and discipline

Children with emotional vulnerabilities are in deep need of empathic caring relationships with adults in order to build the resiliency they need to survive and flourish. Personal connections with family members, neighbors, teachers, and other stable adults build trust and resiliency and serve to mitigate childhood behavioral disorders such as violence and substance abuse. Noddings argues that we cannot afford to limit our educational goals to academic rigor, competency, and cognitive development, but must embrace the moral responsibility to educate all children for caring and loving as well as technical competency. Educating for caring only occurs when a child feels cared for by the educator.[36]

Caring practices begin with a clear awareness of one's own feelings, beliefs, biases, emotions, and intentions. Carefully constructed on the foundation of awareness, caring then moves to the problem of empathy. Empathy has perplexed human beings throughout history, namely: "How does one begin to approximate the inner experience of another?"[37] Caring in education combines the consciousness of one's own emotional reality with the intention and sensitivity to attempt to understand the other person in the context of the other person's own worldview.

Issues of classroom management and discipline become complex and challenging when considered from a caring perspective. When an at-risk youth enters a classroom, the effects of poverty, chronic illness, low self-esteem, neglect, abuse, and stress are carried through the door. The child's behavioral response to the hostile environment in which he or she is living may be necessary for survival. However, the same actions in a classroom may be termed "misbehavior." Rather than acknowledging the source of the "misbehavior", teachers may feel threatened and react with an attempt to control and dominate the young person's behavior with the goal of creating an effective learning environment.

The work of caring is complex and may be emotionally threatening to some. It is, however, the heart of a moral response as an educator. According to Noddings, the context of caring in educational relationships becomes the model of moral ethics for young people. The growing child is a daily witness to adults who struggle to live out an ethic of care. This modeling challenges students to contribute to that relationship in the form of engrossment in the learning activity.[38]

To live out the ethic of care, teachers must receive the training and support to understand and manage personal emotional issues in order to respond morally to the behavior of highly challenging students. The emotional intelligence developed by a teacher is available to students through modeling and integration of lessons for emotional competency in the curriculum. How a teacher handles one difficult student is a lesson for thirty.

Competencies of caring for the teacher who wishes to be a model of self management and discipline include self-awareness, knowing the relationship between feelings, thoughts and emotions, skills in personal decision making, managing feelings, and handling stress. In relationships with students, teachers need to refine their process of empathy and develop the ability to understand the per-spectives and feelings of others. Practices of reflection need development in order to examine actions and acknowledge the consequences. The development of these abilities are a professional moral necessity for a teacher today and will profoundly affect the moral socialization of children.[39]

Researchers have neglected the effect of school exper-iences on the moral socialization of children. We know more about the discipline strategies used by parents that have been effective in children's moral development. In studies of the parental role, children's moral development has been directly linked to the type of discipline used by the adult.

In researching two styles of parental discipline, induction or power-assertion, induction related positively to moral internalization and power-assertion related nega-tively. Inductions are the statements that point up the harmful effects of the child's behavior on others while respecting the young person's sense of self-esteem. Inductions clarify that a child caused another's distress and encourage empathy. In contrast, disciplinary tech-niques of power-assertion or love-withdrawal, similar to dominator-behaviorist styles of discipline in the class-room, can produce fear, anxiety, and resentment in children and interfere with the ability to process induc-tions or teaching.[40]

In order for inductions to be considered valid and reasonable forms of discipline, it is essential for teachers today to return to a focus on interpersonal relationships and the creation of a caring environment in the classroom. Noddings describes schools where caring is a fundamental priority. In schools of care, the teacher is open to the perspectives, feelings and attitudes of students toward specific learning experiences, setting aside her own needs, listening and joining in the child's perspective. Through this caring union, Noddings believes that students are empowered to sort out confusion, set priorities, and open to new dimensions of learning. This engrossment need not be time consuming; a brief moment will suffice with a glance or a simple word that conveys the message that understanding and care is present.[41]

Because caring occurs in the context of classrooms, situations, and relationships, it is difficult to describe with abstract, analytical language. It is also difficult to describe in logical, sequential arguments. Caring is a process of learning, a way of relating to a student that encourages mutual growth and development. It is concrete and emerges interpersonally, drawing us, as educators, out of ourselves and into authentic relationships, weaving our lives into the tapestry of community. Caring in the classroom is dynamic, increasing through time and trust, deepening the bonds between teacher and student, as well as in groups of learners. In the educational environment, caring adds intention, vitality, purpose, and engagement to the mission of learning and development. But above all, caring in the classroom reintegrates emotion and cognition, creating the setting for the most effective learning.

The conflict of caring and control

Novice teachers exploring the implications of caring relationships with students find a conflict with their desire to assume a professional, authoritative role. It is in the interaction between caring and control where the moral issues surrounding power emerge. Classroom management or discipline is often interpreted as controlling a classroom rather than a need to learn about better ways of teaching. In a number of studies cited by McLaughlin, student teachers became more controlling as time went on. They created "distance" from students and more harsh penalties for infractions. In the conflict with the need to control, control won out over caring.[42]

Yet there is no necessary conflict between care and control. McLaughlin found that when student teachers were able to reflect carefully about events in the class-room in order to improve their teaching, they were able to develop a complement between control and caring. A caring classroom community emerged when teachers were open with students, had an intention to establish reciprocal relations, and affirmed the students. Control exercised mechanically and behaviorally can never be reconciled with care, no matter how strongly the teachers claim to care. They model, instead, bureaucratic distance and efficiency, not the morality of care.[43]

Professional ethics of the educator: Justice and care

Judicious Discipline, as developed by Gathercoal, offers a framework of respect for human rights that can be understood as a moral imperative from the perspective of the ethic of justice. From a feminist orientation, the ethic of care in schools is a moral necessity. An ethic of care fleshes out the skeleton of justice, adding relationship, motivation, and meaning to the educational mission. The ethic of justice forms the crucible for practices of care.[44]

Both the ethic of justice and an ethic of care need to be differentiated and articulated in order to imagine the valuable insights each has to offer to teachers. The ethic of justice is externally visible in practices and behavior while the ethic of care is fundamentally inside the one-who-cares and the one-cared-for. This "insideness" of care is not initially visible to an observer, but remains a highly potent aspect of the relationship. The ethic of care does eventually become observable in the growth of belonging, motivation, and empathy in learners.

Distinctions between the ethic of justice and ethic of care include differences in understanding human relationships, differences in ways of knowing, and different guides for moral behavior.[45] In the ethic of justice, human relationships are reciprocal between separate individuals where conflicting claims are mediated. An ethic of care relies on an understanding of relationships in a connected way that entails a response to the learner in his or her own terms and contexts. In other words, fairness is the principle concern in the morality of justice, while connection and relationship are paramount in the morality of care.

Differences regarding ways of knowing in each ethic involve processes of thought and the environment of learning. In the ethic of justice, thinking is highly cognitive. Knowledge is gained through logical analysis and abstract reasoning. Emotions are marginal. In the ethic of care, on the other hand, thinking is subjective, contextual, and takes into account both the cognitive and affective experience of all people in the relationship. Knowledge is developed through dialogue and discussion with the goal of establishing understanding and empathy. Belenky describes this way of knowing as "connected learning," an interdependent style of creating knowledge, within which learners come to know through listening and imagining a world outside of themselves, the world as experienced by others. Emotions are highly valued in the ethic of care.[46] With an ethic of justice, the educational environment is adversarial, based on reasoned arguments. In environments of mutuality, critical thinking and reasoned arguments are productive; however, an adversarial style can feel unfair to students when a teacher holds more authority and power in the relationship. A moral conflict in an ethic of justice exists when rules have been broken, authority challenged, and established moral traditions violated. The educational environment in an ethic of care is characterized by connections of human concern for the subtle and affective dimensions of relationship. A moral conflict in the ethic of care is viewed as a breakdown of relationship, a time when trust is broken, a space where alienation and isolation develops.

The primary distinctions between the ethic of care and the ethic of justice are centered in the use and abuse of power. In the ethic of care, authority is used with great caution and always in service to the one-cared-for. In the ethic of justice, power is in the hands of an authority, the one who is determining interpretation of rules, fairness, and right knowledge. This creates the potential for the misuse of that power and the possible violation of children's human rights to dignity and respect.

Developing educational caring

Traditionally the teacher is *parentis in loco*, in place of the parent in the educational environment, responsible for many hours a day for the growth and development of the child. A significant, and often invisible, part of caring is inside the mind and heart of the one who cares and the one-cared-for. We can observe and describe actions that seem to be caring, but caring has an "insideness" about it that is difficult to describe. Caring begins first with the intention to serve the needs of the other, and moves into attention, listening even to the "non-verbal behavior" of the children and attempting to decode it to discern the essential meaning. Empathic caring in teacher student relationships requires that the teacher be emotionally mature, or at least willing to confront fears and inadequacies and acknowledge mistakes and failures.

At the core of caring is the process of empathy. The English term *empathy* is derived from the German word *einfuhlung*, which means "to acquire insight into . . . to get into the spirit of," and to "grasp the essence of." Empathy is often confused with sympathy, which is the psychological process of identifying one's own feelings with the intense emotions of another. In sympathy there is a simple transference of a state of feeling that does not presuppose any participation or knowledge of the emotions of the other. The feelings of another are unconsciously and involuntarily identified as one's own. Sympathy can come through absorption of another self into one's own or by a process of becoming overwhelmed by another.[47]

Empathy is radically distinct from sympathy. The attention is always with the other, away from one's own feelings. When sympathizing with distressed young people, teachers do feel emotionally drained. With empathy, teachers are able to retain their own emotional peacefulness and become intentional in their attempts to deeply understand children with emotional difficulties. Empathy is an "outreaching" and entry into another's situation that creates an authentic transcendence of one's own self.[48]

In true empathy, there is no reference to one's own feelings. We are not joyful on another person's account, we savor their joy. We do not embrace the sadness of another's life, we acknowledge it as their own experience. Empathy is an intentional choice to imagine the essence of what another may be thinking and feeling, the ability to discern oneself from the other, and be prepared to act for his or her welfare. Rather than depleting, empathy is renewing. Borman and Greenman remark,

> perhaps counterintuitively, empathy appears to be precisely the source of the self-concept and indeed of self-expansion. . . . Without the capacity to feel for the other we do not fully know or develop ourselves. It is not just that we become better selves through empathy, then, but that we become selves at all.[49]

My hunch is that we try to stay safely ensconced in an impersonal abstract way of relating to children because we fear the effects of sympathy, the feelings of childhood emotional distress. We are afraid to take on the suffering and pain of depressed and traumatized children with good reason. We need to keep our emotions stable and centered in order to be effective as educators.

Skills in the development of empathy require that one learn to be conscious of the unconscious ways of sympathizing with others. We can begin to discern more clearly where our emotions are merging into our assumptions regarding the emotions of others. With this skill, we become conscious of the boundaries of our own feelings and protect children from the outbursts and punitive strategies that come from a fear of emotional identification.

A simple reflective protocol called the Encounter Process was used to discern emotional identification from empathy, by consciously imagining the perspective of another. Perspective taking is the active, creative process by which the teacher is able to imagine the situation from the perspective of the learner. With this protocol, the teacher is able to bracket personal emotions and point of view and creatively explore the possible interiority of the other. Reflection on the encounter enables the educator to discern the meaning and significance of the information gleaned in perspective taking.[50]

Developing the discipline of caring

As with any discipline, a teacher's ability to offer an empathic caring response must be carefully developed and sustained. A habit of reflection on the ordinary daily encounters with others encourages teachers to develop, monitor, and deepen the ability to serve the needs of students with care. When teachers were encouraged to reflect on encounters with students that were uncomfortable, confusing, or disturbing, and recalled these interactions at the end of the day, they noted their own perceptions as well as what they imagined to be the perceptions of the child. This simple reflective practice had the effect of making visible much that was experienced mindlessly and vaguely, and deepened the mutual bonds of understanding.[51]

A high school teacher using this process described the effect of writing reflections: "We have become larger—we are more, there has been a small transformation."[52] Through reflections on another's point of view a person becomes open and receives the experience of another expanding personal knowledge. Through reflection, individuals are able to shift perspectives in gradual, intuitive ways. These small but significant shifts effectively reform beliefs, expose unconscious biases and prejudice, and alter outdated habitual patterns.[53]

In the process of reflection we are able to make choices and clarify our intentions, and take account-ability for our interactions with others. Reflection opens the individual to a more optimistic and hopeful perspective, while providing the opportunity for the discernment of meaning in the situation.

With a reflective practice, educators can learn to articulate their own personal inner world and distinguish it from the inner world of the learner. Taking time after an interpersonal encounter with a student to imagine, reflect, and remember what was seen, felt, and heard sharpens the perception and awareness of future experiences.[54]

Canning reports that teachers who wrote in journals for professional purposes where able to more effectively access prior professional knowledge, expand a sense of self, and develop creative alternatives and actions to changing situations. In another study on teacher reflection, educators were able to progress in their thinking from personal feelings to high social and ethical perspectives.[55]

Caring involves maintaining the space

In both the student-teacher relationship and social system of the classroom, issues of trust and safety affect learning. In social systems marked by deep trust, the sense of failure, pain and inadequacy that a child may feel are able to be transformed. Wounds of betrayal, abandonment, and neglect are healed.

In a caring environment the educator is the one who maintains the physical, emotional, and intellectual boundaries for learning. Disruptions and violations of those boundaries become opportunities to teach learners new ways of emotional coping. How the teacher handles the intense anger of a student is a lesson in anger management. The response to disappointment, loss . . . even death, teaches children how to grieve and mourn in healthy ways. When teachers approach learning problems with confidence, courage, and patience, lessons of emotional intelligence are taught.

Caring encourages the development of knowledge

As individuals learn to identify their own limited perspective of themselves and others, they find that barriers to new knowledge dissolve. When we let go of having to be "right", we become open to the possibility of learning from multiple perspectives. In a caring atmosphere, each of us is able to develop awareness of our own abilities and gifts as well as an appreciation for the unique personhood of other individuals. In an atmosphere of awareness and appreciation, human beings share in a way of knowing that transcends cultural and individual boundaries. The connection through knowing is the core of human bonding and understanding. In the active connection of meaning and knowledge, the educator reaches out to the alienated student and brings them into a space of human caring. It is a critical crossroads of human knowledge, this meeting of two views, two perspectives where the learner is offered a contrasting perspective to his current view. The contrasting perspective offers the learner a discontinuity in a habitual pattern of perception and an interpretation that challenges previous interpretations.

In an atmosphere of trust, caring, and empathy, learners can open their hearts and minds to new knowledge, change old patterns of behavior, and develop a vision of how they can relate in caring, responsible ways to the world.

Conclusion

As the psychological profile of the classroom shifts to include young people at high risk for school failure, dysfunctional behavior and even death, educators are challenged to critique the consequences of traditional systems of classroom management and discipline. As moral professionals, teachers must examine the psychological effects of their attempts to manage and discipline the behavior of students. Careful and conscious choices need to be made to insure the growth and well-being of all students. The challenge to care expands the current educational mission beyond the norms of behavioral conformity and cognitive development to the critical task of educating young people for emotional intelligence and responsible social participation in the world.

Notes

1. Geoff Colvin, Edward J. Kanieenui, and George E. Sugai, "Reconceptualizing Behavior Management and School-Wide Discipline in General Education" *Education and Treatment of Children* 16 (4, 1993): 362.

2. Susan F. Phillips and Patricia Benner, eds., *The Crisis of Care: Affirming and Restoring Caring Practices in the Helping Professions* (Washington, D.C.: Georgetown University Press, 1994), p. 1.

3. Nel Noddings, *The Challenge to Care: An Alterative Approach to Education* (New York: Teachers College Press, 1992), p. xiv.

4. Phillips, *Crisis of Care*, p. 2.

5. Robert N. Bellah, *Beyond Belief: Essays on Religion in a Post-Traditional World* (Berkeley: University of California Press, 1991).

6. See, for example, Grant Lee and Marvin J. Westwood, "Cross-Cultural Adjustment Issues Faced by Immigrant Professionals," *Journal of Employment Counseling* 33 (1, 1996): 29–43.

7. Phillips, *Crisis of Care*, p. 8.

8. Nel Noddings, *Caring: A Feminine Approach to Ethics and Moral Education* (Berkeley: University of California Press, 1984);

see also Noddings, *Challenge to Care*; Mary R. Belenky, Blanche Clinchy, Nancy Goldberger, and Jill M. Tarule, *Women's Ways of Knowing* (New York: Basic Books, 1986; Harold F. Wolfgramm, "Educational Remediation of Delinquent Youth: A Humane Approach," *Journal of Humanistic Education and Development* 33 (September 1994): 13–20).

9. See, for example, David Capuzzi and Douglas R. Gross, *Youth at Risk* (Alexandria, VA: American Association for Counseling and Development, 1989).

10. Andrew Slaby and Lili F. Garfinkle, *No One Saw My Pain: Why Teens Kill Themselves* (New York: Norton), p. 8.

11. Domiyti G. Papolos and Janice Papolos, *Overcoming Depression* (New York: Harper Row, 1988).

12. Slaby and Garfinkel, *No One Saw My Pain*, p. 4.

13. Papolos and Papolos, *Overcoming Depression*; Slaby and Garfinkle, *No One Saw My Pain*.

14. See Daniel Goleman, *Emotional Intelligence* (New York: Bantam Books, 1995); Capuzzi and Gross, *Youth at Risk*; Denis M. Donovan and Deborah McIntyre, *Healing the Hurt Child: A Developmental-Contextual Approach* (New York: Norton, 1990).

15. Donald Knowles and Nancy Reeves, *But Won't Granny Need Her Sox? Dealing Effectively with Children's Concerns about Death and Dying* (Dubuque, Iowa: Kendall/Hunt, 1983); Donovan & McIntyre.

16. Jane Middelton-Moz, *Children of Trauma* (Deerfield Beach, Fla.: Health Communication, 1987); David B. Waters and Edith C. Lawrence, *Competence, Courage and Change: An Approach to Family Therapy* (New York: Norton, 1993).

17. Colvin, et al., "Reconceptualizing Behavior Management," p. 363.

18. Donald P. Kauchak and Paul D. Eggen, *Learning and Teaching: Research-Based Methods* (Needham Heights, MA: Allyn and Bacon, 1993), p. 357.

19. Robert Sylwester, "How Emotions Affect Learning," *Educational Leadership* 52 (October 1994): 60–65.

20. Goleman, *Emotional Intelligence*.

21. Ibid.

22. Ibid., p. 41.

23. Kauchak and Eggen, *Learning and Teaching*, p. 358; see also Julian Weisglass, "Teachers have Feelings: What Can We Do about It?" *Journal of Staff Development* 12 (1, 1992): 28–33.

24. Riane T. Eisler and David Loye, *The Partnership Way* (San Francisco: Harper, 1990).

25. Forrest Gathercoal, *Judicious Discipline*, 3rd ed. (San Francisco: Caddo Gap Press, 1993.

26. See particularly Alfie Kohn, *Punished by Rewards: The Trouble with Gold Stars, Incentive Plans, A's, Praise, and Other Bribes* (Boston: Houghton Mifflin, 1993).

27. Thomas L. Good and Jere E. Brophy, *Educational Psychology: A Realistic Approach* (New York: Longman, 1990), p. 551.

28. Noddings, *Caring*; Sharon Stanley, "The Development of Empathy in Eductors," unpublished diss., University of Victoria, 1994.

29. Marilyn Peterson, *At Personal Risk: Boundary Violations in Professional-Client Relationships* (New York: Norton, 1993).

30. William Glasser, *Stations of the Mind: New Directions for Reality Therapy* (New York: Harper Row, 1981), quotation from p. 3.

31. Glasser, *Stations of the Mind*; cf. Goleman, *Emotional Intelligence*.

32. William Glasser, *Positive Addiction* (New York: Harper Row, 1976), p.1.

33. Gathercoal, *Judicious Discipline*, p. 28.

34. Ibid., p. 28.

35. Phillips, *Crisis of Care*.

36. Noddings, *Challenge to Care*; see also Middleton-Moz, *Children of Trauma*; Alice Miller, *The Untouched Key: Tracing Childhood Trauma in Creativity and Destructiveness* (New York: Doubleday, 1990).

37. Alfred Marguiles, *The Empathic Imagination* (New York: Norton, 1989), p. 3.

38. Noddings, *Caring*; Noddings, *Challenge to Care*.

39. Stanley, "Development of Empathy in Educators."

40. Martin L. Hoffman, "Moral Development," in *Developmental Psychology:An Advanced Textbook*, Marc H. Bornstein and Michael E. Lamb, eds. 2nd ed. (Hillsdale, NJ: Lawrence Erlbaum Associates, 1988), pp. 497–548.

41. Noddings, *Caring*; Noddings, *Challenge to Care*.

42. H. James McLaughlin, "Wanting to Care and Hoping to Control: An Exploration of Student Teachers' Relationships with Students," in *The Tapestry of Caring: Education as Nurturance*, A. Renee Prillaman, Deborah J. Eaker, and Doris M. Kendrick, eds., (Norwood, NJ: Ablex, 1994), pp. 109–150.

43. McLaughlin, "Caring and Control?" See also George Noblit, "Power and Caring," *American Educational Research Journal* 30 (spring 1993): 23–38.

44. Carol Gilligan, Nona Lyons, and Trudy J. Hamner, *Making Connections: The Relational Worlds of Adolescent Girls at Emma Willard School* (Cambridge, MA: Harvard University Press, 1990); Noddings, *Caring*; Noddings, *Challenge to Care*; Belenky, et al., *Women's Ways of Knowing*.

45. Gilligan, et al., *Making Connections*.

46. Noddings, *Caring*; Belenky, et al., *Women's Ways of Knowing*.

47. Max Scheler, *On the Nature of Sympathy*, trans. P. Heath (New Haven: Yale University Press, 1954).

48. Scheler, *On the Nature of Sympathy*, p..46.

49. Kathryn M. Borman and Nancy Greenman, eds., *Changing American Education: Recapturing the Past or Inventing the Future?* (Albany: State University of New York Press, 1994), p. 304.

50. Stanley, "Development of Empathy in Educators."

51. Ibid.

52. T.R., personal communication.

53. Belenky, et al., *Women's Ways of Knowing.*

54. Marguiles, *Empathic Imagination.*

55. Christine Canning, "What Teachers Say about Reflection," *Educational Leadership* 48 (3, 1991): 18–21; Elaine Surbeck, Eunhye P. Han, and Joan E. Moyer, "Assessing Relective Responses in Journals," *Educational Leadership* 46 (6, 1991): 25–27.

Conclusion

❏

Barbara McEwan

For a very long time classroom management has existed as an afterthought to pedagogical theory. The historical body of knowledge related to discipline, as classroom management has been more commonly known, can be boiled down to two basic measures: maintain a high level of subject matter competency and do not smile until December. When all else fails, teachers resort to punitive practices that serve to intimidate and create fear in their students. Ill-prepared for the range of student needs evident in our classrooms today, educators too often make decisions arising from their own indignation, animosity, bias, frustration, and disappointment. As objects of these decisions, students typically respond with indignation, animosity, bias, frustration, and disappointment in their own turn.

Poor preparation, misinformation, breakdowns between theory and practice—all of these and more are thrown into the conundrum of management decisions that often are as disruptive to the learning community as are the acts of student misbehavior. Largely ignored or misunderstood by educators and the public alike, veiwed with resentment by students who have suffered the results of poor decisions, classroom management is too often assumed to be something teachers do rather than something to be taught.

> Because we have paid insufficient attention to the synergies and antagonies between the components of attractors, we often do not know the circumstances under which some components can exist with others. Take classroom management. It has certainly proved futile to isolate it from other components of teacher behaviour and then try to instruct teachers in the right way to "do it". . . . As Mann pointed out . . . classroom management is part of the curriculum and is coupled with everything else we do and intend to do."[1]

One of the major purposes for this volume is the revitalization of debate and dialogue regarding classroom management. The conversation surrounding reasonable, equitable management has been too long dismissed from serious consideration, ignored as a worthy area of research. The management books available, with a few notable exceptions, typically rehash the conversation that has gone before. Many educators seem to sense that the conflicts and misunderstandings in classrooms between teachers and students are just part of what is to be expected and that change is not possible. So this very complicated and sensitive topic is reduced to the lowest common denominator—kick out all the students you do not like and teach whomever remains. We hope to jump-start the conversation in the direction of critically examining management practices as educators have critically examined the teaching of reading, authentic assessment, and other representations of democratic curriculum.

New teachers set about their work convinced that they are going to change the world of education just by being in the classroom and believing that if they are friends with their students, learning will occur and management will just happen. Disillusionment comes when they discover that education can indeed be changed, but only through very hard work, and that students tend to respect teachers who play leadership as opposed to buddy roles in their lives. Some throw in the towel at this point and leave the profession. Those who do stay respond to the realities of teaching in one of two ways.

Some do the minimum amount of work necessary to get by. They never challenge themselves or their students in any meaningful way and retire as soon as they can. Others roll up their sleeves, work hard, continually find new challenges, and love what they do almost every minute of their professional lives. This latter group typically have far fewer problems with management because they have lots of ideas for working through the conflicts they encounter and they see them as problems to be solved rather than roadblocks.

There is enormous variance between what is typically taught, or at least advocated, in teacher training programs and what actually goes on in the classroom. Some have attributed this breakdown to the mentoring a teacher intern receives, and that influence cannot be minimized.[2] The transference of information from teacher preparation to practice, however it occurs, appears to fit more closely with chaos theory than with an ordered view of the universe. My own observations reveal a close link between life experience and a new teacher's commitment to equitable management. For example, I see far more transference of democratic concepts from theory to practice in those who have previously held personnel or public relations positions in private industry. These individuals have learned that the bottom line rests with good customer practices and employees who feel safe and secure. The mindset having been created, it is an easy step for them to view their students' needs as a primary focus of their professional responsibilities. The issue then becomes how to create that same mindset in everyone else who chooses to become a teacher.

And even those who make an intellectual commitment to being an equitable decision-maker, the culture of the schools to which they are assigned seems to overwhelm and absorb them. Whether equitable or not, the power of the culture is far more persuasive than are the ideals new teachers bring with them.

Despite all the cognitive research and theory to which my students are exposed in the course of our teacher training program, I know that they will more than likely take on the culture of their schools and incorporate misinformation about management into their teaching practices rather than attempt to consistently apply strategies that are widely endorsed by cognitive theorists. The common quest for the quickest path to a quiet classroom typically weighs far more heavily than does any of the pedagogical knowledge they acquired in college classes.

One student recently told me of a visit she made to a primary classroom in a large city. She was delighted by the quiet nature of the classroom and how all the students in the class seemed to be happily on task. She went on to say that there were "lots of names on the board" for late work, students who had to stay in at recess, notes not returned to school and other rule violations. My student said she thought the practice was "all right" since these little seven and eight year olds had decided that such a public display of various problems was appropriate.

The student who related this story to me not only had spent an entire year discussing applications of cognitive theory, but of legal issues in education as well. She had at least an intellectual understanding that students have a right to an expectation of privacy. She had participated in discussions about the importance of keeping records confidential, including behavioral records, in order to make classrooms environments feel safe and supportive for all students.

"Names on the board" is probably the most common form of behavior control and the least defensible. When I ask teachers or my students why they employ that technique, they say it is to help remind the student of the problem. I typically respond, "Do you really think the student will forget there's a problem?" The counter-response is that it helps the teacher remember who has homework missing. And when I ask if that isn't what a grade book is for, the conversation typically grinds to a halt punctuated by rolling eyes or shrugged shoulders. Ultimately, there is only one effect of writing names on boards: humiliation.

Such a public display of a problem serves only to alienate students from peers and teachers. Even Lee Canter, who incorporated the practice of placing names on the board into the Assertive Discipline model he has been promoting for many years, has backed away from advocating public displays of students' names.[3]

My student had considered this practice of writing names on the board from the perspective of law, pedagogical practice, and developmental psychology. Her mentor teacher, with whom she had spent an entire year, runs a free and open classroom that is well managed and more on task than most. Yet, visiting the second grade classroom where the children had invented rules that violated their own rights in school, but that apparently resulted in quiet, provided her with a justification for names on the board despite our critical examination of why that practice is inappropriate.

Even more disturbing to me was her idea that if the students wanted this practice employed in the classroom, a practice that undoubtedly had been previously implanted in them as being the way students are punished in public school, their endorsement made it acceptable. In any other arena of society, people who make up their own rules of what is appropriate behavior, regardless of legal considerations, are usually considered to be criminals. But in some public schools we encourage children to invent their own rules despite the fact that society does not work that way. To leave rule-making in the hands of young children, whose sense of moral conscience is still very much in the formative stage, is to excuse adults from establishing legal and moral parameters for the classroom. A classroom that relies on the reasoning of second graders for its standards of governance abdicates the moral leadership and authority of the professional educator. When I communicated this story to my co-author, in the course of our many e-mail messages, his response hit the nail on the head. "Democratic education," he wrote, "does not mean getting to vote on the form of oppression to which you will be subjected." And that comment frames not only this conclusion, but the intent of this entire book as well.

The crime and punishment mindset represented in writing names on the board teaches nothing about tolerance, equity, respect, or a right to privacy. Allowing students to put such a system in place does not represent democratic practice so much as it represents passing the moral buck to children too young to know the difference. If educators could view the goal of classroom management as the structure that supports equitable participation in the learning process rather than silence which may or may not help students learn, then children inventing rules would seem an incomprehensible idea.

The goal of democratic education should be to create children who are capable of critically examining their roles as citizens rather than institutionalizing docility and the ability to follow rules, logical or not, as the criteria for success.[4] The ability to critically examine anything can only come from a hermeneuutic exploration of the knowledge available to all of us. The assumption that children can become viable citizens in our human society when they are given the impression at a very young age that they can invent rules for governance devoid of any legal, moral, ethical, or pedagogical framework, is to pass along an astoundingly misinformed concept of what is meant by democratic participation.

The chapters included in this volume, drawn from all over the country, stand as testimony to how widespread the misconceptions and misuses of classroom management are. To conclude this conversation, there is a metaphor I will use to examine the nature of the problem as I see it.

The mental templates individuals construct encode previous ways of understanding. And the previous ways of understanding are embedded in metaphors. As the metaphors of understanding are transmitted from individual to individual, the language that is used to develop schema may change the metaphors of understanding and thus alter the mental templates of culture and tradition.[5]

The mental barriers preventing the creation and maintenance of calm and supportive classroom environments can be imagined as a vast and deep chasm. On one side stand educators who view the churning waters below as their fears of failure because their classrooms are occupied by young people who do not care about learning, who come from dysfunctional home environments, and who do not share the values of educators. They feel frustrated, betrayed, and depressed by a system that demands much and gives few rewards for work well done. Standing by themselves on one side of the chasm, they have created their own culture and traditions surrounding their view of the chasm. They share cultures and traditions that are not student-centered and often actively discourage student-centered attitudes in each other.

Students, clustered on the other side, view the chasm as fraught with the dangers inherent in being compelled by law to be there based on the accident of where they happen to live and their economic status. They are thrown together with peers who may or may not like them for who they are, and are continually threatened or bribed or cajolled by the adults in charge into doing hours of work about which they may not care and over which they have little or no choice. They too have their own culture and traditions that can be reduced to student as victim and educator as victimizer. Standing on opposite sides of the chasm, the culture of each group serves only to reinforce its own perspective and limit understanding of the other.

As we have seen in the chapters included in this volume, there are voices trying to make sense of the dynamic relationships that characterize student-educator interactions. However, if we insert these voices into the metaphor, they are found to be on a precipice of their own. Those of us who research and write about democratic education command a view of both groups as well as the chasm. We can observe and comment upon the dangers inherent in the rocks and water below for both educators and students. We view the scene through a lens informed by research and theory. But in our attempts to help other educators view the landscape through the same wide-angled lens, we often feel as if we are shouting into the winds. It is our fear this volume may be the equivalent of shouts into the wind. It is our passionate wish that it is the beginning of a becalmed exchange among all who hold a stake in the future of public education.

Notes

1. Eric D. MacPherson, "Chaos in the Classroom," *Journal of Curriculum Studies* 27 (3, 1995): 263–279.

2. John I. Goodlad, *Teachers for our Nation's Schools* (San Francisco: Jossey-Bass, 1990).

3. Lee Canter, *Lee Canter's Assertive Discipline: Positive Behavior Management for Today's Classroom* (Santa Monica, Cal.: Lee Canter and Associates, 1992).

4. Henry A. Giroux, *Schooling and the Struggle for Public Life: Critical Pedagogy in the Modern Age* (Minneapolis: University of Minnesota Press, 1988).

5. Paul Gathercoal, "Judicious Discipline and Neuroscience: Constructing a Neurological Rationale for Democracy in the Classroom," in Barbara McEwan, ed., *Practicing Judicious Discipline: An Educator's Guide to a Democratic Classroom*, 3rd ed. (San Francisco, CA: Caddo Gap Press, 1996), in press.

Contributors

Kathleen Knight Abowitz is an Assistant Professor in the Department of Educational Leadership at Miami University of Ohio. Her doctoral studies at the University of Virginia focused on philosophy of education. She is currently working on a book on the educational implications of the communitarian/liberal debate.

Landon Beyer, Associate Professor of Education and Director of Teacher Education at the University of Indiana, has written numerous books, articles, and papers on education, including *The Curriculum: Problems, Politics, and Possibilities* (1988); and *Critical Reflection and the Culture of Schooling: Empowering Teachers* (1989).

Jackie M. Blount is an Assistant Professor at the University of Iowa. She received her undergraduate and graduate degrees from the University of North Carolina. Her dissertation, funded by a Spencer Foundation Grant, explored the history of women school superintendents throughout the twentieth century. Her current research focuses on the history of gendered divisions of labor in American public schools.

Ronald E. Butchart, Professor at the University of Washington Tacoma, has won teaching awards and recognition for service to education. Trained in U.S. social history at the State University of New York at Binghamton, his scholarship has ranged from the Civil War origins of African American education in the South to the social history of teachers, teaching, and classroom practices.

Forrest Gathercoal, Professor of Education Emeritus at Oregon State University, is the author of *Judicious Discipline* (third edition, 1993), *Judicious Parenting*, and *Judicious Leadership for Residence Hall Living*. His work is in educational psychology, school law, parenting, and school discipline.

Sue Ellen Henry is an assistant professor at Bucknell University where she teaches sociology of education. Her interests include democratic education, social conflicts in education, and moral order in schools.

Brian M. McCadden is an Assistant Professor of Education at Southern Illinois University, Carbondale. He received his Ph.D. from The University of North Carolina, Chapel Hill, where he studied social foundations of education, particularly sociology of education and qualitative methodology. His primary research interests lie in linking the sociology of knowledge with moral education, in understanding the roles of ritual in schooling, and in reclaiming narrative ways of knowing.

Barbara McEwan, Associate Professor of Education, directs an innovative Master of Arts in Teaching program at Oregon State University. She has conducted research, written, and spoken extensively on issues in classroom management and equity. Her book, *Practicing Judicious Discipline*, is in its second edition. She has most recently completed *On Being the Boss*, an adaptation for the business community of her concepts of managing through ethics and equity.

Ginny Nimmo is a school psychologist in southern Minnesota.

Sharon Stanley, as an educator and psychotherapist, seeks to integrate research from counseling psychology with the practice of pedagogy. She earned a Ph.D. in Counseling Psychology from the University of Victoria. She is a counselor at the University of Washington, Tacoma.

Index